UNNAM'D FORMS

William Blake, Unnam'd Form.

UNNAM'D FORMS
BLAKE AND TEXTUALITY

Edited by
Nelson Hilton
and
Thomas A. Vogler

University of California Press
Berkeley
Los Angeles
London

University of California Press
Berkeley and Los Angeles, California

University of California Press, Ltd.
London, England

©1986 by
The Regents of the University of California

Library of Congress Cataloging in Publication Data
Main entry under title:
Unnam'd forms.

   "Essays in this volume grew out of a conference entitled
'Blake and criticism' held at the University of California,
Santa Cruz, May 20–21, 1982"—Ack.
   Bibliography: p.
   Includes index.
   1. Blake, William, 1757–1827—Criticism and interpreta-
tion—Addresses, essays, lectures.   I. Hilton, Nelson.   II.
Vogler, Thomas A.   III. University of California (Santa
Cruz)
PR4147.U56   1986   821'.7   84–16330
ISBN 0–520–05298–6

Printed in the United States of America
1 2 3 4 5 6 7 8 9

Cet innommable est le jeu qui fait qu'il y a des effets nomi-
naux, des structures relativement unitaires ou atomiques
qu'on appelle noms, des chaînes de substitutions de noms, et
dans lesquelles, par exemple, l'effet nominal «différance» est
lui-même entraîné, *emporté, réinscrit, comme une fausse*
entrée ou une fausse sortie est encore partie du jeu, fonction
du système.

Jacques Derrida, *Marges de la philosophie*

Where shall we take our stand to view the infinite &
    unbounded
Or where are human feet for Lo our eyes are in the
    heavens

William Blake, *The Four Zoas*

Contents

List of Illustrations

Key to References

Am	*America a Prophecy*
ARO	*All Religions are One*
BA	*The Book of Ahania*
BL	*The Book of Los*
BU	*The [First] Book of Urizen*
DC	*A Descriptive Catalogue of Pictures*
Eur	*Europe a Prophecy*
FR	*The French Revolution*
FZ	*The Four Zoas*
GP	*For the Sexes: The Gates of Paradise*
J	*Jerusalem* (the alternative plate number is supplied in brackets where necessary)
M	*Milton, a Poem in 2 Books* [MIL/TON]
MHH	*The Marriage of Heaven and Hell*
NNR	*There is No Natural Religion*
PA	*[Public Address]*
SE	*Songs of Experience*
SI	*Songs of Innocence*
SIE	*Songs Of Innocence and Of Experience*
SL	*The Song of Los*

Thel   *The Book of Thel*

VDA   *Visions of the Daughters of Albion*

VLJ   [*A Vision of the Last Judgment*]

Quotations of Blake's poetry and prose, unless otherwise indicated, are from *The Complete Poetry and Prose of William Blake*, ed. David V. Erdman, newly revised edition (Berkeley and Los Angeles: University of California Press, 1982), abbreviated as E. In general, citations are to plate and line number for the illuminated works and either to title or page number for the others.

Acknowledgments

The essays in this volume grew out of a conference entitled "Blake and Criticism" held at the University of California, Santa Cruz, May 20–21, 1982.* From the many fine papers presented at the conference, the editors have selected those that seemed to them—though in quite different ways—to come under the general rubric of "Blake and Textuality." The authors have revised their original papers with the more specific goals of this volume in mind. Robert N. Essick's essay "How Blake's Body Means" has been added, along with two new essays by the editors. The contributions of David Simpson and Geoffrey H. Hartman began in the form of impromptu responses to the conference as a whole, but their comments seemed pertinent to the general focus of this volume, and they kindly consented to revise and edit their recorded comments to serve as a frame for the other essays.

We wish to express our gratitude to the National Endowment for the Humanities, which provided a substantial portion of the funding for the conference, and in particular to David Wise for his guidance of the project from its initial form as a grant application through its final endorsement by the NEH. Additional funds were provided by the Humanities Division of the University of California at Santa Cruz, whose dean, Helene Moglen, gave the project both institutional and personal support. Claire Braz-Valentine, Lynn Galiste, and Jill Geisel, staff for the Board of Studies in Literature at UCSC, provided invaluable attention to detail at every stage.

---

*In addition to the authors represented in this volume, the participants included Hazard Adams, Michael Fischer, W. J. T. Mitchell, Morton Paley, Daniel Stempel, Morris Eaves, Margaret Storch, Alicia Ostriker, Jackie DiSalvo, Jerome McGann, Gerda Norvig, Anne Mellor, and Hayden White.

Introduction

Not so long ago, a reviewer of a collection of essays titled *Blake's Vi-sionary Forms Dramatic* wrote that the volume announced "a new pe-riod of Blake criticism" and that "although a few problems remain, may always remain, on the whole we understand Blake's *meaning* well enough. What remains to be done is an immense amount of exciting work on structure, style, iconography, and the relationship of Blake's poetry to his designs" (Paley 98–99). But "the Eye altering alters all," and the interpretive strategies that arrived in the intervening period have made it more difficult to be sure that the meanings we attribute to the works are "Blake's"—not to mention what "well enough" might mean in this context.

Perhaps the most significant alteration of the eye comes with the self-consciousness inherent in the conception of "interpretive strate-gies," which contests from the beginning the idea of *a* meaning well-enough understood. More likely, the "meaning" of a text is something derived from a technique of reading. Certainly strategies of reading emerged as typical of the Blake Industry when it moved from the cot-tage to the factory mode of production, and chief among them has been the understanding of Blake by describing his work in relation to his (supposed) intention and personality.

At the beginning of the 1970s the student of Blake confronted the trilithon of Northrop Frye's genius of archetypal symbols, David Erd-man's social critic, and Kathleen Raine's ventriloquist of the "hidden tradition." The prevailing "meaning" of Blake would seem to have been for many—as Geoffrey Hartman writes later in this volume—"what Frye taught us, after Damon, or what Bloom carried through." Nonetheless each strategist offered a claim to most-authentic-mean-ing by presenting a comprehensive context for Blake's work and ac-

1

complishment: through symbolic coherence, complete with Orc and Jesus cycles, or historical relevance on the grandest and most particular scale, or a "tradition" that supplied a rich if cultish background. These interpretations, although seemingly strange at first, became familiar through practice and had the general effect of making Blake and the study of Blake acceptable, and of establishing his longer poems as masterpieces within the received traditions of Western literature. They also illustrate the inevitable fact that it is not an author alone who is canonized, or the works, but new ways of reading. Developing techniques for reading Blake had the curious effect of producing an organized set of "texts" that form a canon-within-a-canon, simultaneously confirming the status of an author whose works "were intended to form an exclusive and definitive canon" (Frye 6). For Blake this career from chaos to coherence, from mad artist to artist in full control, is the product of collaboration between not only interpretive but also editorial strategies, resulting at last in "AN APPROVED EDITION" of *The Complete Poetry and Prose of William Blake*.[1] *The Marriage of Heaven and Hell* prefigures this whole maneuver by describing "the method in which knowledge is transmitted from generation to generation" as a process in which "Unnam'd forms" eventually "took the forms of books & were arranged in libraries" (*MHH* 15).

The co-canonization of Blake and his texts rests on a number of assumptions that include or imply the existence of something like Eliot's notion of an "ideal order" of literary works considered as "monuments." The literal sense of "canon" requires a fixed measuring rod, against which individual authors and their works can be measured and "canonized" if they fit, themselves becoming rods against which to measure subsequent authors and their works. By joining the ranks of the canonized, authors are removed from the realms of ordinary discourse, isolated and elevated above the social and temporal limits that give us the "measure" of the ordinary. Their texts become "monuments" served by dedicated interpreters in the acceptable forms of worship by the faithful, in a practice that combines features of a secular guild solidarity with those of a religious consciousness. The ideological bases of canon formation, especially

1. A more detailed consideration of this collaboration may be found in the Santa Cruz Blake Study Group review of Erdman's 1982 edition of Blake.

within the academic discipline of literature, have received increasingly intense scrutiny during the past decade, with a growing awareness of how the act of inclusion within a canon requires innumerable acts of silent exclusion (of interpretations of works as well as of works themselves) that *define* the boundaries of acceptable academic fields and of discourse within those fields.

At this stage of literary endeavor we must consider that the manipulation of canons may be of more use to the institutionalized study and processing of literature than to an adequate understanding of literary works in the broader context of human history. We must also face the irony that Blake, who scorned "Hirelings in the Camp, the Court & the University" (*M* "Preface"), may like Milton have written works that can be "adopted by both parties" (*MHH* 5). We must put side by side assertions like those of Harold Bloom, who, after dismissing new approaches to Blake, celebrates instead the "generation of readers who have achieved a loving and accurate understanding of Blake's poetry and prose within the traditions of Western literature" (2), with claims like Michael Riffaterre's that "explication of texts is really a machine for taming a work, for diffusing it by reducing it to habits, to the reigning ideology, to familiar mythology, to something reassuring" (2–3). Perhaps Eliot's confident assertion that "the ideal order" formed by the existing monuments is "modified by the introduction of the new" should be qualified to read "*can be* modified." It is not at all clear that the ideal order of the canon has been modified by the introduction of Blake. It may rather be that Blake has been modified so that he and his works can "fit" preexisting canonical assumptions.

Such matters might make an interesting chapter in an historical work devoted to the sociology of the text and of our relations to the text—a work that considered the conventions of reading in different communities in their interactions with the techniques of conservation, reproduction, diffusion, deletion, and suppression that determine the *availability* of texts. Such a work would focus on the ways in which our acts of understanding and response are social and sociolinguistic, taking place within an economic and political matrix of reading, the practice of which requires books as material facts that must also take their place in that matrix. It would consider how the dominant totalizing interpretations of the 1960s combined with the practical need for new dissertation topics and new academic "careers" in a great expenditure of interpretive energy that, by elucidating minute particulars, aimed to make a heaven of meaning well-enough understood. During this period the common goal seems to have been to link Blake's "signifiers" to the appropriate conceptual pole of the "signified" in order to fulfill the expectations of those who *would* see a sign.

The essays in the present volume form part of the matter for a subsequent chapter in our hypothetical study, for during the 1970s, coming from "the east, distant about three degrees," *nouvelle critique* and its various epigones were "advancing toward us with all the fury of a spiritual existence" (*MHH* 18). While this volume presumes to represent the "new," it cannot pretend to have escaped social and material constraints any more than the generation we have been relativizing. Not in the least, for one of the common threads running through contemporary tangles with textuality is the desire to flex reflexive self-consciousness, making one's own critical assumptions themselves part of the field of inquiry.

Considering that Blake literally took more care with the writing of his writing than any other author in our canons, we are tempted to displace Jacques Derrida's description of Hegel onto Blake, seeing in him the last poet of the Book and the first poet of writing (cf. *Positions* 77). Or, if one distrusts the term "writing," let us call Blake the first epic poet of "print consciousness"—and hence "media consciousness"—which we now begin to appreciate as the legacy of the printing press (itself bearing the first repetition—hence consciousness—of the shock of script). We are perhaps better able to appreciate this now as we begin to adapt to a comparable revolution in media technology, moving from mechanical print to electronic pulse, from the literal to the digital. Such a vision locates Blake at the culmination of a century of English satire against the economy and culture of print that begins with *A Tale of a Tub* and continues through *The Dunciad* and *Tristram Shandy*, all playing with and exploring the limits of the medium of typography as a socioeconomic and artistic form.

Blake's concern with the whole institution of print is reflected in the bookishness of *The Marriage of Heaven and Hell*, and in particular in the next to the last chamber of the "Printing House in Hell," where we find the "Unnam'd forms, which cast the metals into the expanse." These anonymous *forms* suggest, on one level, the printer's "bodies of type, secured in a chase, for printing at one impression" (*OED*), the "type" that in the preceding chamber is cast from the lead-like living fluid of molten metal. The "Unnam'd forms," like unnamed signifiers, exist only to cast what they have to tell "into the expanse" where, as has already been told, "they were reciev'd by Men . . . and took the forms of books & were arranged in libraries."

The "forms of books" embodying our various types of learning, art, and criticism, though neatly ordered in bibliographic grid, may still bear the impress of their production via unnamed forms. One such form comes close to identification in *The Book of Urizen*, plate 4. There, in the impress of the etched metal, we may read Urizen's writing in a form not reproduced by any typographic edition of Blake.[2]

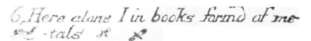

Perhaps it is we who take "the forms of books," or impose those forms as we practice our interpretations, while the forms that cast their me-tals and that arrange bookpeople remain unnamed. The essays collected here attempt to wrestle with these possibilities, asking the question that occurs at some time to every would-be lover of Blake's text: "Why dost thou come to Angels eyes in this terrific form?" (*Am* 7.7).

The authors of these essays agree that the historical author, the person, is a much less well-understood phenomenon than previous Blake criticism assumes. Accordingly, they try to meet head on the power of social structures like language, avoiding the temptation to center understanding of the art on the artist. Likewise they do not invoke the myth of the myth "of" Blake, producer of a universe that belongs to him. These authors reject a Blake who existed *before* language, the Humpty-Dumpty Blake who can make words mean whatever he wants; they recognize how easy it is to regard Blake and his work as a kind of dictionary, one that we write for him, pretending—as with all dictionaries—only to find and *define* what was already *there*.

> So profound were his researches in the *terra incognita* that he may be hailed as the Columbus of the psyche. . . . So novel was everything in this new world that no vocabulary was prepared for him. But these

2. From *The Book of Urizen* (copy C), pl. 4, detail (Paul Mellon Collection, Yale Center for British Art).

psychic forces were so real that he *had* to name them. Thence arose his special mythology, for these forces were living creatures.

(Damon, *Dictionary* ix)

To let go of this vision of Blake as a poetic Adam naming his creatures is to let go of a vision of Blake as the founder of a poetry of nouns that must be translated back into their meanings through a process of *definition*.

These essays also share the conviction that the material traces of Blake's writing practice do not have just an accidental relation to his poetry and its meanings, but instead are evidence of an inevitable materiality of all language-as-writing and an integral part of whatever artistic meaning can be read in Blake's texts. Thus more attention is given here to those material traces of Blake's written language than has been common. Some of the essays suggest the emergence or discovery of a syntax of concrete ideas in the practice of an art that seeks to write the "Divine Revelation in the Litteral expression" (*M* 42.14). Finally, these essays take seriously the inevitable plurality of meanings, so that the interpreter must take some responsibility for producing a meaning that can never recover the consciousness of the poet at the time of writing. This plurality of meanings does not imply that the text can mean *anything* we want it to mean, any more than it can mean *only* what Blake intended it to mean. The wager is that even though Blake's burning bright signifiers can give rise to a range—perhaps even an "infinite & unbounded" range—of meanings, the myriad ways they do so illuminate and can be illuminated by our attempts to frame them.

David Simpson begins by characterizing Blake as most open to analysis in terms set forth by Derrida. He wonders whether these terms do not in fact suggest "a common *history* against which Blake's specific deviations may be plotted," giving rise to the possibility that what we are dealing with is "a history and not a critical 'theory' or critical 'method.'" But such a possible history rests on our perceiving the ground of the frequent desire to "celebrate" Blake, to ride a projection of "him" into some self-referential sublime. Beyond celebration waits the cerebration of "the play of *powers* in the *structuring* of the *historical* psyche (which may indeed take the *form* of a self-engaging play)." Our first unnamed form, then, includes the play of politics, history, sexuality and the yearning to surpass its own textual *extasis*: "less than All cannot satisfy Man" (E2).

"Blake's interest in how people do things to one another with words" prompts Gavin Edwards' study of performative utterances in "London" and of Blake's "proverbial" utterances. Both are repeated formulae, both present a particularly inextricable relation between meaning and use, and both, in effect, "try to conceal that they are acts of speech among others." Speech acts here become the ground of history, as in "London," where the social conditions to which "charter'd," "ban," "curse," and "mark" refer, as well as the words themselves, "appear as the mark of acts performed." To become conscious of the structure of such acts brings some liberation, but the complicity of the "I" in the poem's performatives "simultaneously substantiates and subverts its observation." In a similar way the antiproverbial, specific nature of Blake's "Proverbs" calls into question the generic, repetitive character of experience associated with everyday proverbs. From "Repeating the Same Dull Round" we move to an awareness of relations between specific and generic, between the Blakean speech act and the social discourse. "Reading becomes an endless threading of one's way through an intricate and disconcertingly mobile taxonomy of categories."

The next essay takes us into "*The Book of Urizen* and the Horizon of the Book," into the web of a Derridean "always already" and "nothing outside of the text." Paul Mann finds in Blake's figure of the archetypal maker of books a critique of "the book" itself as "the fallen world," our "Genesis." "Bookish forms confront us everywhere" in this text, which "is precisely a book: not songs, vision, prophecy, dream or emanation." Mann explores the implication of Blake's equation between Fall and Book, testing the hypothesis that "the book is an ontological horizon, the *horror-zone* of the fallen world," and raising the possibility that *any* book necessarily will be implicated and bound within this horizon. He also questions the degree to which criticism must "employ methodologies that allow it the illusion of objective distance from the text, a distance *Urizen* challenges and absorbs." If criticism always reinscribes Urizen, then perhaps, like the later version of that form, it must turn against itself in order to undergo self-annihilation.

History returns in Nelson Hilton's attempt to construe a context for the *Visions of the Daughters of Albion* out of its evident intertextuality and out of the curious personal histories of Henry Fuseli and Mary Wollstonecraft in the period immediately preceding Blake's writing of the poem. This reconstruction reopens a text until now canonically sealed by the assumption that Oothoon "speaks Blake's truth"—an assumption shared both by traditional male critics who endorse that "truth" and by feminist critics who object to it. Far from conveying some "message," the *Visions* reflects (in reflecting on itself) our own desire to make a subject, a desire that reflects Blake's in the context this essay develops.

Donald Ault's "Re-Visioning Blake's *Four Zoas*," the fifth chapter, combines models of the act of reading and something analogous to Freud's idea of *Nachträglichkeit* (as deferred or retrospective insight), arguing that the "deeply sedimented perceptual structures" of the text work through the reader "to subvert normal processing of perceptual and conceptual information and to construct new ways of grouping information." Opposing the "Newtonian" desire for unity and textual order, Ault identifies a variety of subversive narrative processes by which "the reader and text are able to transform one another mutually." But, far from being a realm of free play, such transformations are effected by a narrative that "can be mapped as a complex symmetrical pattern."

In the essay by Thomas A. Vogler, a consideration of hearing and naming leads us to re-cognize Blake's *Milton* as *MIL/TON*, a broken name that signals a deferral of "naming" in all of its various implications. The essay offers itself as an example of a different mode of engagement with the poem—a mode that seeks, with the poem, the possibility of descending through, of breaching, the patriarchal Symbolic Order (imaged by "Milton") to some unnamable "place" or "source." This "place" is historically associated with the "feminine"; so in the "emphasis on voice and sound associated with Ololon" we may trace "a change in the symbolic topography of the feminine for Blake." Since it is "'representation' itself, understood as a psychic process, that will protect—or prevent—us from re-enacting or re-experiencing the breaching" of the Symbolic Order, Vogler focuses on our perceptions of the material form of that representation.

Emphasis on the materiality of the text looms large in the following essays as well. Beginning with the oft noted but usually unexplored fact that each "copy" of an illuminated work differs from all others,

Stephen Leo Carr moves us "Toward a Logic of Difference" in Blake's illuminated printing, a logic "set into play by technical processes of inking, printing, and coloring whose effects are never perfectly determined [and] continually open to new possibilities of meaning that are articulated as individual variants." In the continual differentiation of detail (with the related issue of *how* one identifies a "significant" variant) we recognize "the ultimate impossibility of determining some underlying authoritative structure." Just as "the stereotyped 'original' on the etched plate exists only as an idealized abstraction," so Blake's pages are not transparent media for some canonical Vision. Rather, our reading comes to "originate" in the play of differences between versions, a play that enacts Derridean *différance* and the condition of language it characterizes. Thus no single reading—just as no particular variant—is final or complete, and we face "an ongoing, open-ended production of meanings rather than a representation of an original meaning."

Robert N. Essick responds to Carr's "logic of difference" with a more historically oriented view of graphic production that emphasizes the "deliberation of the medium" and a consequent "dispersal of intentionality." He attends to the ways in which the instability of Blake's printing procedures both subverts and complements the hypothetical repeatability of his copperplate stereotypes, leaving deictic traces that may "signify" nothing more than the work of production that went into their making. For Essick, an end to the "hegemony of verbal signification" is essential if many features of Blake's graphic works, including most of the differences among impressions, are to become part of their meaning. This goal would require a reconsideration of "meaning," since such material effects make no gestures toward forms or concepts existing outside of and prior to themselves. The possibility of a material semiosis, a semiosis of "technique" itself, would seem to be required for an adequate reading of Blake's material traces. Such an alternative semiotic would be "phenomenological and incarnational rather than structural and transcendental," and it would respect Blake's efforts "to prevent his readers from separating out a 'soul' of verbal meaning and leaving the body behind."

V. A. De Luca also engages the problematic of a reading that is always under the control of and at the service of a verbal commentary on the work. He argues that "the true autonomy of Blake's designs inheres not in the likelihood that they 'mean' something that the text also means, but that they break the text, provide it with spacing, that is, open spaces within it to an antitextual universe." Such altered vision allows us to confront Blake's "Wall of Words" and to experience "The Sublime as Text." The insistent iconic and material quality of Blake's printed text leads us to experience the trope of "blockage and elevation" as "the differentiation between the Intellectual Powers and the Corporeal Understanding . . . that Blake holds to be the defining characteristic of the sublime art." "A critique of Blake's sublime and an exposition of textuality's role in his work," writes De Luca, "comes to much the same thing." Here we are far from the conception of a Urizenic horizon of the book, for "heaven is textuality." Confronting a discourse that "represents . . . not merely 'things' but language itself," we see that Blake's sublime involves the self-recognition of textual process. So we return to a Derridean world (and its rhetoric of sublimity) but one made different by the transcending subject of its own intellectual potential.

Geoffrey H. Hartman's concluding remarks, "So Many Things," turn to the perils of our undertaking, which may run the risk of fleeing "the clenched fist of logic, and positivism" only to be caught up in "the open or outstretched hand of rhetoric, the weltering, or floating, or swagging of indeterminacy." Marking differences between the "known and understood," the "known and not understood," and the "not known, yet understood," he points to the *peri bathous* of interpretive attempts to "ground" Blake or to find his "bottom," and considers the ways in which we may still be under the authority of Blake without knowing how to gauge it. So, with the reader's essays at "putting things together lightly, trying to find the 'poetical' logic of Blake," our collection ends.

And begins.

1

Reading Blake and Derrida—
Our Caesars Neither
Praised nor Buried

DAVID SIMPSON

The Blake conference of May 1982, in which this volume had its
origins, was largely carried on in speech rather than in writing, or
perhaps in a mixed genre of speaking from writing. Critics always
have been and always will be divided over the gains and losses accru-
ing when the piper, however humble, sits him down to write. One
might lament the laying aside of the raised eyebrow and the prospective elation of the successful joke, seeing in the passage from the spoken to the written a kind of fall, a loss of a community of immediately
confirming imaginations. A second might applaud the same movement as bringing about the rule of reason over passion, taking on
with pleasure the "arrows ready drawn" of footnotes and acknowl-
edgments. A third might try to turn the printed back into the spoken
word, reinscribing into the *text*, as far as possible, the plays and possibilities of *voice*, whose introduction therein brings with it a series of
problems, syndromes, and satisfactions familiar to all who are engaged in the interpretations of literature, and particularly Romantic
literature.

This third option has become a familiar one among the exponents
of the various literary criticisms founded upon the texts of Derrida. It
is a heady and beguiling mode in which analysis is replaced, both
stylistically and theoretically, by some form of reiteration. The two papers, now become essays, to which I had the pleasure of responding
(by Paul Mann and V. A. De Luca), have been very helpful in focusing

the issues raised by such a criticism. I would like here to pursue the implications of a Derridean reading of Blake, and to relate them to some questions about the operations of the sublime as it can be posited in Blake's writings. The speech-like flippancy of my title alludes to the possibility that both Blake and Derrida, who have gone through cycles in which they have been defiled and then deified, may now be due for a more reasoned reception in which, among other things, their common history might be explored and explained. It is time to address both as something other than oracles of truth and destroyers of shabby metaphysics. And Blake, who is sturdier and has stood the test of time, can help us with the later man, whose obscurities are worshiped or dismissed but seldom clearly challenged.

I shall not be casting aspersions of madness, for on such issues we should be happy to follow James Joyce in disavowing the word as "a medical term that can claim no more notice from the objective critic than he grants the charge of heresy raised by the theologian, or the charge of immorality raised by the police" (220). But I do think it worth pondering whether the gesture of celebration, so often required in the defense of Blake against common sense and its complex assumptions, might not also be blinding us to some significant questions about his writing. And in a fortunate sense some of the initiatives of modern literary criticism are freeing us to ask these questions without risking the demolition of Blake as a worthwhile writer, for in their de-emphasis of the model of a unitary subject "William Blake" they allow the texts and designs to touch upon a wider range of historical and discursive options and allusions than would have been reached by methods using the traditional yardsticks of, for example, biographical reference or meanings demonstrably produced out of conscious free will. In this respect I take the case of Blake to be crucial for our whole construction of Romanticism, making as he does the severest of all demands upon his readership, occupying, particularly, the other extreme of the axis of private and public from Wordsworth. Basically, I shall try to suggest that some of the oppositions we tend to work with—good and bad, radical and reactionary, for and against women, and so on—operate, in part by way of an overly exclusive attention to language in an ahistorical space, to reify Blake and others in ways that they need not be. So:

BLAKE AND DERRIDA

Of all the major writers I know Blake is, along with Smart (in "Jubilate Agno") and Joyce, who himself thought of Blake as "the most enlightened of Western poets" (74–75), the most open to analysis in terms set forth by Derrida. To my knowledge, and with the notable exception of the essay by Paul Mann in this volume, this analysis has not been widely rehearsed, as it has been for Joyce.[1] I shall take, for reasons that will become clear, *Of Grammatology* as my version of "Derrida," and will seek to sketch out some of the ways in which Blake both perpetrates and subverts the mythology of the primacy of speech over writing, and its inferable consequences, as Derrida takes Rousseau to do.

Of Grammatology is Derrida's most conventionally historical book. His translator, Gayatri Spivak, notes that he "never again devotes himself to this sort of textual scholarship" (Derrida, *Grammatology* lxxxv), and her own introduction to his thought indeed presupposes this move away from Derrida as the explicator of significant eighteenth-century texts toward Derrida the successor of Nietzsche and Heidegger, operating in original ways upon modern philosophy and criticism. I am especially anxious to recover the historical foundation for Derrida in the writings of Rousseau—though I thereby risk the accusation of an outmoded concern for origins—because I want to ask some questions about his common *history* with Blake, and because I sense that this relation to the past is not much attended to by those most active in employing his arguments in contemporary literary criticism. Thus Rousseau has been eliminated, so to speak, in favor of Derrida, who makes all things new.

One could speculate usefully about the reasons for this, and we badly need some sort of sociology of the critical divisions and quarrels that are associated with Derrida. Such an inquiry might well include some reflections on the strangely short life of a structuralist criticism in America (if it ever had one), when compared with the more rapid and pervasive popularity of deconstruction and its attack on the forms of objectivity that structuralism promised to revitalize. But I

1. See, for example, MacCabe, *Joyce*, and the other work to which this valuable collection of essays refers.

shall not do that here, except with the obligatory degree of implicitness. Rather I shall lay out three interlocking themes that can be seen in common between Blake and Derrida-Rousseau. I shall myself leave out the presences of Saussure and Lévi-Strauss in Derrida's account.

WRITING AND SPEECH

We can trace clearly in Blake the importance of a model or myth of primary articulation and its fall into writing, or even into language itself. In the "Introduction" to *Songs of Innocence*, for example, the passage from sound to song to writing accompanies the disappearance of the child, who might be thought to stand in the role of an inspiration or immediate audience. And writing is the rule of law in most of the adventures of Urizen. Conversely, we can also identify in Blake (as Derrida does in Rousseau) the other side of the case, where the extreme suspicion of external form is balanced, as it is for most Romantic Protestants, by the recognition that such form is the only means of publicity, survival, and communication, and indeed a gesture demanded of us by our savior: "God becomes as we are, that we may be as he is" (E3). Every child *may* joy to hear, if given the opportunity by being read to, or if so inclined by the free will that is imagination. Albion Blake giantly mediates this potentially rigid paradox, as does Finnegan Joyce, by the deliberate inscription of the traces of writing, as Derrida calls them—those features of the written word that cannot be rendered in speech and therefore signal a plenitude beyond that of the spoken. This mutability of the written word leads us to a whole range of potential etymologies for Urizen, Los, Urthona, and so on, and a variety of possible syntaxes for Blake's protonarrative lines. Such dramatizations of Blake's composition are surely appropriate to his method, in which the painstaking disassembly and reassembly of words and sentences is part of the very technique of relief etching. Perhaps we can even see Blake writing *sous rature*, or "under erasure," in the newly observed features of *The Ghost of Abel* reported by David Erdman in his revised edition:

> A device impossible to reproduce and explain simultaneously is Blake's etching of delete signs fitted to the tops of certain letters in a line in *The Ghost of Abel*, inviting the reader to read the line and immediately revise it.
>
> (Exxv)

The use of overpainting in some copies of the illuminated works, in which letters and words are highlighted by different colors as if to create a text within a text, also appears in this light.[2]

Similarly, but on a larger scale, the text of *The Book of Urizen* incorporates allusions to analogous myths of law and origination—those of Lear, Prometheus, Moses, Abraham, Oedipus, Milton, and so forth—which, in order to be apprehended, depend upon a reading rather than a "being heard spoken," even as they seem to add up perversely to a catalogue of the ways that reading imprisons. Thus, if we are of a scholarly bent, we joyfully discover in Blake's text the traces of the cultural traditions that compose our oppression. The act of reading *Urizen* subverts the closure of the reading theory being described in it. And this move beyond the usefulness of a notion of subjectivity—"Writing can never be thought under the character of the subject," writes Derrida (*Grammatology* 68)—is not a move into an abstract play of linguistic slippage but into a rather precise series of decisions about the status of those cultural traces. Compare Blake's "Mark well my words! they are of your eternal salvation" (E96) and his notice of "Marks of weakness, marks of woe" (E26). The marking is not just that of noticing or observing but that of rewriting, of annotation, of wielding the pen. Which leads us to:

WRITING AND ONANISM

While Milton speaks messianically of "vital fluid infused, and vital warmth / Throughout the fluid mass" (*Paradise Lost* 7.236–37), Blake interpolates another series of pagan creation myths, infusing Urizen with himself:

> the eternal Prophet howl'd
> Beating still on his rivets of iron
> Pouring sodor of iron; dividing
> The horrible night into watches.
>
> 2. And Urizen (so his eternal name)
> His prolific delight obscurd more & more
> In dark secresy hiding in surging
> Sulphureous fluid his phantasies.

(E75)

2. For a description of this technique at work in copy W of "The Little Boy lost," see Simpson, *Irony* 214-15. It can of course be observed elsewhere in Blake's books.

At least, we may assume Urizen as agent, for as copulation is suspended so too is the security of the syntactic copula; this passage could also be read as describing Los hiding Urizen in his (Los') phantasies, or Los hiding Urizen's phantasies . . . or all at once.

This figure compounds with Rousseau, more famous as a masturbator even than Leopold Bloom, with the folds of his curtains and silent pillows drawn back for public inspection first by himself and then again by Derrida (*Grammatology* 165ff.). Derrida's reassembly of the key moments in Rousseau's ethic of civil society further suggests the point of the connection between writing and masturbation. If writing is a fallen form of public *speaking*, then it is a replacement of the speaker's actual and present *demos* by an absent or at best phantasized public, one that may or may not come into being as the author decides to release his book, and as they decide to take it up. Thus the author-reader relation can never be directly reciprocal in the way that it would be in the more democratic speech relation in a public forum, involving an (ideal) symmetry of speech and civic identity. This myth of immediate reciprocity can never have a place in writing, which is always private (enacted behind the curtain) and deferred in its effect.

As well as finding a confirmation of this model in the figure of Urizen, we can also implant its converse, seeing a counter-mythology in Blake's writing in which the dictatorial or irrational power of direct speech is implicit—for every Demosthenes a Burke—and according to which the democracy of writing is asserted through its being meditated at a pace chosen by one's own reason or imagination. The sin of privacy is then also a requirement of the Protestant ethos, for it is there that one finds the privacy to be with God, though risking always his being supplanted by selfhood. Extreme forms of Protestant self-consciousness even celebrate the distance provided by writing, by which we gain distance also from the confusions and false tendencies of the immediate. Friedrich Schleiermacher comments:

> What takes the place of miracles for our time is our historical knowledge of the character, as well as of the scope and the duration, of Christ's spiritual achievements. In this we have an advantage over the contemporaries of the Redeemer, and a witness whose power increases exactly in proportion as the impressiveness of the miracles is lost.[3]
>
> (448–49)

---

3. Compare the arguments in Kierkegaard's *Philosophical Fragments*.

Again Blake contains both admission and refutation (or qualification) of privacy and solipsism, which is why the both positive and negative estimation of Urizen is so hard to get convincingly right. In the Rousseau-Derrida version of these notions, one can sense the importance of the model of small, self-sufficient communities that may be credibly described as marked by the immediate conversion of word into deed without the necessity of the mediation of writing (compare to Wordsworth here)—a show of hands in the *agora*. Which leads us to:

North and South

Here we are introduced to Urizen:

> *Of the primeval Priests assum'd power,*
> *When Eternals spurn'd back his religion;*
> *And gave him a place in the north,*
> *Obscure, shadowy, void, solitary.*
>
> (E70)

Urizen properly belongs in the south, but it seems to be his task in life to conquer the north, and the trouble starts when he does so (see *M* 19.15ff., E112). It is interesting to see Urizen's displacement in the tradition of Grecian verses Gothic, a polarity that runs right through eighteenth-century thinking about the origins and ideals of civil society.[4] Here again is Derrida on Rousseau:

> Rousseau would like the absolute origin to be an absolute south . . . the place of origin or the cradle of languages . . . closer to childhood, non-language, and nature, . . . purer, more alive, more animated. . . . In [the northern languages] one can follow the progress of death and coldness.
>
> (*Grammatology* 217–18)

South is to north as passion to need, love to law, energy to clarity, desire to work, song-speech to writing (*Grammatology* 224–26). The north is the place of Blake's books of brass. But once again Blake is complicated. We know how he elsewhere resolved the polarity: "Gothic is Living Form" and the place of the imagination, against the mathematic ratios of the Greeks (E270). The return of analytical reason to the south, if that is what Blake aims at, would in terms of

---

4. Its nineteenth-century continuation is incisively delineated by Marilyn Butler (113–37).

Derrida-Rousseau be the introduction of a writing tradition where it is supposed to have had no place, and correspondingly an insistence upon the abolition of a potent polarity in Blake's intellectual environment.

One could go on with parallels between Blake and Derrida. Derrida's citation of Rousseau's notion of the ideal originary language—in which there is variation of sound, accent, rhythm, and a use of composite words and aphorisms (*Grammatology* 243)—sounds at least in part close to the declaration of stylistic perversity with which Blake opens *Jerusalem* (E145–46). Derrida's remarks on the implicit relation in Rousseau between the incest prohibition and the alienation of the "father" by the letter of the law invite renewed attention to the terms of the Los-Enitharmon-Orc-Urizen relation, and so on.

The point is that Derrida's Rousseau opens up a series of avenues for the reading of Blake, for example in the areas of the relations between writing and speech, writing and masturbation, north and south, and in so doing simultaneously raises the question of a common *history* against which Blake's specific deviations may be plotted. This history might be expanded to contain Joyce, Pound, or perhaps others, but it would remain a history and not a critical "theory" or "method." Such terms seem to signify approaches created by our institutional eagerness to deprive Derrida of his own historical coordinates, to subsume Rousseau and others into the original and radical presence that is "Derrida." The real reasons for this are not to the point here, but the effects tend to be the creation of more north-south polarizations, both between deconstruction and the rest of the trade, and within deconstruction itself. Thus, in the first instance, Derrida has come to be identified with a critique of all forms of historicism (this is ironic since that very gesture itself has a history) so that he can thus be invoked to remove all possible mediations between the "new" and the "old" ways of doing things. In the second instance, deconstruction itself can sometimes seem to hold within itself an unmediated oscillation between omnipotence and impotence. The will to power, which is conscious, consists in the invocation of a language that is outside institutionally repressive norms and *therefore*, it is said, subversive of those norms (more of this later, in relation to Blake); the will to impotence, sometimes but not always conscious, consists in the reciprocal suspicion that in the adoption of such a language, a verbal sublime, we conspire in our own supersession by the very powers we purport to be fighting. These things, needless to say, need not be as opposed in fact as they seem to be in theory. Their profiles may be traced in two elements of Derridean thought that often seem particularly popular. The first is the selective encoding of play, and the second is the rhetoric of self-implication.

On the matter of play, I cite Gayatri Spivak's shrewd observation that it is "curious that, although Derrida often speaks of Nietzsche's explosive and affirmative and open play, he speaks rarely of Freud's own analysis of play as a restrictive gesture of power" (Derrida, *Grammatology* xlv). She goes on to qualify this point, but let us register here the comparative lack of encouragement that Derrida offers for a consideration of the negative or falsely conscious play. Play is for him rather a pleasure, a joyous perversity, a standing outside the limits of order. This may be a making virtue of necessity in that the second element, the rhetoric of self-implication, tells us that we *have no* place to stand, no alternative form of order that is not itself undercut. Thus Derrida writes that

> operating necessarily from the inside, borrowing all the strategic and economic resources of subversion from the old structure, borrowing them structurally, that is to say without being able to isolate their elements or atoms, the enterprise of deconstruction always in a certain way falls prey to its own work.
>
> *(Grammatology* 24)

This moment of confession and others like it (for it is of course built into the method) tempts forth a whole litany of self-underminings; I take, almost at random, Stefano Agosti's introduction to Derrida's *Spurs: Nietzsche's Styles*, which refers to itself as "a bit of magnetized and commemorative jetsam, tossing in the wake of a ship," speaks of a "textual and semantic drift" that renders us "powerless to fix or seize hold of it," and intimates that the reader of Derrida might "with his own eyes, touch . . . and be blinded "(25, 9, 3). Play thus becomes the random play of incapacity, embracing the idea of total psychic contamination and finding relief only in a moment in which self-intelligibility may be put aside. This is what Paul Mann refers to, eloquently, precisely, and perhaps a little too celebratively, at the end of his essay as an "after-life of the selfhood" produced perhaps by "accident, by counter-error, by an involuntary twitch that leaves one suddenly writing blindly in the rough basement." Beyond ideology, beyond system, beyond the figurative umbrella known as the "book," the ear is closed to its own destruction because it operates at random. In the twitch we are free, but the price of freedom is the isolation of linguistic effect per se as the single place of a merely celebrative play.

BLAKE AND THE POLITICS
OF THE SUBLIME

I begin with Burke, whose *A Philosophical Enquiry into the Origin of Our Ideas of the Sublime and Beautiful* (1757) has been aptly discussed by Stephen Land (*Signs* 36–50). If I may summarize his emphases: Burke denies the need for the calling up of referential images in the mind's eye, or for the decomposition of complex ideas into their constitutive simple parts, to ensure the success of the verbal sublime. The sublime plays on the relation between language and the mind, and reference to nature has no part in it. Poetry might lose much of its effect if it made such reference, moreover, for "we find by experience that eloquence and poetry are capable, nay indeed much more capable of making deep and lively impressions than the other arts, and even than nature itself in very many cases" (Burke, *Enquiry* 334). Blake and Burke in many ways must seem an infamous coalition, and it may be doubted that Blake would have placed eloquence and poetry in the same category as Burke does here. Nevertheless, we are reminded of how Blake saw Wordsworth to be fettering himself, poetry, and the human race: "Natural Objects always did & now do Weaken deaden & obliterate Imagination in Me" (E665). This is an astute insight into the complications Wordsworth necessarily invokes by employing natural objects as the vehicles of the essential human imagination, compelled as he then is to agonize over the fetishistic possibilities latent in such a decision.[5] But for the moment we may note simply that Blake's

---

5. However, this emphatically does not mean that he simply repeats or endorses such a deadness. Often the Wordsworthian speaker is presented dramatically as the perpetrator of misunderstandings that the argument of the poem as a whole is meant to expose. I have tried to show Wordsworth's sense of this, in its relation to his theory of mind and his views of the human and natural environment most proper to it, in *Wordsworth and the Figurings of the Real* (1982).

comment, and indeed his practice, is in line with Burke's idea that the proper place of the sublime is the mind itself. This supersession of a reference to an outside world of natural objects that might be thought to be held in common between poet-speaker and audience entails a risk or choice. On the one hand (let us call it the pole of eloquence, in Blakean terms), we register the potential for deceit implicit in such a sublimity. The famous passage in *King Lear* (4.4) that pretends to look down from the cliffs of Dover is of course a *lie*. The blind Gloucester is deceived by *language* ("Methinks the ground is even") into thinking that he stands at the top of a cliff. There are no crows, no choughs, no midway air, except in the rhetorical abundance of the verbal sublime. Blake cannot be accused, I think, of choosing this pole; rather we find him occupying the pole of imagination, in which the excision of the natural object is designed to stimulate the powers within. But there is a very narrow category of self-election into this imaginative society—though we should never forget that the softening first appeal of Blake's designs is an inducement to a relaxation of the Protestant intensity of true vision. Generally, however, the poet takes risks with his audience in such a cutting off from what they habitually recognize as nature; moreover, it is part of his purpose that he does so. W. S. Walker, reviewing in 1821 Shelley's *Prometheus Unbound*, by Blakean standards a rather accessible poem, comments as follows:

> All is brilliance, vacuity and confusion. We are dazzled by the multitude of words which sound as if they denoted something very grand or splendid: fragments of images pass in crowds before us; but when the procession has gone by, and the tumult of it is over, not a trace of it remains upon the memory. The mind, fatigued and perplexed, is mortified by the consciousness that its labour has not been rewarded by the acquisition of a single distinct conception.
>
> (Barcus 254)

Here is the same critic again:

> They argue in criticism, as those men do in morals, who think debauchery and dissipation an excellent proof of a good heart. The want of meaning is called sublimity, absurdity becomes venerable under the name of originality, the jumble of metaphor is the richness of imagination, and even the rough, clumsy, confused structure of the style, with not unfrequent violation of the rules of grammar, is, forsooth, the sign

and effect of a bold, overflowing genius, that disdains to walk in common trammels.

(263–64)

I would not wish to be seen to be siding with the rotten rags of memory and the rules of grammar against either Shelley or Blake, but I want to make the point that such contemporary criticism ought to make us wary of reposing in the myth that the single function of Blake's texts "is" (and the present tense tells all) to make us joyously aware of the usefulness of difficulty in the achievement of valuable forms of self-consciousness. Such modern critical recuperation misses a whole series of questions about the politics and indeed the theology (for we are dealing with the literature of self-election) of the sublime. Kant, among others, stressed that the sublime is always a cultivated taste; to the ordinary consciousness it is merely terrifying (*Critique of Judgment* §29). Not only might Blake's books have terrified many readers, if he had had them, it is part of his very *purpose* that he did not. As with Blake, so for Derrida?

We know that times were hard in England after 1794, and that it was dangerous to say anything in public that could even be interpreted as democratic. Working as we now can with a "Blake" who is free from the chains of a unitary or monolithic subjectivity and its existential dichotomies (this being as I have said the most valuable contribution of the Derridean movement, though not unique to it), we can understand the obscurity of Blake's writings without any accusation of bad faith. My sense is, however, that we tend to go to the opposite extreme, making Blake the yardstick of right thinking in an age when so many others can be seen to be making compromises with the establishment. Because his *text* is radical, sublime in the aesthetic sense, we move, in a gesture that surreptitiously inscribes the importance of our own discipline of exegesis, to a radical Blake. The radical text was very possibly written on the assumption that it would not be read, and indeed it was produced in such a form that it could *never* have had mass circulation or radical effect (unless we make an argument for the policy of changing the minds of the rich and powerful). Even today we seldom read Blake but have to make do with variously inadequate facsimiles, a subject on which Essick's and Carr's essays in this volume comment in detail. The real Blake is locked away in museums, a prey to the very social tendencies we assume that he opposed. Or did he? For Blake was never "there" for the taking, ignored by a merely ignorant or prejudiced public. Most of his books were incapable of being mass-produced, given the coloring process, and they were too expensive for most potential readers.

Perhaps I am laboring the point, but the radical Blake, as we know him, may be a consequence of our allowing the space vacated by the old-fashioned subject "William Blake" to be reoccupied by text or language *alone*, imaged as an autonomous organism generating a self-engaging play, rather than language as the repository of the play of *powers* in the *structuring* of the *historical* psyche (which may indeed take the *form* of a self-engaging play)—a language allowing in, in other words, the play of politics, history, sexuality, and all the things that give language a content in the traditional sense of the term—a play that might bear the question of a false consciousness. This cannot be good for Blake, for Romanticism, or for criticism. We must work to complicate the reified contrast, which still appears, between Blake and Wordsworth as radical and reactionary. It is not enough to say that Blake is "radical" because his *text* is so, while Wordsworth is somehow reactionary because he writes a language more nearly approximating to that of ordinary social intercourse, or because his poems are in some unanalyzed aesthetic sense "unachieved." These confusions may embody their own meanings, their burdens of political and imaginative crisis or alienation; in our myth of Blake's aesthetic wholeness there may be something we should suspect.[6]

Derrida and many of his disciples seem to offer precious little in the

6. See, for example, Aers, Cook, and Punter. This important series of essays is organized around a Blake-Wordsworth opposition, very much along the lines I am here questioning (apart from some arguments for Blake's assimilation of some of the mythologies he opposes in the sphere of sexuality and patriarchy). Wordsworth is made unitary in his tendency to "dissolve the social and political dimension of individual life and to lead the reader towards affirmative and reconciliatory attitudes to current modes of social control" (5). Again: "Unlike Blake, Wordsworth is not concerned with the creation of a poetic form which can imaginatively convey the reader into the reality of contradictory perceptions of the social world" (59). What this really says is that Blake's text is more apparently complex than Wordsworth's; at least, it misses the signs of alienation in Wordsworth's apparently more easeful manner. When Blake is the stick with which Wordsworth is beaten, we do neither poet much of a service. Similar and greater problems arise in Glen (1983), where the inexplicit category of the "imaginative" and the language of "embodiment" are wielded to show Blake the better (or more moral, human, imaginative) poet. Until such terms are traded in once and for all for humbler goals such as more historical documentation and more critical sophistication, one reader's man of property will always be another reader's rick burner.

way of incentives to move the analysis beyond the surface of the text, back into the historical powers that constitute its play. Such a movement is indeed usually dismissed by Derrida's disciples as metaphysically improper, a social blunder in the direction of the old beliefs in "substance." This dismissal confuses subjectivity with the powers that constitute and pass through subjectivity. The former is certainly to be posited as fluent, but the latter are very substantial; they are the historical constituents of identity. Only when this is admitted can there be any *rapprochement* between critical Marxism and deconstruction, whose ossified popular forms are certainly incompatible (is that the logic of the profession?) but whose theoretical, mutual exclusion is unnecessary once language is recognized as one of the areas in which the powers identified by Marx make their (often secret) appearance.

Blake, I think, offers more incentives for the move *behind* the text, and invites reference to a substantial archive to which the text may be related. Like many Romantics, and unlike many moderns, he insists always on the existential seriousness of superficiality when it does occur. Blake, like Kierkegaard, sees despair *and* joy, and a great many implications for both, where many a deconstructionist would tend to rest comfortably with a demonstration of the infinite artificiality of text. In particular, Blake and many of his contemporaries write a language through which a highly sophisticated political energy may be discovered to be latent, and occasionally obvious. The recovery of this energy of course takes *research*, in the old-fashioned sense; it cannot be expected to emanate from a mere exercise in "reading the poem," however ingenious. Putting the case simply and crudely, we may demonstrate the question of Blake's *textuality* in the form of a paradox, the elucidation and specification of which would entail a sophisticated and extensive historical inquiry. On the one hand, the irrationalist movements in whose orbits Blake can be situated can be read as democratic, taking the creation of significant meaning out of the control of established institutions (Parliament and the Church of England). On the other hand they can seem to reinforce the status quo by focusing all oppositional energies in a language so deflected and esoteric that it only registers as a fringe phenomenon (if at all), a Hobbesian nightmare or scrambling of all sociable codes.

This volume entertains various speculations about the future of

Blake criticism. No one seems to see Blake as a future Dryden, now alas all too often a stranded whale on the beach of literary history. I have enough of the celebrative impulse in me to hope that this will never happen. Perhaps I have been guilty of stating the obvious in outlining a move away from celebration, and many will feel that they have already made that move. It is a truism to all of us that undergraduates no longer read on library walls that the tigers of wrath are wiser than the horses of instruction, and it is a further truism that we are as the times are. But this matter of celebration (along with its opposite, serious historical self-consciousness) does pertain to the presence of Derrida in contemporary criticism, and the reasons for and consequences of this are worth pondering. Perhaps there will come a time when our successors, if they ever come into being, will look back with scholarly disinterest on the period now ending, or beginning, or continuing. I quote from an imaginary *PMLA*, say the May issue of the year 2125, now electronically flashed up on the wall (is this "writing"?) of every subscriber's home or office:

> The English Christian radical William Blake proved irresistibly attractive to a generation of critics interested, by virtue of apprenticeship in mid-century liberationist movements, in an aesthetic of fertile indeterminacy, irreverence for the past, and the possibilities of a macrocosmic dance to the tune of an exemplary subjectivity. The more imaginative members of the profession found him an infinite provider of epiphanies. . . .

Perhaps this colleague-to-be may also conclude that "signs of change could be seen emerging at the Santa Cruz conference of May 1982, and in the volume of essays emanating from it."

2

Repeating the Same Dull Round

GAVIN EDWARDS

One of the aphorisms in *There is No Natural Religion* says:

> The bounded is loathed by its possessor. The same dull round even of a univer[s]e would soon become a mill with complicated wheels.
>
> (E2)

This metaphorical sense of "round" as routine was already commonplace, already routine, in Blake's time. Blake revives the metaphor and the link between various senses of "round" by applying the phrase to those turning worlds and mills that divine and human creators conceive (think up, give birth to). One implication may be that the process whereby metaphors lose their life through repetition is a part of the process whereby life becomes "everyday" life. To remind us that they are metaphors, acts of imagination, is then an integral part of revealing and contesting the alienated life that the aphorism describes. At the same time that he brings the metaphor to life Blake is revealing that metaphors that are not brought to life take on a deadly life of their own: there is a sense in which the dead metaphor of the dull round comes fearsomely to life as a real mill with complicated wheels.

The aphorism on the "Conclusion" plate of *There is No Natural Religion* says:

> If it were not for the Poetic or Prophetic character, the Philosophic & Experimental would soon be at the ratio of all things & stand still, unable to do other than repeat the same dull round over again.[1]
>
> (E3)

---

1. Most editions now follow Keynes's edition of copy L and put the "Conclusion" plate in the [b] series. Blake probably never assembled the loose sheets of *NNR*; in whichever way we choose to assemble them repetition of "the same dull round" will occur, but of course its significance will be different for each assembly.

Is Blake aware that he has repeated "the same dull round" over again? This is a question I am bound to ask but to which I can give no definite answer. Perhaps Blake's work is implicated in the deadening routine it castigates. On the other hand he may be rousing my faculties to act and to supply the missing quotation marks around "the same dull round."[2] One consequence of this uncertainty is that a problematic relationship is set up between saying something again (repeating) and doing something again (repeating).

Blake was certainly interested in repeated utterances, notably in two kinds of utterance that actively participate in the construction of everyday life by virtue of their repetitious, ritualized character. The first part of my argument will be about Blake's interest in what we now call "performative" utterances, including those performatives that play a central role in the ritual practices of the Law and the Church.[3] The second part will be about proverbs, Blake's interest in proverbs, and his own aphoristic, proverb-like writing.

PERFORMATIVES

"London" (and I am taking the word as the title of the poem beneath it rather than the caption of the picture above it) obviously involves a sequence of voices heard in the street, over and over again. But its interest is wider than that; it includes a whole range of acts of vocalization and scription: sighs and charters and marks as well as curses and bans. Four of Blake's words are particularly interesting in the present context: "charter'd," "ban," "curse," and "mark." They are all words that, in other grammatical forms, can act as performatives. Briefly, performative utterances are utterances that themselves perform the actions to which they refer. Thus:

> Lawyers when talking about legal instruments will distinguish the preamble, which recites the circumstances in which a transaction is effected, and on the other hand the operative part—the part of it which actually performs the legal act which it is the purpose of the instrument

2. This is not simply a competition between rival interpretations. Blake would not be able to rouse my faculties to act in this way (making me author of his punctuation) unless it were impossible for me to be sure that this is what he is doing.

3. For another version of this part of the argument, paying more attention to social contexts, see Edwards, "Manacles" 87–105.

to perform. . . . "I give and bequeath my watch to my brother" would
be an operative clause and is a performative utterance.

(Austin, "Performative" 223)

This example is pertinent for a number of reasons. First, it demonstrates that written discourse (a charter, for instance) can involve performative utterances. Second, "I give and bequeath x to y" is clearly a
formula, a repeated phrase, and it needs to be if the instrument is to
be legally binding. Furthermore such ritual performatives are clearly
always of particular significance where conventional relationships are
being established in a conventional context—such as the fixing of
rights of property and inheritance (charters for the incorporation of
companies or towns), social contracts between rulers and ruled
(Magna Carta), articles of apprenticeship (such as those signed by
James Blake and James Basire), marriage ceremonies (the "I do" of
William Blake and Catherine Boucher, the "I declare you man and
wife" of the parson), and baptisms ("I name this child . . ."). Such situations provide most of Austin's examples, and Blake's poem is overwhelmingly concerned with the overlapping areas of Church, Law,
property, generational inheritance, and marriage.

As for the words themselves, "I curse" would be a performative, as
would "I ban," and the poem also alludes to the banns of marriage,
which gives us the parson's "I publish the banns of marriage between. . . ." Charters are legal instruments that have to involve performative utterances, though I have not come across a charter in
which the word itself is used performatively (as in "I/We charter"). Finally, "mark" is a special case to which I shall return.

Evidently these words in Blake's poem ("charter'd," "ban," and
"curse") are not themselves performative. But as nouns or participial
adjectives, they are what Barbara Johnson has called "deactivated
performatives" (146). And the particular force that seems to animate
them in the poem derives, I believe, from their direct reference to situations in which those same words help to constitute performative
utterances. Austin points out that in performative words there is an
"asymmetry of a systematic kind [with respect to] other persons and
tenses of the *very same word*" (*How* 63). For instance, "I curse you" is a
performative utterance, whereas "he curses you," like "I hear you," is
not since it refers to an event independent of the referring utterance.
The words in the poem—"charter'd," "ban," and "curse"—derive at

least some of their force from how they embody this asymmetry. They refer to conditions in the world outside the poem, but how they so refer is determined by the fact that, as deactivated performatives, they are also existentially linked to actual performative utterances. The poem's words actually do bear the operative power of performative utterance within themselves, in a congealed form. Consequently the social conditions to which the words refer, as well as the words themselves, appear as the marks of acts performed in another grammatical form by the utterance of those very same words. Those social conditions are represented therefore not so much as facts but as *faits accomplis*. The word "charter'd" bears repetition in the poem because of the force to which it is linked. These performatives are uttered in churches and law courts where their force is inseparable from the fact that they have been said before and will be said again.

Blake's use of these words tends to confirm another of Austin's contentions, that performative utterances depend for their plausibility on at least a tacit acceptance by the interlocutor of the conventions involved in their use. Indeed to describe the situations of their use as conventional implies as much. Most of Austin's examples, and these three words from the poem, are concerned with human power relationships. And the poem's use of these words suggests that to be at the receiving end of performative utterances of this kind is to be more than labeled: it is to take the label to heart, to assume it as one's identity, even unwittingly. The religious and juridical act of christening could be taken as exemplary in this respect. It is an act of labeling imposed arbitrarily on the basis of our father's name and our parents' wishes that we take as the sign of our personal identity. The achievement of the poem is to register such acts as the imposition of arbitrary labels that are nevertheless not external to those who receive them: as marks inscribed by authority that are also signs of an inward condition, marks "of weakness and of woe."

There is only one actual performative in Blake's poem, and that is "I . . . mark." Of course, one sense of the verb *mark* in the poem is "to observe." In this sense the word reports on the poet's action as he walks the streets and is not performative. But since the same word used as a noun in "Marks of weakness, marks of woe" refers to physical alterations of the human body, and since the practice in which the poet is actually engaged involves inscription on paper and the subsequent biting of the copper plate by acid to reveal the letters in relief, then surely there is also a reference in "I . . . mark" to itself. Insofar as "I . . . mark" means "I observe," the relationship established between the marked faces and the poet who marks them is of the fatally reflexive kind that Heather Glen has so accurately described. Blake, she argues, shows us what it means to be both at odds with and yet conditioned by one's cultural ethos:

> The relentless, restricting categorising which stamps the Thames as surely as it does the streets is like his own mode of relating to the world. He may "wander" freely enough, but he can only "mark" one repetitive set of "marks" in all the different faces before him.
>
> ("Poet" 6)

And this is still the case if one admits the sense of "mark" as an act of perception involving a registering or noting of what is perceived. The writer and reader implied by that registering are still caught within the same kind of specular relationship, in a poetic utterance that presents itself as an unmeditated survey of the reality it simply repeats. But insofar as "I . . . mark" refers also to itself as an act of inscription, all those mirror-relationships are fissured, marked, rendered problematic. The best way to explain this effect is in terms of the different forms of the present tense that the ways of reading "I . . . mark" imply. The poem employs a generalizing present tense, one that describes not "what I am doing" but "what I do" (repeatedly). But insofar as "I . . . mark" is self-referential, it introduces the present tense of "what I am doing," and this has a number of consequences. First, it links the poetic utterance existentially to the writing self, in a way that can be associated with the existential link that I have argued for between the deactivated performatives and the actual performative utterances to which they refer.[4] But, second, this self is not the unitary entity that its grammatical name, "first person singular," suggests; it is not the anterior source of the utterance. "I . . . mark" is self-referential both in the sense that it refers to the self and in the sense that it

---

4. In both cases this existential link shifts the poem toward Peirce's "indexical" mode of signification. Roman Jakobson discusses the pronoun *I* as an "indexical symbol" (*Shifters*). My discussion of subjectivity in language is also indebted to Emile Benveniste. A semiological study of Blake's composite art would also take account of Vincent A. De Luca's insights (in the present volume) into the "iconic" aspects of the verbal text.

refers to itself. "I . . . mark" describes me in the act of scription, but it also *is* the act of scription. Consequently the present it reveals is not a moment but a movement, and there is no governing subject but a continual differentiation in which the subject of the act of writing and the subject of what is written never finally coincide or separate.[5]

The presence in the poem of actual and deactivated performatives is part of its concern with the power of discourse to effect (in both senses) the development of physical life and human relationships.[6] This power is most strikingly evident in the case of a curse, which not only performs the act to which it refers but whose action is the creation of a real future. Moreover, curses are classically, as they are in the poem, about generation (in both senses). It is families, lineages, "houses" that are traditionally cursed, to the *n*th generation. Thus in Sophocles, as Geoffrey Hartman puts it, "The oracle takes away, from the outset, any chance of self-development: Oedipus is redundant, he is his father, and as his father he is nothing, for he returns to the womb that bore him" (*Beyond* 348). The Oedipus myth does seem peculiarly apposite to Blake's final stanza. So that Hartman's comment that "the marriage-bed is the death-bed" is another way of saying "Marriage hearse." And the last line of the poem is so powerful partly because (to adapt another Hartmanism) we converge on the final word like a Greek tragedy on its recognition scene: "hearse" appears on the horizon of our expectations simultaneously with the word—"bed"—

5. The following relevant formulation provides a link with my subsequent discussion of "to Generalise is to be an Idiot":

In the utterance "I am lying," for example, it is evident that the subject of the proposition is not one with the subject of the enunciation of the proposition and vice-versa; the "I" cannot lie on both planes at once (dream, lapsus, and joke are so many disorders of the regulation of these planes, of the exchange between subject and signifier). From here . . . the question can be posed as to the foundations of knowledge in the homogeneity of the self-reflexive consciousness, a question to which the discovery of the unconscious replies by the demonstration of a division, of a work, of the constitutive impossibility of a cohesion between the *énoncé* (what is said) and the *énonciation* (the act of saying) as the simple identity of the subject ("the only homogeneous function of consciousness is the imaginary capture of the ego by its specular reflexion and the function of misrecognition which rests attached to it"—Lacan).

(Brewster, Heath, and McCabe 86)

6. In "The Little Girl Lost" Blake's etched sentence claims the force of a legal sentence, but in a punning process that separates the imperative and the indicative even as it presses them together: "(Grave the sentence deep)."

whose place it usurps. It represents the reappearance of those blights and plagues that we thought we had left behind at the beginning of the line.

Heather Glen and Edward Thompson, in their comments on Blake's "charter'd," refer to the significance that charters have for Edmund Burke and Tom Paine (Glen, "Poet"; Thompson, "London"). They suggest that Blake uses the word in a bitterly ironic reversal of its laudatory Whig sense, to imply (perhaps following Paine) that charters represent a *licensed* freedom, a freedom that is exclusive and granted by authority, rather than universal and of right. I would only add that it is also characteristic of charters to commit future generations, on both sides of the relationship. Thus James I, in the Third Charter of the Virginia Company (12 March 1612):

> We therefore . . . of our royal power and authority, have therefore, and of our special grace, certain knowledge, and mere motion, given, granted, and confirmed, and for us, our heirs, and successors, we do by these presents, give, grant, and confirm, to the said company of adventurers and planters of the city of London for the first colony of Virginia, and to their heirs and successors, for ever, all and singular those islands whatsoever, situate and being in any part of the ocean seas bordering upon the coast of our said first colony of Virginia.
>
> (Jensen 248)

This aspect of chartering is at the forefront of the argument for both Burke and Paine. "From the Magna Carta to the Declaration of Right," argues Burke,

> it has been the uniform policy of our constitution to claim and assert our liberties as an *entailed inheritance* derived from our forefathers, and to be transmitted to our posterity.
>
> (*Reflections* 119)

To which Paine counters:

> I am contending for the rights of the *living*, and against their being willed away, and controlled and contracted for, by the manuscript assumed authority of the dead.
>
> (64)

Paine magnificently establishes the authority of the living through performative utterance: "I am contending. . . ." I would not want in any way to condescend to Paine's self-confidence, or its proven power to elicit self-confidence in others, but Burke's argument was by and large victorious in practice. *One* reason for that must be that Paine is mistaken in his idea that human generations are autonomous and that manuscript-assumed authority is a paper tiger. Blake, wandering through the London streets, finds everything—"the man-made streets, the freely flowing Thames," as Glen puts it (7)—always already owned and named, trademarked, an abstract and schematic geography where everything is already (with the help of the *OED*) char*ted*, marked out. According to one of the passages from Revelation quoted by Thompson and Glen, the "marks" are anyway both charters and inscribed names:

> And he causeth all, both small and great, rich and poor, free and bond, to receive a mark in their right hand, or in their foreheads:
>   And that no man might buy or sell, save he had the mark or the name of the Beast, or the number of his name.
>
> (Rev. 13.16–17)

All the people are, fatally, sons and daughters of the one Father, bearing his name: Albion and Dombey Incorporated.

The allusion to Revelation is undoubtedly significant, given the radical Protestant context in which Blake moved. But it is sectarian, and an allusion that would have been more generally available is surely to the marks ("x his mark") that many of the people whom Blake sees in the street would have used as their signature, registering their names in, and thereby giving their assent to, legal instruments such as certificates of marriage.[7] Both these allusions to marking as naming are therefore to situations in which one accedes to a kind of freedom, an identity as a human subject and center of initiative, by virtue of one's subjection to a name (see Althusser 123–73). As with the name of the Lord, "whose service is perfect freedom," so it is by virtue of the inscription of the name of the Beast that individuals are freed to buy and sell themselves and their products in the free market, in weakness and in woe. Thompson concludes his discussion of the poem by arguing that there is

---

7. Catherine Boucher/Blake signed her wedding bond with an "X" (see Bentley, *Records* 23–24).

an ulterior symbolic organisation behind the literal organisation of this street-cry following upon that. . . . And the symbolic organisation is within the clearly conceived and developing logic of market relations. . . . "Charter'd" both grants from on high and licences and it limits and excludes; if we recall Paine it is a "selling and buying" of freedom. What is bought and sold in "London" are not only goods and services but human values, affections, and vitalities.

(21–22)

However, "market relations" is not a sufficiently specific description of the kinds of interchange involved. For instance, charters may represent a "selling and buying of freedom," but they also represented a deliberate restriction of market relations in the interests of corporation and lineage. Moreover, acts of discourse, of licensing and crying, are fundamental to the character of the social relations that the poem reveals. People who advertise themselves and their wares for sale in the streets, crying their own subjection over and over again, thereby name themselves: "weep weep weep weep," as Blake puts it in "The Chimney Sweeper" (*SI*).

The second and third stanzas of the poem are evidently concerned with acts of discourse that in themselves effect material change. The poet hears

> How the Chimney-sweepers cry
> Every blackning Church appalls,
> And the hapless Soldiers sigh
> Runs in blood down Palace walls
> (E27)

Glen suggests that "the cries, in two startlingly surrealistic images, have *become* marks" (11). But it may be said that whereas charters and curses are ritual utterances that can literally effect material change, these are metaphorical, indeed assertively so. As images of almost magical transformation, their effect is to emphasize the vast difference between the charters and bans of authority on the one hand and the powerless voices of the oppressed on the other, the repetitiveness of whose cries signals their impotence. Indeed, there are numerous, often contradictory, implications of these lines, none of which can be completely ruled out. The variety of critical interpretations put upon the lines testifies to their ineradicably unstable and multiple significance, an instability and multiplicity that it has been the ideological function of literary criticism to resolve, conceal, or condemn.[8]

It is the nature of the images themselves, their extraordinary combination of concreteness and abstraction, that makes all single-minded and unequivocal interpretations so inadequate. And this would be true of any interpretation that amounts to a translation of the lines into a hypothetical real-life sequence of cause and effect. On the other hand it is inevitable that one should be drawn into this activity of translation; it is inseparable from the activity of reading, and I have obviously spent hours doing it myself with this poem, helped by the literary critics I have just criticized. But what all these different critical interpretations (with their often startlingly different moral and political implications) testify to is this: it is the same characteristics of Blake's lines that require us to translate them and that so successfully prevent any of us from doing so in a way that carries much conviction for anybody except possibly ourselves.

This impasse has to do with the combination of extreme concreteness and extreme abstraction in the lines. They play in a particular way with the relationships that can be set up in language between the literal and the figurative, between cause and effect, between the material, the less material, and the nonmaterial. The various interpretations essentially involve different decisions about how to read the images in these respects: whether to read them as rather more or rather less figurative, and whether to read the lines of cause and effect between the terms of the action as traveling in one direction rather than in another.

Blake makes "sigh" and "blood" immediately and magically correlative in a way that suggests the active exclusion of chains of cause and effect that might *really* link them. This polarization of a complex set of relationships, excluding intermediate links so as to produce a dramatic condensation of its terminal points, is accomplished by various methods, for instance by the substitution of "Church" and "Palace" for the people and relationships that utilize them. The condensation of "hearse" and implicit "bed" in the poem's final line is a similar case. The difficulty of course is to know *how far* these are figures of

---

8. See Edwards, "Manacles," for a more detailed discussion of the variety of interpretations.

speech. Real blood is very likely involved, and by definition the blood of both the soldiers and their enemies. Yet they are clearly also figures of speech, powerfully condensed "ways of saying" something else, such that Damon can read the blood flowing down the palace walls as "a stain upon the state" (*Blake* 283). What is finally at issue is the relation between such figures of language and modes of substitution intrinsic to nonlinguistic forms of social activity. After all, walls *do* stand, and they stand *for* princes and states.

The other image in the stanza, of the chimney sweeper's cry, provides another fascinating example of how we are led to construct incompatible "real-life" narratives out of the lines. Glen quite reasonably claims that the word "appalls" suggests, "in a submerged pun, the pall-like appearance of the blackened walls" (11). But if that is so we must surely be equally aware, in a splendidly impossible mental perception, of the sense of "appalls" as "to go pale" or "to make pale." And that radical ambivalence has to do with how the syntax of the lines allows alternative readings of the relations of cause and effect and the degree of figurativeness involved: does the cry appall the blackening church, or does the cry blacken the church?

I have suggested that this third stanza links utterance and material change in a way that is assertively problematic. But perhaps this is true also of "the youthful Harlots curse." I am surely wrong to have written of the harlot's curse as if it were really a curse in the theological and oracular (or Muggletonian) sense. It certainly invokes that ancient practice, and that concept, but only by fusing two quite different meanings of the word: on the one hand a blasphemous expletive (one of the cries heard in the streets) and on the other a figure of speech— "the harlot's curse"—naming venereal disease. Or, to look at it another way, by using the unitary concept in this context Blake produces fission within it (or reactivates a fission that already existed in common usage). The split in the word takes place, what is more, exactly between the two elements whose inseparability is the *differentia specifica* of the ancient curse considered as a method for doing things with words: utterance and physical effect. Finally, what gives the lines their extraordinary power is precisely the fateful combination that sustains the narrative logic of the ancient curse, between aggressive and repetitious utterance deprived of material effect and a physical condition that has all the contagious power, the power to repeat itself through generation/s, of the ancient curse. The very splitting of utterance and physical life gives a new lease of life to the metaphysical violence of the ancient curse, whose unity it bifurcates. Utterance and physical life, like marriage and prostitution, are bound together, but back to back like Bromion and Oothoon. Relations of cause and effect go in both directions, not as a reciprocity but as a moral and epistemological impasse. The "Marriage hearse," which is part of the "ancient curse" in "An Ancient Proverb," is threatened and/or sustained by the "Harlots curse." And the internal bifurcation of that "curse," which "An Ancient Proverb" uses in its unitary sense, is linked to the problematic redistribution of that poem's terms. The separation of utterance and physical life that removes the *ancient* curse is such as to give it a new lease of life.

The Magna Carta (1215) contains passages such as the following:

> Know that we . . . in the first place have granted to God and by this our present Charter have confirmed, for us and our heirs in perpetuity, that the English church shall be free, and shall have its rights undiminished and its liberties unimpaired; . . . And the city of London is to have all its ancient liberties and free customs by land and water.[9]
>
> (Holt 317, 321)

In his analysis Austin suggests that the characteristic grammatical form of the performative is the first-person singular present indicative active: "I give, grant, and confirm . . .," where the grammatical form in a sense advertises the performative character of the utterance. But the notable thing about the Magna Carta or James I's charter to the Virginia Company is that elements of the grammatical form that Austin stipulates are mixed with the first-person *plural* and the *past* tense, without the utterance being any less performative. Thus "we . . . by this our present Charter have confirmed" is in fact one man speaking, and his speech is an act of confirmation. But he uses a certain rhetoric, speaking *as if* he were the embodiment of an authority larger and

---

9. The original Latin is as follows:

Sciatis nos. . . . In primis concessisse Deo et hac presenti carta nostra confirmasse, pro nobis et heredibus nostris in perpetuum, quod Anglicana ecclesia libera sit, et habeat jura sua integra, et libertates suas illesas. . . . Et civitas Londoniarum habeat omnes antiquas libertates et liberas consuetudines suas, tam per terras quam per aquas.

(Holt 316,320)

less personal than himself and were reporting on an action that had already taken place. Emile Benveniste has pointed out that the so-called first-person plural pronoun is never really a pluralization of the first-person singular (202–3). It does not name a plurality of "I"'s but is always a combination of "I plus you" or "I plus he (or she, or it, or they)." And the fact that a king is addressed to his face as "your majesty" suggests that the royal "we" is in fact a combination of "I" and "it," where "it" is "majesty."[10] I suggested at an earlier stage of this argument that a crucial feature of performative utterance is the internal differentiation it introduces into the first-person pronoun "I," as subject of the act of saying and as subject of what is said. The significance of the rhetorical form of the performative in the charters is that it gives a degree of explicit embodiment to the elements of this differentiation that neutralizes some of its effects. The royal "we" and the past tense of "we . . . by this our present Charter have confirmed" put the speaker together with the reader in position as spectators of an event in which the speaker is also a participant. Insofar as this can be done, the "I" that is nothing but the subject of the utterance in which the word "I" is uttered is continually suppressed, appearing as an entity external to the discourse, the spectator of an action in which "I" figures as the subject. By such a mechanism as this we participate in the production of a state of affairs that has all the character of a given.

But we do not have to go back to the seventeenth century and the royal charters to discover these mechanisms. A characteristic eighteenth-century idiom puts us in position as spectators of our own lives conceived as a kind of third-person narrative. This is not necessarily an external view in the limiting, modern sense of that word. Rather, our capacity to see things as they really are is taken to be the capacity to see our own lives, inner as well as outer, in the same form as we see the lives of others. The idiom could be said to be dominated by the quasi-personal pronoun "one," considered as a unity of the subject of the narrative and the subject of the act of narration. Correlatively, the tense that contains this idiom is the universal and morally normative present tense of "what one does," or of "what is done" in the good-manners sense of the phrase. Of course, a great deal of eighteenth-century writing, notably satirical writing, emphasizes the gap

10. Benveniste talks about the "Royal We" in rather different terms from my own.

between quotidian experience on the one hand and its moral and artistic ordering (Poetic Justice) on the other. But that gap, that distance can also be what is required if we are to see that reality as it *really* is, to get it "into perspective," as it were. Such writing is able to assert, via the alibi of perspective, both its separation from and its identity with a reality prior to representation.

This idiom is by no means a purely literary matter, even in the wider sense of literature then current. This putting of the self into position as the spectator of a narrative in which the self also figures is akin to the process shown to be at work in charters and which defines the work of performative utterances in the exercise of social power. What we are talking about when we concentrate on the written literature of the eighteenth century, and the character of its language, is not only a certain implicit conception of narrative and character and their ethical function. We are beginning to define the historically specific position that literature may have held among other forms of social relationship, specifically its overwhelmingly, and perhaps crucial, ideological function, its role in the forging of manacles. We are concerned not just with a certain idea of narrative but, as Martin Golding puts it, with "a narrative idea of the moral life" in which "character" as personal identity and "character" as figure in a narrative are identical meanings.[11]

Blake's poem emerges from this idiom, and it represents a particular testimony to its crisis.[12] The poem's generalized present tense and its generic definite articles suggest its allegiance to that idiom. Yet it is precisely the generic, repetitive character of experience that is at issue ("In *every* cry of *every* Man") even as the poem itself lives within it ("*the* hapless Soldiers," "*the* youthful Harlots").

In Samuel Johnson's *The Vanity of Human Wishes* each one of us is credited simultaneously with the clearsightedness of "Observation" (which involves the ability to see ourselves in terms of the same categories we are all too willing to acknowledge as applicable to others) and the blindness of Vanity (which involves a systematic misrecognition of the world in the image of our own hopes and fears). That ex-

---

11. This section of my argument owes a lot to discussions with Martin Golding; the quotation is from an unpublished essay.

12. For other manifestations of the crisis see Edwards, "Politics," and Everest and Edwards.

traordinary simultaneous placement of each of us in the positions of Truth and Vanity is only possible by virtue of the concealed proximity of the epistemological characteristics attributed to each. How that proximity is concealed I cannot properly go into here, though one crucial factor is the availability of an attenuated Heaven. But Blake's poem can be seen as making that latent tension within the inherited mode patent. The complicity of the Observing "I" in the systematic social estrangement it observes simultaneously substantiates and subverts its Observation. The eighteenth-century alibi is revealed as such, in all its strength, as a fearful hall of mirrors. Johnson's "Observation" does not distinguish between seeing and the making of statements; Blake's poem makes that relation—the relation between distinct senses of "I . . . mark"—visible and problematic. The process whereby we are put into position as Spectators of ourselves as "genre-figures" (in Golding's phrase) is revealed, in a liberating movement from offstage, as a work of scription and vocalization, an inscription of written characters.

PROVERBS

Blake's work with proverbs and proverb-like statements goes beyond the "Proverbs of Hell" and collections of aphorisms such as *There is No Natural Religion*. Much of his poetry is written in proverb-like sentences; for instance, the argument between Oothoon, Theotormon, and Bromion in *Visions of the Daughters of Albion* is really a contest between strings of aphorisms.

The normal function of proverbs is to bring novel or confusing situations into focus as examples of what has already been experienced and understood.[13] They employ, or imply, the universal and morally normative present tense of "what is done," the tense of good table manners by means of which the imperatives of authority disguise themselves as the indicatives of "common sense" and a homogeneous "tradition."[14] Barthes writes of "this peremptory *because* which par-

---

13. My understanding of proverbs is indebted to conversations with Geoffrey Blunden and Deborah Ferris.

14. Proverbs characteristically imply that there is such a thing as "tradition," whereas in fact there are only traditions, including antinomian (antitraditionalist) traditions. In all hitherto existing societies the most powerful traditions have been the ones that say there is such a thing as "tradition."

ents in need of knowledge hang above the heads of their children" (*Mythologies* 155). Proverbs are a form of personal address, embedded in dialogue, but their aim is to rise above dialogue and put a stop to it. In proverbs "you" can always be translated as "one."

But if this is the case—if, as Barthes contends, proverbs are associated with "universalism, the refusal of any explanation, an unalterable hierarchy of the world" (*Mythologies* 154)—then Blake's commitment to them is paradoxical, particularly when what Blake's proverb-like statements are constantly talking *about* is difference and incomparability. And though we may come to the conclusion that his aphorisms are anti-proverbs, we should not jump to it. For instance, the statement that "To Generalize is to be an Idiot" (E641) is as Cretan a paradox as "I am a liar." It is a statement that contradicts what it says about statements. If it is true it is false. It must be a member of the class ("generalizations") that it names and must not be a member of it. It is the kind of statement to which Russell's Theory of Logical Types is addressed, and according to that theory (which says that a class cannot be a member of that class) Blake's statement is simply "meaningless." But of course it is not just a statement; it is an energetic annotation of Reynolds' *Discourses*. Gregory Bateson, who developed his theory of the double bind from the Theory of Logical Types, emphasized that

> in the psychology of real communications [the discontinuity between a class and its members] is continually and inevitably breached, and that *a priori* we must expect a pathology to occur in the human organism when certain formal patterns of the breaching occur in the communication between mother and child.
>
> (202–3)

Blake's interest in how people do things to one another with words is very much an interest of Bateson's kind. But the insight needs to be turned on Blake's own work. At any rate there is no doubt that Blake can be invoked as an authority by an authoritarian libertarianism that says (to give one of the classic examples) "be spontaneous!"

A large number of Blake's proverb-like statements involve analogies, as do other proverbs. David Simpson, in a discussion of Blake's attitude to figurative language, has suggested that Blake prefers analogy to simple metaphor because "the moment of analogy *starts out* in a state of division"; analogy directs our attention to "the *activity* of making connections" (*Irony* 159–60, 158). The explicit or implicit analogies in normal proverbs and in Blake's proverb-like writing are very often between human beings and animals. In these cases it is the sharp class distinction between the human species and animal species, or between one animal species and another, that is the initial state of division to which Simpson refers. But Blake's animal aphorisms are also as often as not *about* the *in*comparability of particular beings or relationships. The paradoxical effect of this is to undermine the initial categorization of animals into species, and the sharp distinction between animals and humans, on which the analogies rest.

Here are three examples:

> have not the mouse & frog
> Eyes and ears and sense of touch? yet are their habitations.
> And their pursuits, as different as their forms and as their joys:
> (VDA 3.4–6)

> The bird a nest, the spider a web, man friendship.
> (MHH 8)

> One Law for the Lion & Ox is Oppression
> (MHH 24)

Oothoon later pleads, "How can one joy absorb another? are not different joys / Holy, eternal, infinite! and each joy is a Love" (*VDA* 5.5–6). And in her earlier speech she is looking for examples to illustrate this view of life, analogies for her situation that she can show to Theotormon so that he may help them both break out of their vicious triangle. The "differences" with which Oothoon is concerned in her example, however, are not between individual beings or relationships but between species, between *the* mouse and *the* frog. She implies a similarity between that difference, on the one hand, and the difference between different human individuals or relationships, on the other.

A similar permutation of similarity and difference is made beautifully explicit in "The bird a nest, the spider a web, man friendship." "One Law for the Lion & Ox is Oppression" implies that the difference between the two animal species can stand for the difference between any two creatures or kinds of creature (including human beings and kinds of human beings). But can you say it when you want to talk about the difference between lions? The problem is that the incomparability and uniqueness that these passages talk about seem to cast doubt on how all mice and frogs and lions and oxen are herded under their generic definite articles. Why doesn't incomparability apply to them too? How do you know but *every* bird (and not just every *kind* of bird) that cuts the airy way is an immense world of delight closed by your senses five? And if the similarity between all mice disappears, if it is not really possible to abstract from all individuals to produce a general category, then of course the *difference* between mice and frogs on the one hand and humans on the other is blurred. If analogical proverbs reveal similarity against a background of prior difference, Blake's are about difference to a degree that must emphasize the similarity and continuity between the beings who are initially distinguished. Blake establishes a kind of self-subverting taxonomy in which similarity subverts difference and difference subverts similarity.

Perhaps Blake believes that blindness is at any one moment a condition of insight. It has proved all too easy for people not to see that "To Generalize is to be an Idiot" is a paradox, and therefore to be enslaved by an act of discourse camouflaged as a programmatic statement. But the list of proverbs in the "Proverbs of Hell" actively prompts readers to read individual proverbs in numerous contexts. Any one proverb can be read in a variety of partial contexts (the contexts, say, of other proverbs about "fools," of other proverbs colored in the same ink in the version you are reading, of the contiguous proverbs, and so on). Reading becomes an endless threading of one's way through an intricate and disconcertingly mobile taxonomy of categories. "The bird a nest, the spider a web, man friendship" appears in a list that is introduced by

> How do you know but ev'ry Bird that cuts the airy way,
> Is an immense world of delight, clos'd by your senses five?
> (*MHH* 7)

And while we may be as confident in the solidity of the category "man" as we were in "*the* bird" and "*the* spider," that confidence is shaken if we look at what the same word means in the previous proverb:

Let man wear the fell of the lion. woman the fleece
of the sheep.

(*MHH* 8)

If proverbs normally aim at common sense, Blake's know that there is no common sense of the word "man," any more than there is of "Mercy" or "Pity" (see Glen 23).

Is one law for all lions oppression? Somebody might reply that the proverb is not really *about* lions in that sense, but aren't lions even allowed to be examples of the truth they are required to demonstrate? By a curious coincidence a lion plays an important part in Barthes' analysis of myth as a form of speech that disingenuously employs a first-order sign as the signifier of a second-order (mythical) sign. The phrase "quia ego nominor leo" would be, originally, part of a fable: "I am an animal, a lion, I live in a certain country, I have just been hunting. . . . I award myself certain shares for various reasons, the last of which is quite simply that *my name is lion*" (*Mythologies* 117–18). But all the meanings of this phrase (historical, zoological, literary, and so on) are put at a distance when the phrase appears in the context of a Latin grammar, as an example to illustrate the agreement of the predicate:

> The meaning loses its value, but keeps its life, from which the form of the myth will draw its nourishment. The meaning will be for the form like an instantaneous reserve of history, a tamed richness, which it is possible to call and dismiss in a sort of rapid alternation: the form must constantly be able to be rooted again in the meaning and to get there what nature it needs for its nutriment; above all, it must be able to hide there. It is this constant game of hide-and-seek between the meaning and the form which defines myth.
>
> (*Mythologies* 118)

"Myth tends towards proverbs," concludes Barthes, and what Blake seems to be doing, with some of his proverbs, is disrupting the game of hide-and-seek by slowing down the rapid alternation. Blake's proverbs can draw our attention to the mechanisms by which, in using other proverbs (including some of his own), we *exploit* the literal sense. Consider

The cut worm forgives the plow.
(*MHH* 7)

A worm has a compartmentalized body so that, unlike most animal species and unlike human beings, both parts can survive if it is cut in two. In this sense the cut worm can be said to forgive the plough. This peculiar fact (it is far more peculiar to the worm than "you can lead a horse to water but you can't make it drink" is peculiar to horses) urges us to search for a figurative sense for the statement, in order that we may envisage contexts for its use as a proverb, but it also makes it difficult for us to find such a sense. Perhaps we can understand (and therefore use) the proverb to mean "Opposition is True Friendship": openly expressed wrath is better than deviously inflicted wounds. Or we could read it in the quite different spirit of the Clod of Clay. Or, if we respond to the sexual connotations of "plow" and "worm," we can translate the "cut worm" as the vagina and see the proverb as a curious Freudian allegory of sexual differentiation, pleasure and fertility—in which case the proverb is also another form of popular speech, a riddle (see Dundes 103–18). However we interpret it this proverb is a kind of riddle, with various and scarcely compatible solutions. In effect, the peculiar fact to which the proverb literally refers continues to force itself on our attention as it goes on forcing us to attempt translations (the similarity to Blake's strategy in the third stanza of "London" will be evident). It is scarcely possible to find anything that can be substituted for "worm" ("starfish"?). Perhaps then this is the meaning of the proverb, the clue to the kind of occasion on which it might be appropriately used: when you want to say that an unbelievable, apparently incomparable event is indeed incomparable—it is like the fact that the cut worm forgives the plough! Has Blake found a foolproof way of saying that to generalize is to be an idiot?

Proverbs, unlike performative utterances strictly defined, are not self-referring. But they are an exericise of power. And like the performatives of religious and legal ritual they are quotations, acts of speech that gain their authority from having been said before and whose only function is to be repeated at appropriate moments, though the definition of the appropriate moment is not so clear for proverbs as it is for ritual performatives. Proverbs do not perform the acts to which they refer, but to know their meaning in any real sense is to know the occasions on which they may appropriately be spoken. So for both proverbs and performatives there is a peculiarly inextricable relation between meaning and use. This is notably the case for those proverbs that imply, or seem to imply, an analogy between humans and (other) animals: the nature of the analogy with human situations is always *waiting* to be clarified. Some of Blake's proverbs—unlike most normal proverbs—aim to reveal that this is the case by *keeping* us waiting.

Of course, Blake knew very well that he was producing aphorisms and not proverbs. He ironically emphasizes the gap between the two by inventing a society in which his aphorisms become proverbs by utopian fiat:

> As I was walking among the fires of hell, delighted with the enjoyments of Genius; which to Angels look like torment and insanity. I collected some of their Proverbs: thinking that as the sayings used in a nation, mark its character, so the Proverbs of Hell, shew the nature of Infernal wisdom better than any description of buildings or garments.
>
> (*MHH* 6)

This is Blake playing at field-work anthropologist. He is drawing attention to the gaps between the elite and the popular, the invented and the inherited, sayings and writings, proverbs and aphorisms—by denying them. Of course these are distinct distinctions, and none of the distinctions is an absolute one. Authored aphorisms like Blake's can get into general circulation, to be handed down from generation to generation, becoming proverbs. And within the field of proverbs themselves there has always been interchange between oral and written transmission. The Book of Proverbs itself was probably a collection of existing sayings that were then spoken back into popular English usage by generations of parsons and readers. These heavenly proverbs joined a popular proverbial wisdom that was often less conservative, ethically black and white, patriarchal. Blake draws on these more flexible and ironic sayings to produce, in his *Marriage*, a written parody of the services of the Book of Common Prayer.[15] The title page announces the work as a marriage ceremony, and it turns out to be the script for a *rite de passage* in which the liminal phase expands uncontrollably.

Proverbs are that form of artistic speech most widely diffused in everyday discourse; they are part of conversation. But they are a part of conversation designed to put a stop to conversation, replies that do

---

15. A comparison of the increasingly complex and ironic senses of the word *fool* in Proverbs, *The Oxford Dictionary of English Proverbs*, and Blake's *Marriage* is instructive in this context. Blake's most direct work on Proverbs is, appropriately, about discursive power: "A Poison Tree" surely grows out of "A soft answer turneth away wrath."

not ask for replies. The speaker does not take responsibility for his speech but lays claim to its power by virtue of being the mouthpiece of "what is said." In working with proverbs and answering them Blake is not simply proposing alternative proverbs—proverbs of hell against proverbs of the church; he is questioning the finality of proverbs as such, refusing their authority, insisting on replying to these replies, on revealing what proverbs try to conceal, that they are acts of speech among others. Consequently his own proverbs, unlike most real proverbs, are evidently questionable answers. They rouse the faculties to act, provoking argument not just within our minds but between us. Malcolm Bradbury demonstrates this very nicely in *The History Man* (109, 163), where Howard Kirk and Miss Callender each attempts to claim the authority of "sooner murder an infant in its cradle than nurse unacted desires" (*MHH* 10) for themselves and discover that Blake refuses to provide a common sense, a proverb. Both of them want, quite inevitably, to believe that the proverb is a way of saying something else: even the self-styled libertarian Howard does not believe that, in invoking the proverb, he is really talking about infanticide. David Simpson, in his fascinating description of his own experience of reading this aphorism, concludes:

> The point is, of course, that there is no simple reading, and recognising the reflexiveness of this line may well be the closest we can get to its author's purpose. As a performative aphorism, it demands a context to decide its credibility, what Austin might have called its "happiness", and we must bring that context with us. In other words, we become its author.
>
> (*Irony* 85)

I would only add that Bradbury is right to have set the aphorism loose in the sexual and political conflicts of his novel where people in relationships become its authors, and where neither a common sense nor a range of senses to suit all pockets turns out to be available. To "interpret" such a proverb is to do what an orchestra does to a musical score or actors do to a play text rather than what critics think they do to a piece of literature. Perhaps the best analogy is with Blake's own method of producing and distributing his illuminated books. As Stephen Carr writes elsewhere in this volume, no "original" version of a Blake plate can be established, so there are no "copies"; even "the stereotyped 'original' on the etched plate exists only as an idealized ab-

straction." It is as if, in the kind of relationship that his method establishes between stereotype and "copy," Blake is aware in advance of
the figurative sense that the word *stereotype* was to acquire. And his
work with performatives and proverbs suggests that he was also
aware in advance of the semantic history of the word *cliché* in English
as it first gained its sense of "a stereotype block" and later became "a
stereotype expression, a commonplace phrase."[16]

16. These are entries under *cliché* in *The Shorter Oxford English Dictionary*. Christopher Ricks has many useful observations on this subject.

3

The Book of Urizen and the Horizon of the Book

PAUL MANN

If you have formd a Circle to go into
Go into it yourself & see how you would do

FIRST BOOK

A revision of the biblical Genesis, *The Book of Urizen* is also a book about books.[1] Bookish forms confront us everywhere: in the books Urizen engraves and half offers, half withholds (plates 1 and 5), in the bicolumnar text that replicates the printed forms of bibles and the two-up format of open books.[2] *The Book of Urizen* is precisely a book: not songs, vision, prophecy, dream, or emanation. It extends concerns articulated in *The Marriage of Heaven and Hell*, with its infernal printing house and its plates on the making of plates, and anticipates the persistent implication of Urizen in books in Blake's later work. Urizen is the inventor, the archetypal maker of books, and through Urizen Blake examines the ontology of books. But why press the ontology of books in a revision of Genesis, a book about the world's origin? Is Blake investigating the Urizenic and therefore potentially oppressive features of all bookmaking and book culture—the book's historical power to "impose"? Is he being self-critical about his own complicity in book culture? Is this a question of a creation myth that appears

---

1. Certainly *The Book of Urizen* has a much wider allusive reach. My focus on Genesis is meant not to deny these connections but as a means of focusing on "first" books. For more on *Urizen*'s links with Genesis see Tannenbaum (201–24).

2. I have used copy G of *The Book of Urizen,* in the convenient edition of the Eassons, for my discussion.

in a book, the "First Book"—*the* Book, the Bible? Is Blake calling into question all creative enterprises, whether they be of universes or of books?

Mallarmé: "Tout au monde existe pour aboutir à un livre" (Everything in the world exists to end in a book). Perhaps because it began in a book. Islam speaks of a "people of the book," and one could take that preposition in one of the senses of the preposition in Blake's title, *The Book of Urizen*: made of, generated from. *The Book of Urizen* involves a critique of Genesis *as* biblical, a creation not only in but *of* the Book; and since, as many commentators note, Blake's revision of Genesis identifies it with the Fall, Fall and Book are also identified. The question of Genesis intersects that of the genesis of books as an investigation of origin itself as a ground of loss.[3] In the genetico-historical word-world of *The Book of Urizen*, to *unfold* dark visions of torment is necessarily to *explicate* Urizen as a book, and as the book of loss. This essay will consider that mutual implication, the folding into each other of Urizen and books in a book concerned with human origins. The hypothesis I will test is that the book is an ontological horizon, the horror-zone of the fallen world. The question that must follow from this hypothesis is whether any conception of the horizon— strictly speaking, any book—will itself be implicated and bound within the horizon.

BIOBIBLIOGRAPHY

In the frontispiece Urizen sits on a book, rests his arms on books, holds the tools of bookmaking in either hand. His "wings" are mosaic

---

3. In an epilogue to an unpublished lecture, Harry Berger, Jr., writes that the Old Testament grows and changes "during the period of the divided kingdom, during the Babylonian exile and captivity, and after the return and rebuilding. Its message to all those who possess the promised land, or who long for it, is clear: to possess the land is to lose the promise. Possession is loss; *ergo*, loss must be a kind of possession, a kind of promise; losing the land must be a condition for regaining the promise. The text enshrines the loss for us to see, for us to have, for us to share." A community of loss is founded, and furthermore it is "the text that supplants the promised land. The text is the first Book of Loss, presenting itself to us as the abiding revision of what it abidingly absentiates. . . . In the portability of the text lies the seed of the one community that abides, that can gather metaphorically around the metaphoric center, that can fold itself up into the scriptural sheepskin, into the holy of holies, and keep moving on." See also Easson and Easson *Urizen* 81.

tablets and/or illegibly engraved (in-grave) tombstones and/or the doors of a stony cavern, the entrance to the book through which the reader passes. The bilateral symmetry and spatial organization of the frontispiece seem, at first, projections of the physical geometry of Urizen's own embodied form: the book as human representation. But the frontispiece declares what will not begin to occur until plate 10, when Los binds Urizen into that bodily form. This is more than a matter of foreshadowing or narrative convenience, more than a result of the fact that the artist needs to imagine Urizen before Urizen can shrink into his body. The very insistence on books in the frontispiece gives the book an eerie precedence, as if to say: to take on a body, Urizen must first be a book. Urizen is bound inside these doubly bordered pages; they constitute his horizon. To be imprisoned in stone ("astonished," plate 4) or to float in the waters of materialism (the fallen world in general, but also the "wash" with which plate 6 is colored); to strain at the page's margins only to find oneself in another page, pushing its englobed horizon back into yet another page (plates 23 and 24): in various ways every plate replicates the strictures of the frontispiece. Book-space must be organized before Urizen can be conceived, and he is conceived within it.

In the first chapter, the Eternals are heard but not seen. Their state must be described largely through negatives ("Earth was not: nor globes of attraction," plate 3). They are faceless and fading echoes, unembodied, precisely invisible. But to them it is Urizen who grows increasingly obscure. As he comes into focus as a fallen form—that is, as he becomes increasingly clear to the reader, who is thereby also defined as fallen—as he divides, measures, and paginates the space that will become his own and human reality, the Eternals see him as a shadow, a vacuum, a void. By setting himself apart from the Eternals, Urizen makes himself the space of Eternity's absence; his book, marking its difference from Eternity, also conceives itself as an absence. Eternity is a perspective from which the book is seen as a hole torn in the seamless fabric of Eternity; from its own side, the book eclipses Eternity with its shadowy volume. As Geoffrey Hartman writes, "The Bible's 'in the beginning' [is] a limiting concept, which tells us not to think about what went before" (*Fate* 119).

As Urizen falls outside Eternity—indeed, causes "outside" by enclosing and creating his interior space—so Eternity is excluded, thrown outside the horizon of the book.[4] Inside and outside—in the Bible, creation involves a series of divisions: light separated from darkness, females from males, one generation from another. In *Urizen* horizontals and verticals are pushed apart (plate 15), right- and left-hand columns are divided, pages occur in a series; fallen space is organized as a system of enclosures.[5] This organization displaces Eternity. Urizen usurps Eternity by leaving it; he defines it as outside, prior, lost; he establishes the mutual absence of Eternity and fallen reality. What was seamless and present is now made divided and prior by Urizen's violent creative activity.

Again, book and body continually intersect. Urizen is bound (by Los and as *Urizen*); Los's eternal life is ob-literated (15); "shrinking" may encompass a pun on inking, and Urizen "hiding in surging / Sulphureous fluid his phantasies" (12) seems a typically Blakean allusion to the acid bath of platemaking (also, as David Simpson notes, an image of masturbation); in plate 3, Urizen's thunders "str*etch* out across / The dread [dead/read] world." The globe of blood section (16–18) can be read as a parable of papermaking: paper is a weave of "fibres" that becomes an external surface, "Pale as a cloud of snow," onto which mental activity is projected. Even the geological upheavals of the early plates are associated with books. One need only note that the flat-sided steep of *The Marriage of Heaven and Hell* (6–7) is both mosaic tablet and copper plate—*Urizen* speaks of "books form'd of metals" (plate 4, copy C)—to recall Blake's intense awareness of the materiality of his production. In *The Marriage* Blake proposed a phys-

---

4. Note the insistent syntax of interiors, for instance on plate 5: "In living creations," "In the flames of eternal fury,'" "In whirlwinds & cataracts of blood," "In fierce anguish & quenchless flames," "in incessant labour," "In howlings & pangs & fierce madness," "in burning fires," "In despair and the shadows of death." "And a roof vast petrific around, / On all sides he fram'd: like a womb": literally solid ground, metaphorically the human skull, finally the copper plate itself.

5. *Songs Of Innocence and Of Experience* involves a meditation on the dual nature of enclosure. Innocence is enclosed as a protected state. The frontispiece of *Innocence* depicts a sheltering wood; the echoing green is hedged round and contains inward-turning rings of children under an overarching tree; the infant of "The Cradle Song" is contained in its canopied crib, surrounded by draperies and hovered over by its mother. These enclosures are images of Identity in its infant state, Eternity as the in-itselfness of individuals, the infinite in the finite. But in *Experience* enclosure is all restriction, imprisonment, and it is not distinguished from the open space of its own frontispiece: Newtonian absolute space is the most restrictive prison of all.

ical, sensual enjoyment that is, in part, the enjoyment of *The Marriage* itself and a mode of spiritual activity. In *Urizen*, however, Blake explores the terror of book and body as a "wide world of solid obstruction" (plate 4, copy C). What the engraved book and body obstruct is Eternity, and they obstruct it as writing over speech. If *Urizen* begins as a series of speeches—indeed, opens as a *call heard* gladly and taken as dictation—it turns rapidly into narrative.[6] The Eternals' voices, always only echoes, fade and die out. (Urizen himself speaks only in plate 4, copy C, a plate dropped from most other copies. Curiously, this is also the plate that directs itself most explicitly to the constitution of his book.) Writing, specifically book writing, both traces and displaces eternal *logos*. Urizen's Book obliterates Eternity, defines it as what has been lost (from the Book).

Perhaps we encounter here something like what Derrida encounters in Rousseau's *Confessions*. *The Book of Urizen* describes a lost and equivocally lamented origin, but an origin that the book itself obscures and, ultimately, erases. "The universe (which others call the Library)" (Borges 51) is an exclusive and "dangerous supplement," a horizon in which

> [t]here has never been anything but writing; there have never been anything but supplements, substitutive significations which could only come forth in a chain of differential references, the "real" supervening, and being added only while taking on meaning from a trace and from an invocation of the supplement, etc. And thus to infinity, for we have read, *in the text*, that the absolute present, Nature, that which words like "real mother" name, have always already escaped, have never existed; that what opens meaning and language is writing as the disappearance of natural presence.
>
> (Derrida *Grammatology* 159)

And thus from Eternity . . . the disappearance of eternal presence: for by writing, that presence is "always already" lost beyond the book's

---

6. "Eternals, I hear your call gladly, / Dictate swift winged words." If the Preludium contradicts my sense of the effacing of speech, it does not do so unequivocally. I find this (mock?) heroic invocation of *logos* qualified by three details: 1) the sources of *Urizen* in books—the invocation itself is a bookish trope, learned from heroic literature and, most importantly, from *Paradise Lost*; 2) by the "time" Blake "hears" this call, the Eternals are themselves fallen—*The Book of Urizen* continually calls into question their perspective on Urizen; and 3) the plate's illustration, which depicts a maternal figure leading a naked babe *into* the fallen world of the book.

horizon. It is suddenly as if Eternity were not only prior, but never was. (Thel could not retreat into Innocence because her passage into Experience effaced it; her regression could only reproduce Experience.) Urizen's procedure is always to bind (be bound), enclose (be enclosed), construct (be constructed as) an interior space and, once inside his text-body, *"there is nothing outside of the text"* (*Il n'y a pas de hors-texte*; Derrida *Grammatology* 158). Eventually, in plate 16, the Eternals themselves will be netted within this horizon, and one of them will engrave the englobed surface of the page.

BINDING URIZEN

Seeing Urizen as a void, the Eternals "avoid / The petrific abominable chaos" (3). Their revulsion is the co-author of Urizen's vacuity. Moreover, by failing to embrace him the Eternals are themselves voided. They become the absence they behold. Binding Urizen backfires.

Los seems at first the agent of the Eternals' desire to contain Urizenic chaos, but he turns out to be Urizen's unwilling agent. By creating the fallen world (book, supplement, horizon) Urizen provides for and indeed generates Los's activity. Los's antithetical posture toward Urizen is belied by the fundamentally Urizenic nature of his activity. Since separation, isolation of selfhood, and containment were invented by Urizen, binding Urizen is Urizenic. Los inscribes Urizen in a horizon circumscribed by and as Urizen himself. If one sees Urizen as various discourses of the fallen world—a "universe of discourse": epistemology, theology, morality, history, psychology, physics, politics, aesthetics, etc.: a sort of primal episteme—Los learns the language of these discourses and writes Urizen in it. If Urizen seems an Old Testament Jehovah it is partly because Los, a co-author of the Bible, has written him thus, in forms generated from Urizen himself. Indeed, one can easily imagine the Preludium written by Los: he is the "first" writer to take Eternal (as it turns out, fallen) dictation; he unfolds dark visions of torment by explicating the Urizenic body.

What this means, clearly, is that Los "becomes" Urizen. The bond between them, their mutual mirroring (witness plate 13) has often been noted. Los is "smitten with astonishment" (10): he becomes what he beholds, a stone, as stony Urizen. His own postures frequently ape the visual vocabulary of Urizenic contraction: squatting, hunkering, straining against bonds. In Blake's text we must reunite the mental and biological meanings of the verb *to conceive*: reality is that which we conceive (fallen reality is a "conceit" of the selfhood). By conceiving Urizen urizenically, Los establishes his essential complicity with Urizen, enters the horizon, and is lost.

> 2. *All the myriads of Eternity:*
> *All the wisdom & joy of life:*
> *Roll like a sea around him.*
> *Except what his little orbs*
> *Of sight by degrees unfold.*
>
> 3. *And now his eternal life*
> *Like a dream was obliterated*
> (15)

"And now . . . was," as if to say: Los is immediately past. By (re)writing Urizen, in effect by taking Urizenic dictation, Los ob-literates and los-es himself. By binding Urizen he binds himself. "No more Los beheld Eternity" (20): now he groans and rolls like Urizen, smites and is smitten; "The Eternal Prophet & Urizen clos'd" (c-los-d); Los stands divided before the death-image of Urizen that he himself (re)created and which serves him as a mirror (10–16). And this activity continues: Los bears his own divided image in Enitharmon and binds his son, Orc, the third generation of the Fall. The forms are constant.

In *The Book of Urizen* the divine *fiat* is Urizen's bibliogenetic conception, not a pure and unequivocal utterance of *logos* but origin precisely as supplement and fall. Urizen falls from logological presence *as* the Book. The biblical *fiat* is properly, tautologically, translated as the *fiat* of the Book. Fallen reality is fundamentally tautological: Genesis is genesis. The world is a representation and what is represented in it as cosmogonical origin is bound in Urizen's shadowy, obstructive volume.[7]

---

7. The problem of origin is addressed in a highly relevant manner by Leslie Brisman (224–75). Brisman is chiefly concerned with the five accounts of the Fall in *The Four Zoas*, and concludes that the accounts are not only belated, retrospective, but also prospective and (re)generative. Paraphrasing Foucault, he writes, "Origin, for Blake, is . . . the way in which man in general—Albion—articulates himself upon the already-begun" (228). *The Four Zoas* is an exploration not only of the Fall but of the potential for resurrection as well, a potential rigorously excluded from the grimmer confines of *The Book of Urizen*. Whereas the Zoas try to regenerate spiritual unity through their accounts, the Eternals relate to division by revulsion, confinement and mutual exclusion. There is no articulation of a hoped-for resurrection upon the already-begun in *Urizen*; projection is not (re)generation but only the replication of error.

REPRODUCTION

The Urizenic genesis is the production or rather the continual reproduction of selfhood. What Urizen invents are, in effect, the mechanisms of reproduction. Urizen's body is a reproduction of chaos; Los's
reproduction of this chaos is the "first" moment in a historical series
of reproductions in and from *The Book of Urizen*. The construction of
Urizen's body reproduces the violent geological upheavals of the
early plates; in every case the response to perceived chaos is binding.
The binding of Orc proves that Los's response to Urizen is not anomalous, that binding will continue indefinitely. In the Orc cycle each
generation of sons is bound by its fathers and becomes a generation
of fathers binding its sons; in bibliological terms, each generation is
encoded as a people of the book and in turn reproduces reality in
terms of the book. The Hebraic week of Chapter IX is a contracted
repetition of Urizenic embodiment. Derrida: "Everything begins as
reproduction" ("Freud" 92); in *The Book of Urizen* everything begins as
Urizenic reproduction.

The Los of *Urizen* is a writer caught in the intertextual nets of what
he has read, and he recasts those nets around him—netting, along
the way, Blake. In *The Book of Urizen* Blake considers his complicity in
Urizen's project, mirrors himself in both Urizen and Los. The production of *Urizen* is a critique of the production of Urizen (the reverse
may also hold true). Blake implicates himself in Urizenic reproduction: if the writing of origin is itself the obliteration of origin, if the
Book necessarily conflates origin and fall, then Blake writing *Urizen* is
Blake repeating Los's errors, urizenically (re)conceiving the Fall and
himself as fallen; we the readers follow in his wake. In the text's
words, Urizen creates globes of attraction, inky black holes into
which all forms, all formal activity will be drawn.

The reader also falls: the later equation, "they became what they
beheld," includes us. If we tend to imagine ourselves outside the
book, looking in, we are very much like the Eternals. The outside is
excluded; *Urizen* has deconstructed it. In *The Book of Urizen* all action
is reaction and paradoxically synthetic: not a matter of individual,
subjective literary response, of my reading as distinct from your reading, but of determined response, readers generated within a horizon
of response. Barthes:

This "I" which approaches the text is already itself a plurality of other texts, of codes which are infinite or, more precisely, lost (whose origin is lost). . . . Subjectivity is a plenary image, with which I may be thought to encumber the text, but whose deceptive plenitude is merely the wake of all the codes which constitute me, so that my subjectivity has ultimately the generality of stereotypes.

(S/Z 10)

The Book of Urizen conceives (of) books in their fundamental and perpetually replicated forms, and it conceives reading in the same manner; even as we read *Urizen* it is reading us. *Urizen* sees the reader within its own horizon: humanity is collective, reduced to the "generality of stereotypes," an undifferentiated mass of replicated bodies powerless to do anything other than what culture dictates. The reader is conceived as one atom in the race of the people of the book, one moment in a vast, historical, determined and determining, reproductive succession of readings, always inscribed within the horizon.

HUMAN FORM DIVINE

If *Urizen* sees humanity as a chaos of representations, it seems to see itself as unique. *The Book of Urizen* is very much a book, it participates in the history of book-forms, but it is also special, unlike any other book in history. Blake's method of bookmaking, as Stephen Carr emphasizes elsewhere in this volume, insists on difference: no one has ever made books in precisely this way, and no two copies of *Urizen* are exactly alike.

One of the histories generated from Urizen is repetition by division in the book trade, the reproduction of Urizenic forms in the industrial, economic horizon of the publishing industry. Blake's method of engraving and his production of handmade, limited editions, each copy of which tends to differ in significant details from the others, have often been taken as a critique of the mechanical reproduction of art.[8] But in this "First Book" uniqueness might be problematic: *Urizen* is nearly as isolated as Urizen himself. The unique book is quite pos-

---

8. See, for example, Morris Eaves, "Blake and the Artistic Machine: An Essay in Decorum and Technology." Much has been made of the differences between Blake's books and industrially produced books, but often at the expense of noting essential similarities. The self-criticism evidenced in *The Book of Urizen* might also function at this level.

sibly a version of Urizenic selfhood. It is as if Blake's very reluctance to reproduce his book in industrial forms reproduces it in Urizenic forms, binds it into a Urizenic body.

There is a more hopeful reading. If the book is a body, it is also possible that Blake saw it not simply as Urizen but as a version of an incarnated Jesus, a "human form divine," words made flesh. This reading should still face the argument of obliterated origins, flesh effacing the word, but one does find in Blake's text a certain indifference to the more doctrinal features of the incarnation of *logos*: "God only Acts & Is, in existing beings or Men" (*MHH* 16). Blake's books were limited editions; Jesus spoke directly to few men but gave rise to a global religion whose promise is resurrection. Resurrection is prefigured, at the very least, in two worldly forms (visionary art would be the third). On one hand, Jesus is resurrected as the Church: communion is a kind of *sparagmos,* a division that annihilates the physical body in order to reorganize it as a spiritual body, the body of the faithful, the "members" of the Church itself. On the other hand, the second body is the Book—flesh made words, so to speak—the Gospel disseminated rather as bread and wine among its readers. The problem in both cases is one of mediation, legal regulation, encoding, interpriestation: witness the parable of the Ancient Poets in *The Marriage of Heaven and Hell.* But *The Book of Urizen* puts the problem in more radical terms: it is not simply that communion-reading degenerates through the interference of priestcraft but that the "first" book is Urizen's and already stipulates that all subsequent incarnations will be Urizenic reproductions.

Urizen sees all books, all bookish bodies, as dangerous supplements, all human forms bound in books, the Urizenic horizon as inevitable; it also implicitly maintains its connection with the human form divine. It situates itself in an Old Testament universe of fall and diaspora and in *Paradise Lost,* but other books are foreshadowed, conspicuous in their absence: the New Testament, *Paradise Regained. The Book of Urizen* is, in other words, at least twofold: both a horror-zone of selfhood and a *saving remnant,* a limit of contraction. The body is trapped in a horrible horizon but holds, in seed form, the hope or potential for progress toward Eternity or Organized Innocence. *Felix culpa.*

The text's force is that both implications are kept constantly, and rather unequally, in play. The very isolation of the book's body proposes it as a saving remnant, but the saving remnant is continually challenged, seen continually as generating more and more sophisticated forms or strategies of constriction. It is a limit of contraction, but that limit can reproduce itself indefinitely. This is not either/or but an insistence that the saving remnant is indeed horrible—horribly necessary, given the fallen world, but horrible nonetheless. Simply to repeat Blakean maxims about firm bounding lines and minute particulars as if they were purely benevolent is to avoid the persistent threat implicit in bounding and particularization. Bounding is binding. *The Book of Urizen* is crucial to a reading of Blake because it makes this reductive equation, because it both invokes and effaces hope, because poetry itself is seen here as loss, obliteration, absence.

The task then is to comprehend the limits implicit in delimitation, in human lineaments, in the covers of beautiful books; to grasp the book's sacrifice to space and time, to a succession of divisions and therefore of deaths. The horizon is a prison. If it can also be made to reveal a transcendental exit, *The Book of Urizen* suppresses this hope. This text begins and ends *in medias res*, and Urizen makes it rigorously difficult to discover the end of the golden string. In Night 9 of *The Four Zoas* the escape from the horizon is accomplished in part by Urizen's self-annihilation, the destruction of the body and the end of the book.[9] The overwhelming difficulty of this apocalypse has never per-

---

9. Urizen's self-annihilation should not be confused with any gesture of interpretive modesty, with a criticism that conceals the "I" of its narrative by writing the text or the author as the subject of every sentence (see below, footnote 12). Some of Urizen's guises—modesty, compassion, scientific objectivity, self-effacement—only reinforce his hegemony. As Terry Eagleton writes:

When history begins to 'think itself' as historiography, material production as political economy, quotidian behaviour as philosophy or psychology, the rupture thus established between thought and reality is not the guarantee of a knowledge, though it is the pre-condition of one. It may well be a merely 'provisional' rupture, an opening through which the practice unites more intimately with itself. That this is so, indeed, is particularly evident in the case of criticism. For criticism's self-separation from its object is a kind of feint—a mere prelude to reuniting with it more completely. Its analytic distantiation of its object is the parody of a knowledge—a means of 'possessing' it more closely, dissolving itself into a oneness with it. The end of criticism is to efface itself before the text, vicariously naturalising its own troubled 'artifice' by its power to elicit the 'naturalness' of the text itself. In a spiral of mutual reinforcements, the literary text naturalises experience, critical practice naturalises the text, and the theories of that practice legitimate the 'naturalness' of criticism.

(18)

haps been adequately grasped. But in *The Book of Urizen* the only escape is to close the book, and that is no escape at all.

CORPOREAL FRIENDS

Blake calls the activity that uncovers books, reconceives Eternity, organizes innocence: poetic genius. Poetic genius is the revelatory perception of Eternity through the closed spaces of the fallen world. It is an interpretive act, an act of de-limitation, a definition that de-defines. Not all poems manifest poetic genius: in *The Book of Urizen* the poet Los is recalcitrantly Urizenic, and there are many poems—Wordsworth's, for instance (see Blake's annotations to Wordsworth, E665–67)—that, by Blake's standards, only replicate the fallen condition. Poems such as these require a re-visionary reading capable of seeing through fallen text-nature into eternal alterity. The salient example is, of course, Blake's *Milton*, a revisionary reading of *Paradise Lost*. Poetic genius explicates or unfolds dark visions of torment in such a way that physical bodies are reconceived as spiritual bodies, restrictive horizons or texts as windows. Poetic genius attempts to break through the chaotic, eclipsing shadows of absence into the lost light of presence that they obscure.

One can discover poetic genius in a reading of "Auguries of Innocence," a poem that is largely a series of couplet fragments. Each fragment is the perception of a minute particular; the paired lines counterpose sin or error with punishment or correction; microcosm opens into macrocosm, fall into resurrection. The poetic principle is synecdoche, but the whole is not the poem itself: unity is rather a certain state of seeing-being, a certain spiritual potential glimpsed through the horizon of the poem. To rearrange the poem, as Erdman has done (E493–95), toward the goal of some general editorial unity is essentially to miss the point. We are invited to see the fragments *as* fragments, isolated incidents of wrong- or right-doing that echo from or toward Eternity, and then to read through them. Each couplet is a grain of sand, an eternal hour of reading.

> He who shall teach the Child to Doubt
> The rotting Grave shall neer get out
> He who respects the Infants faith
> Triumphs over Hell & Death

. . . .

The Questioner who sits so sly
Shall never know how to Reply
He who replies to words of Doubt
Doth put the light of Knowledge out
. . . .

A riddle or the Crickets Cry
Is to Doubt a fit Reply
. . . .

He who Doubts from what he sees
Will neer Believe do as you Please
If the Sun & Moon should doubt
Theyd immediately Go out

(E492)

"Auguries" describes the tautological, kangaroo-court system of the fallen world and at the same time prescribes its cure: to choose blessing over cursing, generosity over possession and imposition, integrity over disintegration, faith over doubt. I have cited those couplets that deal explicitly with faith and doubt partly in order to introduce their analogue in *Jerusalem*, the famous counterposition of faith and demonstration (e.g., 45.46), an antinomy that could be translated into poetic genius and Urizenic discourse. The question that concerns me—in a sense, the doubt I wish to raise—is whether they are mutually exclusive.

The Book of Urizen raises this question forcefully. By radically identifying book, body, discourse and fallen world, *Urizen* contradicts the more hopeful dialectic of the "Auguries." *The Book of Urizen* asks whether the very forms in which a visionary poet works are not ultimately futile, whether poetic apocalypse is not a contradiction in terms, whether poets are not doomed from the outset to reproduce Urizen's body and (as) the fallen world. Were "Auguries of Innocence" all that Blake left us such questions might not pertain. But one imagines a poet who throughout his career had to work with the incisive negations of *Urizen*, a poet who seems never to have identified text and resurrection absolutely but always suspected that resurrection to unity might be accomplished only by passing through books and leaving them behind.

Blake's readers frequently seize on the hope suggested in "poetic genius," in a perception of the saving remnant as residual presence and potential resurrection. If this hope is more explicit in the ironic counterstatements of "Auguries," in the sensual energy of *The Marriage*, in the revolutionary enthusiasm of *America* or *Europe*, or in the apocalypse of *Jerusalem* than in the relentless enclosures of *The Book of Urizen*, at least one reader has found hope there as well. W. J. T. Mitchell writes of plate 26,

> Blake's refusal to make any concession to the rules of aesthetic distance or disinterestedness in the final version of his pictorial narrative is only logical in view of the strenuous participation he has demanded from his audience throughout the book, and it is his way of suggesting that he wants something more than the intelligent contemplation of his artifacts. . . . [T]he prophetic tradition refuses to allow the energies of art to be contained in a magic circle of mythic, archetypal irrelevance, and . . . to put them in this magic circle is to reenact the crime of Los and abandon Orc on the streets of London. The abandoned children of the imagination do not need our help so much as we need theirs, a point that Blake makes explicitly when he shows the same orphan . . . leading the aged, crippled wanderer of "London" (1794) and *Jerusalem* 84 (1818). If *Urizen* begins by showing us in the Preludium the child being led into the fallen world by a protective adult, it concludes with a vision of that child alone, now ready to show the adult the way out of that world.
>
> (*Composite* 163)

One might like to believe in the transcendental gesture Mitchell indicates; *Urizen* itself seems rather to enforce enclosure, to insist that all attempts to find a way out of the text-world will only deposit one inside another imprisoning horizon.[10] In plate 26 the double border,

---

10. Another of the preferred escape routes from Urizenic oppression is through laughing it off. Robert E. Simmons, who is as concerned as I am with the text's most restrictive dimensions, also finds in a number of the plates a distinctly satirical or parodic element. "Blake is often, like Joyce, a visionary of the comic, of change, of 'eternal life sprung' (II, 1). The solemn, the painful, the tragic may ultimately be seen as only food for laughter" (167). Certainly a satirical reading is available, but as with all other responses one must question its visionary adequacy and ask if Urizen's recuperative strategies will not succeed against it. When can one be sure that Urizen will not laugh last and best? Much satire can be said to function as a kind of double discourse that identifies us with or as the object of the satire and at the same time allows us to step back from that object by being in on the joke, the ironic truth. But perhaps the most sophisticated satire also works against the smug securities of that separation. In Gulliver's fourth voyage, the Yahoos are a clear parody of human savagery, and Gulliver sees them as such, but he is only a reader of satire of the first order; in the second order the Houyhnhnms and Gulliver himself become satirical targets. There is something in the Houyhnhnms of the Laputan academicians, some satirical undercutting of even the

the bisecting shadow, the closed and framing door, and the intensely rigid and pious posture of this "Orc" child all hark back to the bounded space of the frontispiece, the "original" ground of the Fall. And to pass through this door is, in a sense, only to enter the plate lying behind it and to find oneself with yet another figure of Urizen bound (in nets of religion that define the child's piety), repeating his own posture of plates 4 and 12 and the posture of his own "child," Grodna, rising in plate 24—a posture Orc himself assumes elsewhere as he rises into the fallen world (see *America* 2).

But my point is not that Mitchell has misinterpreted the plate. His reading is valid and, in any case, the son's light when he unfolds it depends on the organ that beholds it. It is also possible that the ex- plicitly negative constructions of *The Book of Urizen* do imply, as it were dialectically, a positive conception that is both conspicuous in its absence here and in relation to other Blake texts. Perhaps Mitchell is even "revising" the plate, as if the plate were the first line of an "Au- guries" couplet and his commentary the second, and this might be precisely the sort of reading *Urizen* calls for.

My primary concern is rather with criticism itself. Mitchell's dis- missal of an archetypal criticism that reinscribes a magic circle around Orc is very much to the point. One might consider much criticism the corporeal friend and therefore the spiritual enemy of the text: a criti- cism that, say, imposes some system on the text in the guise of expli- cating it, that forces the text through an ideological machine, that takes the text as its occasion while covertly signifying its own institu- tional values and practice. The question is whether all criticism must do this. And would it not be naive, in this age so sensitive to the workings of ideology and power, to deny that it must? (And is it not the sophisticated rejection of such naivety that makes one a sly ques-

---

best of eighteenth-century rationalism and ethnocentrism, and Gulliver's maniacal re- jection of his own humanity and rather overly literal embrace of horses is the knife Swift uses to do the cutting.

One may laugh at Urizen, but laughter doesn't necessarily let one off the hook. If Los's depiction-incarnation of Urizen contains strong satirical elements, Los nonethe- less remains bound with Urizen in the circle. To dismiss Urizen as a grotesque buffoon is to spurn him much as the Eternals do, and with similar consequences; which is to say that one is at least partly right about Urizen but wholly wrong about oneself, about the safety of one's distance from Urizen. There is always a kind of bottom-line bracketing of Urizen and his critic; critical methodology is Urizenic epistemology; at the level of *form* criticism cannot but *intend* Urizen.

tioner?) Is the hope that Mitchell or any critic invokes itself defined and bound in discursive forms that *Urizen* conceives as bookish, legalistic, institutional, horizontal? Is critical mediation of hope finally a priestly mode of imposition? Is criticism immune to Urizenic reproduction? How often do critics echo the Eternals' laments about Urizen's universe and, like the Eternals, thereby inscribe themselves in the horizon? How often do critics, like Los, replicate the Urizenic body? To what degree must criticism employ methodologies that allow it the illusion of objective distance from the text, a distance *Urizen* challenges and absorbs? Can poetic genius be taken on faith by discourses that are themselves largely defined as demonstration? If one takes poetic genius on faith, is one not therefore calling into question discourses that are not poetic? Can one, in good faith, demonstrate faith's supremacy over demonstration? Is criticism itself a writing that obliterates (textual) origins?[11] *The Book of Urizen* confronts these questions more directly than has any of its critics.

EXODUS

Urizen denies that the horizon can be transcended. It was Urizen's very desire to "transcend" Eternity that generated the fallen world. In Blake's text in general, most attempts at transcendental projects are doomed to failure. The moment this Genesis begins to open into Exodus, the book comes to a close. Indeed, given the consistently strident tone of the text, its closing lines are remarkably casual. Urizen's sons call him (his bookish body, his text-world) "Egypt, & left it." But this is the penultimate line; in the final line we are back inside originary chaos, englobed in the salt sea of textual *materia prima*; we are thrown back to the first plates and reread.

How then can exodus be conceived? Within such strictures as *The Book of Urizen* imposes, no other question seems so much to matter. But *Urizen* functions precisely as a critique of exodus (of Exodus). It is not a prophecy of evacuation or abandonment but of embrace. Where the Eternals lose Urizen and themselves by spurning him, the text

---

11. *The Book of Urizen* claims to be unreadable. One's very attempt to comprehend it is challenged by plate 5: Urizen tips his book toward the reader, and the reader discovers that its writing is illegible.

dwells with him on his own ground, in his bookish body, in his language. If the text subverts him it does so by representing him, possessing him, trying to out-Urizen Urizen, "With Demonstrative Science piercing Apollyon with his own bow" (*J* 12.14); the text transgresses the horizon by re-occupying it (to re-occupy is to occupy with a difference). Consider *The Book of Urizen* as the sort of text Barthes calls *scriptible*: "You cannot speak 'on' such a text, you can only speak 'in' it, *in its fashion*, enter into a desperate plagiarism" (*S/Z* 22). To do so is to risk self-condemnation to the history of replication, becoming, like Los, Urizen's mirror-image. But it might also be Los's very ability to enter the circle he has formed and see just how badly he does that enables him, in later works, to act differently.

Urizen is a book, and in Night 9 of *The Four Zoas* he must undergo self-annihilation.[12] So too, perhaps, must criticism: always an assumption of power, unable to refrain from reproducing the ideological horizon, criticism may be forced to turn against itself. Blake's persistent self-implication with Urizen and the increasingly atomized nature of his writing—disrupting or abandoning narrative and symbolic coherence, interrupting closure, leaving works in manuscript—

---

12. Blake's identification with Urizen and the later necessity of Urizen's self-annihilation suggest that Blake also sees the necessity of his own self-annihilation *as author*, "that somewhat decrepit deity of the old criticism" (Barthes, *S/Z* 111). (The Eternals paradoxically permit Los to bring Urizen to "life.") But criticism gets in his way: it reincarnates the author in book after book, in essay after essay (including this one), in "Blake Studies," as the subject of countless sentences, in a perpetual nomination (Blake's signature forged, as it were, by the critic) that keeps "Blake" the a priori subject of study. Recently, a more general attack on the subject has been pursued through conceptions of writing, *écriture*, "the end of the book and the beginning of writing," but, as Foucault notes, "the conception of *écriture* sustains the privileges of the author through the safeguard of the a priori; the play of representations that formed a particular image of the author is extended within a gray neutrality. The disappearance of the author . . . is held in check by the transcendental" ("Author" 20).

Foucault proposes to suspend the author in discourse, to anatomize him as an "'author-function' . . . tied to the legal and institutional systems that circumscribe, determine, and articulate the realm of discourses. . . . [T]he subject (and its substitutes) must be stripped of its creative role and analysed as a complex and variable function of discourse" (138). This seems to have something in common with the procedures of *The Book of Urizen*: "Blake" participates in Los's construction of the Urizenic subject but at the same time deconstructs the subject and, by implication, the author-function in which he must participate.

For criticism to engage in such a project it would have to do to "Blake" what Blake does to Urizen. And it would have to do it to itself: criticism would attempt to comprehend itself not as the practice of creative subjects (individual readers) but as a historical institution (assumption) of ideological power. Many writers are working in this area.

taken together with the call for self-annihilation in the later works, suggest that the exodus must pass through the destruction of the Book. No longer integral and identified—a lost emanation (*FZ* 4.7)— the read book becomes a body torn apart and consumed by a violence counter to that violence by which it was incarnated. The book as sacramental body: like Jesus or Osiris, it must undergo its own *sparagmos*. The book becomes a saving remnant by ceasing to be a book, by being read/conceived as a chaos of minute particulars, an anthology of fiery fragments. As Urizen causes a rupture in Eternity by covering it over with his bookish body, so this *ideal* reading would reveal Eternity by tearing holes in the book, anatomizing it for moments Satan cannot find, luminous details that discourse cannot circumscribe.

But perhaps this reading is not just an ideal. Perhaps it exists as a moment in discourse itself that discourse cannot find, a blind spot written and read as if by accident. This reading is by no means a system, a project, a new or jerryrigged methodology, a rhetorical gesture of deference to poetic genius. It is not the reading of some individual more gifted or trained at reading than some other. It is textuality at the level of language, an automatic disruption of ideology and bodily integrity that may or may not occur. Derrida:

> The writer writes *in* a language and *in* a logic whose proper system, laws, and life his discourse cannot dominate absolutely. He uses them only by letting himself, after a fashion and up to a point, be governed by the system.
>
> (*Grammatology* 158)

One cannot *avoid* the system, as the Eternals attempt to do, but at the same time no system is absolute. Urizen weeps because no one, not even Urizen himself, can maintain his laws. He cannot sustain himself indefinitely as his own worst enemy; he continually fails to establish total control. (Is this failure itself "sweet science"?) Language plays through one's writing, and at any moment it can release a safety valve. The pen slips, produces unexpected allusions, unintended puns, flashes of insight that one does not have "in" one and which disrupt, as though naturally, the flow of monological domination.

Derrida proposes a Sadean dialectic of freedom through submission in which "the person writing is inscribed in a determined textual system" (*Grammatology* 160); but by delivering oneself into the wine presses of that system, into the valuelessness of language, one may already be beside oneself, out of control, in the afterlife of the self-hood. Whether or not such a moment occurs in an interpretive essay it is not, strictly speaking, an interpretive moment but rather an anarchic impulse or convulsion by which discourse obliterates itself. Conceivably, in a universe that came into existence through a project of the selfhood, no project of selfhood can escape or transform it. Disruption might only occur by accident, by countererror, by an involuntary twitch that leaves one suddenly writing blindly in the rough basement, the stubborn structure of the language. In Urizen's universe no ideology, no critical system, no book purposely generates this moment. It happens or it does not, and when it does happen one might not even be aware of it.

And yet ultimately this "reading" too is circumscribed, for *textuality* has by now long since been installed in the Urizenic pantheon, and the most deconstructive reading imaginable would still be merely obligatory. In the history of criticism, *il n'y a pas de hors-texte* no longer represents the infinity of writing or even of some tastefully demystified Imagination; it is now nothing more than one of the myriad "signatures" of a dyscourse that has successfully put play to work supporting its own economy. Urizen is the name of an everpresent and overwhelmingly absorptive (Devouring) space, a space of contraction that extends as far as any of the watch fiends who contribute to this book or any other volume of academic criticism can see. In this entropic realm the difference between a positivist/historical and a poststructuralist reading is fictive; any ideological extreme can be circulated quite as profitably as any other. To interpret Blake is to surround him with interpretation, to neutralize him within the horizon; interpretation *is* the horizon, and from its perspective Vision must be equated absolutely with that which remains invisible. For me to indicate the ideality of some counter-Urizenic disruption is already to target it for destruction, in a kind of textual counterinsurgency operation, just as V. A. De Luca's representation of Edenic textuality, elsewhere in this volume, itself exiles Blake's text from the Eden it describes. Hazard Adams has claimed that "there are *messages* in Blake, and Blake scholarship and criticism ought to be involved in making these messages available to a needy world" (400). *Urizen* testifies that interpriestation obliterates the message and further impoverishes the world.

EXODUS

So he took me thro' a stable & thro' a church & down into the church vault at the end of which was a mill: thro' the mill we went, and came to a cave. down the winding cavern we groped our tedious way till a void boundless as a nether sky appeard beneath us & we held by the roots of trees and hung over this immensity; but I said, if you please we will commit ourselves to this void, and see whether providence is here also, if you will not I will?

(MHH 17)

4

An Original Story

NELSON HILTON

But as the Sun in Water we can bear,
Yet not the Sun, but his Reflection there,
So let us view her here, in what she was;
And take her Image, in this watry Glass
　　　　　　　　　　　Dryden, "Eleonora"

Students of Blake's *Visions of the Daughters of Albion,* dated 1793, have long felt that it reflects his reading of Mary Wollstonecraft's *A Vindication of the Rights of Woman,* published in January 1792, and one perceptive critic has argued, already a generation ago, that the poem also expresses "Blake's knowledge of the love affair between Mary Wollstonecraft and Henry Fuseli" (Wasser 292).[1] The poem's reference to the story of Persephone as presented in the translations and commentaries of Thomas Taylor and to the heroine of "Ossian" Macpherson's "Oithona" is generally recognized as well—but received interpretations have yet to coordinate these insights.[2] As Wollstonecraft attains mythic status as "the greatest of polemical feminists" (Moers 38), we might consider more closely how this most anomalous of poems suggests Blake's reflections on the engendering and engenderer of such polemical argument—which entails that we also posit how Blake's work builds on the mysterious tangle of his reading and his daily life, and how, finally, the eye is always more visionary than the heart knows.

---

1. This possibility was noted recently by Alicia Ostriker (130). The commonplace association of *Visions* with Wollstonecraft begins with Damon in *Blake* (100, 106), followed by Murry (109) and Schorer (289–93).
2. See the initial discussion by Damon in *Blake* (105–6) and detailed investigations by Harper, *Neoplatonism* 256–62, and Raine, *Tradition* 1:166–79.

I

Though circumstantial, the evidence that Blake was personally acquainted with Wollstonecraft is compelling. Both were in the circle of the publisher Joseph Johnson (1737–1809), who published all of Wollstonecraft's works and who commissioned a number of engravings from Blake (including illustrations for Wollstonecraft beginning in 1790). Moreover, Johnson appears as the publisher of record on the 1791 page proofs of *The French Revolution*, the closest Blake's work ever got to regular commercial publication. Johnson's liberal coterie—including Dr. Price, Joseph Priestley, Henry Fuseli, Thomas Paine, and William Godwin—met in the pages of his *Analytical Review*, founded in 1788, and at his famous weekly dinners, which Blake is thought to have occasionally attended. Henry Fuseli called Johnson his "first and best friend," and once roomed with him.[3] By the early 1790s, Blake considered himself a close friend to both men: when his close friend John Flaxman went to Italy in 1787, Blake recalled, "Fuseli was giv'n to me for a season" (E707). Frederick Tatham, who knew Blake well, reports that "Blake was more fond of Fuseli, than any other man on earth" (Bentley, *Records* 531). As regards Fuseli's best friend, "J. Johnson St. Pauls Church Yard" appears on the title page of Blake's 1793 emblem book, *For Children: The Gates of Paradise*—and whether Johnson is listed there as copublisher, bookseller, or alternate address, it is the only time Blake joins another name with his in any of the illuminated works. Wollstonecraft probably first met Fuseli in 1788 under the aegis of Johnson, who had taken up her interest and found her a place to live on her arrival in London. Four years later, when the famous author of the recently published *Vindication of the Rights of Woman* avowed her long obvious, self-lacerating love for Fuseli, Blake could hardly have avoided being among the closest of offstage observers.

Wollstonecraft's personality has been discussed in a number of biographies over the last decade. With one emphasis or another, they recount the story of an unhappy, resentful daughter who, as she grew up to realize that no individual would or could relieve her intense needs, turned to writing as a means of projecting (and distancing) her

---

3. Fuseli writes this in a letter to Johnson's nephew, quoted in Knowles (300).

inner conflicts onto the social realm. "All her life," reports one biographer, "she fretted over baffling emotional reactions; a recurring cry of anxiety was her 'I know not myself'" (George 15). A more immediate account of Wollstonecraft's inner life appears in her slight novella, *Mary*, published by Johnson in 1788, perhaps to give the author some income and encouragement as much as for any other reason. The autobiographical implication of the title is seconded in the "Advertisement," which argues that "those compositions only have power to delight, and carry us willing captives, where the soul of the author is exhibited." While "sublime ideas filled [Mary's] young mind," her recurrent experience is of not being beloved: "I looked for some one to have pity on me; but found none!" (52). "The society of men of genius" delights Mary, and her favorites—the description appears twice—are men of genius "past the meridian of life" (19, 54). Prophetically enough, Mary falls in love with a man named Henry and becomes "particularly fond of seeing historical paintings" (27). When they most probably met in 1788, Henry Fuseli, at 47, was eighteen years older than the young author. Blake, 31, was less than a year and a half older than Wollstonecraft.

Wollstonecraft's public reputation began in late 1790, when Johnson published her *Vindication of the Rights of Man*, one of the earliest replies to Burke's *Reflections on the French Revolution*. It is the style that one remembers: "Security of property! Behold in a few words, the definition of English liberty. And to this selfish principle every nobler one is sacrificed.—The Briton takes the place of the man, and the image of God is lost in the citizen"; or, again, "virtue is out of the question when you only worship a shadow, and worship it to secure your property" (24, 44). In 1791 Johnson published a new edition of Wollstonecraft's *Original Stories from Real Life*, which included six illustrations designed and engraved by Blake and dated "Sept. 1st, 1791." In the most satisfying of these plates (fig. 1), Blake replaces the "old" harper sought out by Wollstonecraft's protagonist with an inspired young man playing a harp much like that depicted in "The Voice of the Ancient Bard" in *Songs of Innocence*, perhaps hinting at some fantasy of being sought out on the engraver's part.[4] But by late September of 1791, Wollstonecraft—whose frugal lifestyle and contempt for

4. Blake's illustrations are discussed by Welch (4–15).

*Trying to trace the sound, I discovered
a little hut, rudely built.*

Published by J. Johnson. Sept.ʳ 1. 1791.

1. *Original Stories from Real Life*, pl. 5

2. Fuseli, *The Nightmare* (1792)

dress had conveyed the impression of "what [Fuseli] most disliked in woman [—] a philosophical sloven" (Knowles 164)—took up a more fashionable life within a few blocks of Fuseli's home, and one of her sisters wrote the other that Mary was "brimful of her friend Fuseli" (Flexner 136). During the last months of 1791 she wrote *A Vindication of the Rights of Woman*. The book's several meteorological references to

"November" suggest the author's ready reflection of immediate circumstances.

"The only Man that eer I knew / Who did not make me almost spew," wrote Blake in his *Notebook*, "Was Fuseli he was both Turk & Jew" (E507). Fuseli was, in fact, Swiss and Zwinglian. Impetuous and highly gifted, he had come to England in 1763 after serving a year as a minister in Zurich, a position abandoned following the uproar over his pamphlet attacking a corrupt magistrate. Leaving with him was his longtime friend Johann Casper Lavater, whose *Physiognomy*—dedicated to Fuseli— was to be partially translated by Wollstonecraft in 1788, and whose *Aphorisms on Man*—translated by Fuseli—Blake annotated extensively. Soon after his arrival in England Fuseli became intimate with Joseph Johnson, eventually renting an apartment in Johnson's house in 1769. When the house burned down in 1770, destroying many of his literary manuscripts, Fuseli, advised by Sir Joshua Reynolds, went to Rome for eight years to develop his talent for painting. There, he was later to relate, he would lie on his back day after day musing on the splendors of the Sistine ceiling, and "such a posture of repose was necessary for a body fatigued like his with the pleasant gratifications of a luxurious city" (Janson 27). In later years he would speak freely, even to Wollstonecraft's sisters, of his youthful love affairs and sexual experiences (Sunstein 186). Two years after his return from Rome Fuseli began to exhibit paintings regularly in the Royal Academy Exhibition, and in 1782 he scored his initial—and greatest—success with *The Nightmare*. Among the homages to the painting were Erasmus Darwin's verses in *The Loves of the Plants*, published by Johnson in 1789,[5] and when the poem proved extremely popular, Johnson commissioned Fuseli to paint another ver-

---

5. Darwin writes:

> So on his NIGHTMARE through the evening fog
> Flits the squab fiend o'er fen, and lake, and bog;
> Seeks some love-wilder'd Maid with sleep oppress'd,
> Alights, and grinning sits upon her breast.
> —Such as of late amid the murky sky
> Was mark'd by FUSSELI'S poetic eye;
> Whose daring tints, with SHAKESPEAR'S happiest grace,
> Give to the airy phantom form and place.—
> Back o'er her pillow sinks her blushing head,
> Her snow-white limbs hang helpless from the bed;
> While with quick sighs, and suffocative breath,
> Her interrupted heart-pulse swims in death.
>
> (*Loves* 3.51–62)

sion, which was then engraved to illustrate Darwin's verses. That *Nightmare*, now the best known (fig. 2), was completed in 1792 and hung in Johnson's sitting room, where it might have reminded a reflective visitor of its creator's ambivalent attitude toward women.[6] Blake, at any rate, was no doubt including Lavater's best friend and "cotemporary" Fuseli when he concluded his annotations to *Aphorisms on Man* with the remark that the "mistake in Lavater & his cotemporaries, is, They suppose that Womans Love is Sin. in consequence all the Loves & Graces with them are Sin" (E601).

Fuseli's character was complex. Eudo Mason summarizes many accounts this way: "He seemed always to be in a rage, or on the point of flying into one, or just recovering from one. . . . The language and the gestures of anger became for Fuseli more and more a convenient and stereotyped medium through which to communicate with the rest of the world, and with which, also, to keep it at arms' length; for those who knew him best all testify that he was in reality both diffident and shy" (24). Lavater described him to J. G. Herder as the epitome of "Sturm und Drang": "He is everything in extremes—always an original . . . hurricane and tempest. . . . His look is lightning, his word a thunderstorm [Sein Blick ist Blitz, sein Wort ein Wetter]" (Sunstein 181; Schiff 1:81). Joseph Farrington labeled Fuseli a cynic; Benjamin Haydon felt that "Evil was in him"; and William Godwin pointed to "a caustic turn of mind, with much wit, and a disposition to search, in everything new or modern, for occasion of censure" (89). But part of Fuseli was always the ordained minister—behind his cynical contempt "is not indifference to morality, but a kind of inverted, ineradicable Puritanism" (Mason 188).

Though John Knowles, Fuseli's friend and biographer, writes that Fuseli and Wollstonecraft met in the autumn of 1790, it seems more likely that they were acquainted by mid-1788: both were among Johnson's most frequent visitors, and both were regular contributors to Johnson's new *Analytical Review*.[7] Fuseli would certainly have known

6. Jean Starobinski, discussing the painting in *Trois fureurs*, remarks, "Je préférerais, pour ma part, attribuer au peintre non l'angoisse du cauchemar, mais le plaisir voyeuriste d'en être le spectateur, au moment du tourment le plus intense. Il voit souffrir; il fait souffrir. . . . Les cheveux dénoués de la dormeuse du *Cauchemar* me paraissent donc dire l'abolition complète du *danger* lié à la femme" (143).

7. See Godwin (86); Sunstein (179). After Wollstonecraft's death, Johnson recalled that Fuseli and Wollstonecraft "spent so many happy hours in my house" (quoted in Tyson 151).

about one of Johnson's writers undertaking a translation of Lavater's *Physiognomy*—he may even have suggested it. Knowles may have been inclined to postdate the acquaintance because mid-1788 also saw Fuseli's marriage to Sophia Rawlins. Knowles writes that this artist's model was "a young lady of reputable parentage and of personal attractions" who made "an excellent wife," and leaves it at that; Fuseli's involvement with Wollstonecraft receives considerably more attention, even in the chapter recording his marriage. As recent biographers suggest, it may have been the marriage itself that made Fuseli receptive to Wollstonecraft, since he could thus both reassure himself with the admiration of an intelligent woman and assert his independence from his wife. William Godwin locates the beginning of their attraction in Fuseli's finding Wollstonecraft "a person perhaps more susceptible of the emotions painting is calculated to excite, than any other with whom he ever conversed" (86). He continues, "She saw Mr. Fuseli frequently, he amused, delighted and instructed her." Although Wollstonecraft had spent "upwards of thirty years in a state of celibacy and seclusion," Godwin writes, "the sentiments which Mr. Fuseli excited in her mind taught her the secret to which she was so long in a manner a stranger" (93). Lest the reader misunderstand the character of the woman he had later married, Godwin adds that "no one knew more perfectly how to assign the engagements of affection their respective rank, or to maintain in virgin and unsullied purity the chasteness of her mind." But at the same time, Godwin finds it "singular" that Wollstonecraft produced only a few articles for the *Analytical Review* in the year following the January 1792 completion of *A Vindication of the Rights of Woman*. Here again one may mistrust the biographer, considering that among the materials he had collected for the memoir, Godwin had a note from Johnson that recalled, laconically, how in 1792 "her exertions were palsied, you know the cause" (Flexner 172). According to Knowles, who had access to letters (later destroyed) from Wollstonecraft to Fuseli and to Fuseli's friend William Roscoe, Wollstonecraft "expressed to some of her intimate friends [Roscoe?], that although Mrs. Fuseli had a right to the person of her husband, she . . . might claim, and for congeniality of sentiments and talents, hold a place in his heart; for 'she hoped,' she said, 'to unite herself to his mind'" (165).

In the summer of 1792, Johnson, Wollstonecraft, and the Fuselis embarked on a trip to revolutionary France, prompting one of Wollstonecraft's sisters to comment to another, "Well, in spite of Reason, when Mrs. W. reaches the Continent she will be but a woman" (Wardle 172). The group never reached the continent. At Dover they turned back, possibly discouraged by news of the massacre in the Tuileries (10 August); more probably, Johnson (at least) realized that Wollstonecraft's absorption with Fuseli made the situation impossible. On their return, Wollstonecraft left London for a while. But evidently she could not stop "her ardent imagination," as Godwin puts it, from "continually conjuring up pictures of the happiness she would have found, if fortune had favored their more intimate union" (100).

Knowles offers the only direct testimony to the melodramatic conclusion of the sad affair:

> Fuseli reasoned with her, but without any effect, upon the impropriety of indulging in a passion that took her out of common life. Her answer was, "If I thought my passion criminal, I would conquer it, or die in the attempt. For immodesty, in my eyes, is ugliness; my soul turns with disgust from pleasure tricked out in charms which shun the light of heaven."
>
> At length Mrs. Wollstonecraft appears to have grown desperate, for she had the temerity to go to Mrs. Fuseli, and to tell her, that she wished to become an inmate in her family; and she added, as I am above deceit, it is right to say that this proposal "arises from the sincere affection which I have for your husband, for I find I cannot live without the satisfaction of seeing and conversing with him daily." This frank avowal immediately opened the eyes of Mrs. Fuseli, who being alarmed by the declaration, not only refused her solicitation, but she instantly forbade her the house.
>
> (167)

Fuseli, who had taken to carrying around Wollstonecraft's letters without opening them ("thinking they teemed only with the usual effusion of regard, and the same complaints of neglect," writes Knowles), was doubtless glad to see his wife resolve a situation that no longer interested him. Wollstonecraft immediately made plans to leave and departed for France on 8 December 1792, a little over three weeks later. Thus, a year after the *Vindication of the Rights of Woman*, Mary Wollstonecraft presented Johnson's circle with another lesson on the female soul.[8] Blake must have been a fascinated student of both the public and the private text.

II

Blake's vision begins with the emphatic first word, "Enslav'd." The Daughters of Albion weep, "Enslav'd," but the poem's remaining two references to slavery do nothing to indicate directly why or how the Daughters are in such condition. Slavery, however, *is* the master trope of the *Vindication*. "When, therefore I call women slaves," writes Wollstonecraft, reflecting on the recurrence of that concept throughout her book, "I mean in a political and civil sense" (386); she views "with indignation, the mistaken notions that enslave my sex" (72). The *Vindication* also offers the association that explains the reference to black slavery that some critics have seen—with the contemporary abolitionist controversy—as the essential backdrop of the *Visions* (Erdman, *Prophet* 228–42): "Is one half of the human species, like the poor African slaves, to be subject to prejudices that brutalize them?" (33). The "slaves beneath the sun" that Blake's poem mentions in plate 2 are, like most of its readers, "beneath the sun," shivering "in religious caves beneath the burning fires / Of lust, that belch incessant from the summits of the earth" (2.9–10). For Wollstonecraft, "the mass of mankind are . . . the slaves of their appetites," and, she metaphorizes, "if from their birth men and women be placed in a torrid zone, with the meridian sun of pleasure darting directly upon them, how can they sufficiently brace their minds?" (137, 116). The "black African" that David Erdman sees on plate 2 (*Illuminated* 130; fig. 3) is, inter alia, an "image of Theotormon" on Oothoon's "pure transparent breast"; that is, *through* Oothoon we see the "political and civil," cultural, psychological, and ethnological bases of enslavement.

Wollstonecraft argues, essentially, that since woman has an immortal soul, she must be treated (especially, educated) in the same respect as man. But, she explains, through the doctrine of "sensibility" women are condemned to be "slaves to their bodies," "slaves of ca-

8. Gert Schiff also feels that Wollstonecraft's "debacle with Sophia must have been known, at least in their little coterie" (for this comment and others, I am grateful to Professor Schiff).

The image of Theotormon on my pure transparent breast.

3. *Visions of the Daughters of Albion*, pl. 2

sual lust," slaves "to prejudice," "of sensibility," "slaves of injustice," "slaves to their persons," and to their own "feelings": "they become in the same proportion the slaves of pleasure as they are the slaves of men" (*Vindication* 88, 314, 345, 283, 439, 330, 227, 402). Wollstonecraft has "often been forcibly struck" by the description of damnation, "when the spirit is represented as continually hovering with abortive eagerness round the defiled body, unable to enjoy anything without the organs of sense." "Yet," she continues, "to their senses women are made slaves" (131). Similarly, in an image of individual ontology that also links the *Visions* to the developing cosmology of the other Lambeth books, Oothoon laments:

> They told me that the night & day were all that I could see;
> They told me that I had five senses to inclose me up.
> And they inclos'd my infinite brain into a narrow circle.
> And sunk my heart into the Abyss, a red round globe hot burning
> Till all from life I was obliterated and erased.
> (2.30–34; cf. *The Book of Urizen*, 11.2–4)

In the last of the three overt references to slavery in the *Visions*, Oothoon discovers that Theotormon's commitment to the ethos of "hypocrite modesty" is so neurotically profound that he "is a sick mans dream / And Oothoon is the crafty slave of selfish holiness" (6.19–20). Here, "selfish holiness" comes close to the "doting self-love" that Wollstonecraft identifies (*Vindication* 18) as a dominant component of male psychology, but, more revealing, the line offers the only appearance of "craft" or its variants in Blake's work. Before this nominal indication of a link between Oothoon and Wollstonecraft is dismissed outright, remark Oothoon's opening encounter with the "bright

Marygold," also making *its* only appearance in Blake's work (and, as G. E. Bentley, Jr., notes, capitalized at the significantly laborious expense of altering an *m*, which was "originally etched lower case" [*Writings* 1:105]). According to the *OED*, the spelling of *marigold* with an *i* begins in the fifteenth century, and the last spelling with a *y* that it records dates from 1714. "Marygold," then, for us as for Oothoon, is "now a flower; / Now a nymph!" (1.6–7). In plucking the Marygold, Oothoon seems to gain the soul she had been lacking, since only afterward does she speak of her "whole soul" (1.13). Marygold and crafty Oothoon are thus closely related, and readers who credit the possible operation of a kind of "primary process" of the imagination (as argued in my *Literal Imagination*) may also hear the disembodied name of Mary "Woolstonecraft" (see Taylor, *Vindication*, cited below) behind them as well.

Oothoon's encounter with Marygold, indented from the margin of the poem, asks to be considered still more closely. Before coming upon Marygold, "Oothoon wanderd in woe, / Along the vales of Leutha seeking flowers to comfort her" (1.2–3). Like most of Blake's names, "Leutha" taps several associations. In Macpherson's *Poems . . . by Ossian*, "Lutha"—"a valley in Morven"—is the home of the beautiful virgin Malvina, who is described as a "maid of Lutha" as well as "the maid of the voice of love," and many of the Bard's compositions are presented as being addressed to Malvina, the beloved of his dead son. At one point she utters this self-reflexive soliloquy, with its oblique prefiguration of Oothoon and the Daughters, perhaps even of Wollstonecraft and Blake:

> What then, daughter of Lutha, travels over thy soul, like the dreary path of a ghost along the nightly beam? Should the young warrior fall, in the roar of his troubled fields! Young virgins of Lutha arise, call back the wandering thoughts of Malvina. Awake the voice of the harp along my echoing vale. Then shall my soul come forth, like a light from the gates of morn.
>
> (317)

But the *e* in Blake's "Leutha" may also remind us of Homer's "Leucothea," the "white goddess" who lends Odysseus her veil to preserve him from the wrath of Poseidon in book 5 of the *Odyssey*.[9]

9. Leucothea is the immortal form of Ino, who nursed Dionysos/Bromios; Blake's knowledge of *that* association seems indicated by the opening of *The Book of Los*, which invokes "Eno aged mother, / Who the chariot of Leutha guides" (3.1–2).

Perhaps most suggestive, pertinent, and weird are the name's subterranean links to "Eleusis," site of the mysteries celebrating Demeter and Persephone, and "eleutherios," a Greek epithet of Dionysos cognate with words denoting "freedom," "liberty," and a verb future for "what shall come" (Thass-Thienemann 211).

The description of Oothoon's initial woeful condition echoes Malvina's unhappiness over her dead lover and suggests, as well, Wollstonecraft's lament for "the creature of sensibility . . . surprised by her sensibility into folly": "Where art thou to find comfort, forlorn and disconsolate one? . . . In a dream of passion thou consented to wander through flowery lawns" (*Vindication* 191). Oothoon's comfort, it seems, is found in Marygold's message, with its obvious sexual reference to plucking, deflowering, and the nymph's clitoral "dewy bed"[10]—according to Thomas Taylor in his *Dissertation on the Eleusinian and Bacchic Mysteries*, published a year or two before Wollstonecraft's *Vindication*, "Nymphs are evident symbols of generation . . . and are, therefore, the proper companions of the soul about to fall into its fluctuating realms" (102).[11] The singular "nymph" of *Visions*, a figure who appears nowhere else in Blake, needs more attention. A nymph is, above all, a water spirit—hence the word is used poetically to denote a stream. So, for Blake's literal imagination, she is a *flow-er* ("now a flower; / Now a nymph!").[12] Blake also read in Taylor that "the flowing condition of our body . . . like an ever-running stream, is continually rolling into the dark sea of matter, as into the abyss of non-entity" (*Vindication* 43). (And Oothoon will end up "wailing on the margin of non-entity" [7.15]). These associations lend additional resonance to Leutha's connection with the Ossianic vale of Lutha, which name, we are told, means "swift stream." We may sense, as well, a text concerning the writing of the *Vindication* and the realizing of Mary's golden message. Wollstonecraft aspires, for example, to "rouse my sex from the flowery bed on which they supinely sleep life away!" (273), for,

10. "I see thee now a flower; / Now a nymph! I dare not pluck thee from thy dewy bed!" *Nympha* was the common classical term for the clitoris, used by Galen and numerous other medical writers through the eighteenth century (see Kanner 228–33); in English, *nymphae* still denotes the "labia minor" (see *OED*, s.v.).

11. Blake was already well acquainted with speculation concerning the Eleusinian mysteries and the myth of Persephone from his work engraving views of the Portland vase for Erasmus Darwin's *The Economy of Vegetation* in 1791.

12. The "flowing" possibility connects subliminally to the later images of the "dewy bed" (as in a stream bed), and the message that "another flower shall *spring*" (my emphasis).

she reminds her readers, "the body . . . enshrines . . . an improvable soul" (279). After the nymph closes "her golden shrine," Oothoon places the "Sweet flower" between her breasts, like Hera with Aphrodite's sex-arousing "cestus" (*Iliad* 14.214ff.). Only then does she speak of her "whole soul," completing the poem's early embedding of "soul" as one of its key referents: "the soft soul of America," for which Oothoon wandered in woe, and "the soul of sweet delight" that, Marygold says, "can never pass away." If Oothoon had known her Proverbs of Hell, she might have pondered the fact that the nymph does *not* say, "The soul of sweet delight, can never be defil'd" (*MHH* 9).

On gathering her flower, Oothoon becomes one with Persephone and Wollstonecraft, to be gathered by the gloomy Dis of Bromion and her own unconscious (cf. *Paradise Lost* 4.268–72). Blake would have read in Taylor's *Dissertation* that "Proserpine, therefore, or the soul, at the very instant of her descent into matter, is, with the utmost propriety, represented as eagerly engaged in plucking this fatal flower; for her energies at this period are entirely conversant with a life divided about the fluctuating condition of body" (106). Taylor, Blake's age, was already making a name for himself as "the Platonist." Blake probably heard his lectures on "Platonic philosophy" at Flaxman's house—presented sometime in the mid-1780s—and at one point even studied geometry with him.[13] As G. M. Harper notes, the plot of the *Visions* "fits almost exactly" the brief summary of the Persephone myth that Taylor supplies: "The soul . . . descends Corically, or after the manner of Proserpine, into generation, but is distributed into generation Dionysiacally; as she is bound in body Prometheiacally and Titanically: she frees herself therefore from its bounds by exercising the strength of Hercules; but she is collected into one . . . by philosophizing in a manner truly cathartic" (*Dissertation* 61–62). It is another curious instance of the small world of personal acquaintance just behind the *Visions* that Mary Wollstonecraft had lodged in Taylor's house a decade before Blake's poem (Harper, "Wollstonecraft" 461–63).

Various critics have noted the evident reference of the name

---

13. See King (153–57); on Flaxman and Taylor, see Harper, *Neoplatonism* 41–45, and Taylor's own "Biographical Account," reprinted in *Selected Writings* (114–15).

"Bromion" to the Greek *bromios*, meaning "sounding, noisy, boisterous," and to *bromos*, "thunder." "Bromios" is also one of the names of Dionysos, most memorably in Euripides' *Bacchae*, another vision of feminine plight in a maddening male world.[14] The calculatedly classical reference might remind us of Fuseli's great reputation and ability as a Greek scholar, ever declaiming that "the Greeks were Gods, the Greeks were gods!" Through Joseph Johnson, Fuseli became entrusted with correcting, revising, and annotating William Cowper's translation of Homer and was of such assistance that, at the close of his preface, Cowper acknowledges "the learned and ingenious Mr. Fuseli . . . the best critic in Homer I have ever met with." The translation was published by Johnson in 1791 and lists "Mr. W. Blake, Engraver" among the subscribers. Blake's knowledge of the mythological context surrounding Bromios/Dionysos is evident in the "jealous dolphins"—these, again, unique in Blake—that Bromion orders to "sport around the lovely maid" (1.19). Such information could easily have been had from a friend who "loved to annoy certain of his companions with the display of his antique lore" (Cunningham 249).[15]

That Theotormon is in some way intimately related to Bromion is evident on his first appearance, folding "black *jealous* waters round the adulterate pair" (2.41). (And why does "adulterate" also appear only here in Blake's work? Is the pair, "Bound back to back," genuinely adulterous, or merely a "spurious, counterfeit" pair? And why, to anticipate, does Blake inscribe the jealous water "black"?) Theotormon's name also relates him to the thunder-wielding Bromion, since, as Macpherson explains in *Ossian*, the proper name "Tormon" means "thunder"; the name of course invokes other associations, particularly, "God-tormented." J. M. Murry, who felt that the *Visions* "faintly concealed the personal story of Mary Wollstonecraft," was the first to suggest that Bromion and Theotormon could be aspects of the same

14. In *Jerusalem* 73.42, Euripides appears with "Virgil Dante Milton" in a select list of artists created by Los.

15. See also Fuseli's many paintings on mythological subjects catalogued in Schiff, *Heinrich Füssli*. The story of Dionysos and the Tyrrhenian pirates changed to dolphins appears in the Homeric Hymn to Dionysos and in Ovid's *Metamorphoses*, book 3. In view of David Erdman's more political interpretation of *Visions*, one might note George Sandys' comment on the episode in his wonderful 1632 translation, *Ovid's Metamorphoses*: "These *Tyrrhenians* for their pyracies and power at sea, and for that they had transported divers Colonies to sundry parts of the world [like the English, then], were surnamed Dolphins" (167).

person, representing "the divided soul of a single man" (109–10). If the *Visions* strongly conceals a personal story, the logical candidate for that uneasily fused man would be the "Turk & Jew" Fuseli.

The graphic designs of *Visions*, at any rate, ask us to think of Fuseli from the beginning. On Blake's title page (fig. 4) Oothoon flees from his adaptation of Fuseli's idea for *The Fertilization of Egypt* (fig. 5). The figure's left wing connects with heavy black rain, while its right one joins the ring of dancing "creatures of the element," reminiscent of a similar dancing group of dreams in Fuseli's *The Shepherd's Dream* (fig. 6).[16] Plate 1 (fig. 7) has figures armed with bows and arrows taken, appropriately, from Blake's engraving of Fuseli's *Falsa Ad Coelum Mittunt Insomnia Manes* (fig. 8),[17] while the male figure at the bottom of the plate refers us to Bottom in Fuseli's painting of *The Awakening of Titania* from *A Midsummer Night's Dream* 5.1 (fig. 9). In that design, Bottom has a "nightmare" flying over (out from?) his head, which may account for the quotation of his form in *Visions*, plate 1, next to the female figure posed (as Erdman notes) "like the woman in Fuseli's *Nightmare*" (*Illuminated* 129).[18] The sexual nature of the whole scene, as David Erdman has discovered, is additionally signaled by the design above the *i* in "Visions"—a female vainly daydreaming (like "the maiden" in "The Angel" [*Songs of Experience*]) rides astride the tip of a cloud-penis, the *V* of "Visions" falling from her hand like a neglected rein. Plate 1, it seems, is laden with graphic references to dreams, false or unpleasant, and to Fuseli.

Macpherson's "Oithona," in *Poems of Ossian*, offers another intertext for the *Visions*. While her true love, Gaul, is away, Oithona is carried off by Dunrommath, a rejected suitor, "into Tromathon, a desert island, where he concealed her in a cave" (133). Gaul eventually follows and defeats Dunrommath, only to discover, in the midst of the

16. Fuseli's 1793 painting closely follows his 1785 pencil and chalk sketch of the same subject. David Erdman does not note this association in his discussion of the *Visions* title page in *The Illuminated Blake*, although it is directly suggested by his discussion of emblem designs in Blake's *Notebook*. *The Illuminated Blake* directs us to the drawing on page 30 of the *Notebook*, which, says Erdman, shows "a scarf dance of three fairy 'creatures of the element'" (126), and *that* discussion urges us to compare the sketch on page 114, which "can be understood as Blake's interpretation of *Paradise Lost*, I, 781–88 of a shepherd's dream" by Fuseli.

17. On the dating of this plate (c. 1790), see Essick, *Plates* 175–76.

18. Peter Tomory notes that "the propinquity of this Awakening to the realm of the Nightmare is demonstrated . . . by the demon rider" (101).

battlefield, "the wounded Oithona! She had armed herself in the cave and come in search of death" (138). "Oi-thona," a note explains, signifies *"the virgin of the wave,"* "Trom-thon, *heavy or deep-sounding wave"* (242–43). After plucking the Marygold, Oothoon takes off "over the waves," that is, "over Theotormons reign."[19] Theotormon is consistently associated with waves: after Bromion "rent" Oothoon, "then storms rent Theotormons limbs; he rolld his waves around" (2.3), and while he sits at the threshold of "Bromions caves," "beneath him sound like waves on a desart shore / The voice of slaves" (2.7–8). Bromion also appears a kind of ocean god, with his "stormy bed" and dolphins. The question of what exactly happened to Oothoon is illuminated by Tharmas' behavior in *The Four Zoas:*

> *in a Wave he rap'd bright Enitharmon far*
> *Apart from Los. but coverd her with softest brooding care*
> *On a broad wave in the warm west. balming her bleeding wound*
> (49.4–6)

This bizarre incident can be related to the story of Tyro in the *Odyssey,* who was ravished by the ocean god, Poseidon (11.242ff.). During the rape, "around a spacious arch of waves he throws" (Pope's translation), and afterward the god tells Tyro that she shall give birth "when nine times the moon renews her horn"—"Oothoon shall put forth in the nine moons time," says Bromion. The illustration to plate 4 shows Oothoon arched in (as) a wave over Theotormon.

After her encounter with titanic irrational life in the form of Bromion,[20] "Oothoon weeps not; she cannot weep!":

> But she can howl incessant writhing her soft snowy limbs.
> And calling Theotormons Eagles to prey upon her flesh.

> I call with holy voice! kings of the sounding air,
> Rend away this defiled bosom that I may reflect.
> The image of Theotormon. . . .
> (2.12–16)

---

19. Over Theotormon's "rain" as well, as in the title page; compare also the reference to Theotormon's "salt tears" in *Europe* 14.24.

20. According to Taylor, "our irrational life is Titannic, under which the rational life is torn in pieces. . . . But when we establish ourselves in union with this Dionysical or kindred form, then we become Bacchuses, or perfect guardians of our irrational life" (*Dissertation* 145–46).

4. *Visions of the Daughters of Albion,* pl. ii

5. *The Fertilization of Egypt*

6. Fuseli, *The Shepherd's Dream* (1793)

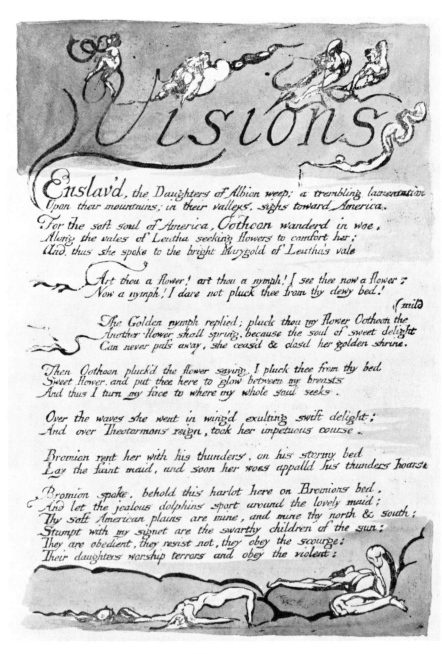

Enslav'd, the Daughters of Albion weep; a trembling lamentation
Upon their mountains; in their valleys, sighs toward America.

For the soft soul of America, Oothoon wanderd in woe,
Along the vales of Leutha seeking flowers to comfort her;
And thus she spoke to the bright Marygold of Leutha's vale

Art thou a flower! art thou a nymph! I see thee now a flower;
Now a nymph! I dare not pluck thee from thy dewy bed!

The Golden nymph replied; pluck thou my flower Oothoon the mild
Another flower shall spring, because the soul of sweet delight
Can never pass away, she ceas'd & clos'd her golden shrine.

Then Oothoon pluck'd the flower saying, I pluck thee from thy bed
Sweet flower, and put thee here to glow between my breasts
And thus I turn my face to where my whole soul seeks.

Over the waves she went in wing'd exulting swift delight;
And over Theotormons reign, took her impetuous course.

Bromion rent her with his thunders, on his stormy bed
Lay the faint maid, and soon her woes appalld his thunders hoarse

Bromion spoke. behold this harlot here on Bromions bed.
And let the jealous dolphins sport around the lovely maid;
Thy soft American plains are mine, and mine thy north & south;
Stampt with my signet are the swarthy children of the sun:
They are obedient, they resist not, they obey the scourge:
Their daughters worship terrors and obey the violent:

7.   *Visions of the Daughters of Albion,* pl. 1

8. *Falsa Ad Coelum Mittunt Insomnia Manes*

9. Fuseli, *The Awakening of Titania* (c. 1785–90)

"I call with the firm tone of humanity," announces the first sentence of the *Vindication*, dedicating the work to Talleyrand, "for my arguments, sir, are dictated by a disinterested spirit—I plead for my sex— not for myself" (iii). We perhaps may wonder, with Blake, exactly how clearly Wollstonecraft could reflect on her sex and herself in a work that, as Emily Sunstein writes, "was also an address to Fuseli, the man who currently personified masculine rejection of women like herself in favor of conventional femininity" (214). "The Eagle," says a Proverb of Hell, is "a portion of genius,"[21] but the "Eagles of heaven," according to the arch-reactionary Duke of Burgundy in *The French Revolution*, "must have their prey." Oothoon later discovers that after "nightly prey" the Eagle "lifts his golden beak to the pure east," and, finally, that it "scorn[s] the earth & despise[s] the treasures beneath" (5.39). But in response to her call, the Eagles "descend & rend their bleeding prey," repeating the rending action of Bromion's thunders and Theotormon's storms. Oothoon is, evidently, "bleeding" or "full of anguish from suffering" (*OED*): as in Thomas Creech's translation of Lucretius, "vexing love" and "fierce cares" are "the eagles that still tear [her] breast" (3.993–94). The introductory moment of the poem concludes as

> Theotormon severely smiles. her soul reflects the smile;
> As the clear spring mudded with the feet of beasts grows pure & smiles.
>
> (2.18–19)

Severity marks Theotormon's moral condemnation, but more revealing in this poem of echoes and repetition is the reflection of Oothoon's no longer whole soul and its result.

The relation of reflection and purity is further put into question as Oothoon asks Theotormon, "How can I be defil'd when I reflect thy image pure?" (3.16). For Wollstonecraft, "purity of mind . . . is the delicacy of reflection" (*Vindication* 187); "reflection is the noble distinction of man . . . an instrument to raise him above his earthly dross" (249); "the power of reflecting" is "the grand privilege of man" (345); and reflection on the Supreme Being "must give rise to the wish of being pure as he is pure!" (294). Reflection, then, is an essential

---

21. Wollstonecraft writes in the *Vindication* of the "eagle eye" of genius, "the glowing minds that concentrate pictures for their fellow-creatures; forcing them to view with interest the objects reflected from the impassioned imagination" (261).

power for change and liberation held out by the *Vindication*. But, of course, as soon as we realize the constructing role of reflection in Wollstonecraft's thought, all of the problems with the dynamic of specular images leap into view. Wollstonecraft, that is to say, reflects male ideals of "purity," "religion," "God the Father," and "reflection" even as she attacks the effects of those ideals as slavery. Quotations we have just considered from the *Visions* suggest that Blake found the following passage from the *Vindication* an emblem of Wollstonecraft's contradictory reflections and a source of Oothoon's:

> Religion, pure source of comfort in this vale of tears! How has thy clear stream been muddied by the dabblers, who have presumptuously endeavoured to confine in one narrow channel the living waters that ever flow toward God—the sublime ocean of existence! What would life be without that peace which the love of God, when built on humanity, alone can impart? Every earthly affection turns back, at intervals, to prey upon the heart that feeds it; and the purest effusions of benevolence, often rudely damped by man, must mount as free-will offering to Him who gave them birth, whose bright image they faintly reflect.
>
> (369–70)

For Blake, Wollstonecraft did not reflect enough; so she is left like one of the female spirits "pining in bonds of religion" (*Am* 15.23), arguing to Fuseli that if she thought her passion criminal she would conquer it and so maintain (as Godwin wrote) "in virgin and unsullied purity the chasteness of her mind." So Oothoon's theo-tormented reflection that "the soul prey'd on by woe" is "sweetest" (3.17) leaves her only the blank self-consolation that "I am white and pure to hover round Theotormons breast" (3.20). Wollstonecraft, we noted above, wrote that she was "often forcibly struck" by the image of a damned soul "continually hovering with abortive eagerness round the defiled body" (*Vindication* 130).

The repeated and ineffectual assertion of purity asks us to ponder the psychic state that chooses to hear itself mouth such assertions: it asks us to seek motivation rather than strategy behind such rhetoric. Realizing, after the two male lamentations, that she is still unrecognized, Oothoon exults in flights of Blake's most unrestrained rhetoric; flower springs after rhetorical flower, to put it in Marygold's terms. And herein lies what has so long been the paradox of the *Visions*; for, rather than continuing to confront motivation, critics (mostly male) themselves succumb to the seemingly rapturous power of Oothoon's voice.[22] It must rank as a form of rape, seizure by power, to hear what one wants in a speech without reference to the motivation(s) and context of that speech. Rape all the more *spectacular* when self-inflicted on one's own motivation. So in her *Vindication*, for example, we can sense with Blake that Wollstonecraft's "I" is the flowering of a rhetorical *persona* (a mask, *that through which one speaks*): "I shall disdain to cull my phrases or polish my style;—I aim at being useful, and sincerity will render me unaffected; for, wishing rather to persuade by the force of my arguments, than dazzle by the elegance of my language, I shall not waste my time in rounding periods, or in fabricating the turgid bombast of artificial feelings, which, coming from the head, never reach the heart.—I shall be employed about things, not words!" (7–8). "Sincerity," "integrity," or whatever we might call the attributes of a "whole soul" are belied by self-reflexivity, by writing, just as they are by Oothoon's drawing attention to herself in the third person ("But Oothoon is not so . . .") or by her use of histrionic, abortive performatives ("I cry, Love! Love! Love! happy happy Love!"). Who or what prompts "I"?

III

Elissa S. Guralnick has recently characterized the more remarkable aspects of the "rhetorical strategy" of the *Vindication* as consisting of "the unphilosophic nature of its persona; the frantic flamboyance of its style; and the vehemence of its vicious attack on Rousseau—unprecedented and unrepeated in Wollstonecraft's other work" (174). The applicability of the first two of these descriptions to Oothoon should be evident, but what of the third? Guralnick is most puzzled by the fact that Wollstonecraft, who "had been, and would again be, an enthusiastic admirer of Rousseau . . . descends to a vicious attack on Rousseau's sexuality." "What," she asks, "prompted Wollstonecraft's despite?" The answer, according to the dynamic proposed here, is that Rousseau was Fuseli's favorite modern author. Soon after arriving in England, Fuseli had composed *Remarks on the Writing and*

---

22. A refreshing exception is Damrosch (197–201). David Erdman carried his admiration so far as to dedicate the *Concordance to the Writings of William Blake* "To Oothoon."

Conduct of J. J. Rousseau—published by Johnson—which one modern critic calls the only contemporary publication reflecting "a critical understanding" of Rousseau's philosophy (Guthke i). Fuseli's reputation as a Rousseauist guides Godwin's description of the literary taste of Wollstonecraft's first love: "The nearest rival of Homer, if Homer can have a rival, is Jean-Jacques Rousseau. A young man embraces entire the opinions of a favorite writer, and Mr. Fuseli has not had leisure to bring the opinion of his youth to a revision" (88). In the *Vindication*, Wollstonecraft's *ad hominem* attack comes after a discussion of the "unintelligible paradoxes" of *Émile*:

> But all Rousseau's errors in reasoning arose from sensibility, and sensibility to their charms women are very ready to forgive! When he should have reasoned he became impassioned, and reflection inflamed his imagination instead of enlightening his understanding. Even his virtues also led him farther astray; for, born with a warm constitution and lively fancy, nature carried him toward the other sex with such eager fondness, that he soon became lascivious. Had he given way to these desires, the fire would have extinguished itself in a natural manner; but virtue, and a romantic kind of delicacy, made him practise self-denial. . . . He then sought for solitude . . . merely to indulge his feelings.
>
> (202)

What Wollstonecraft sees as this "epicurism of virtue—self denial" (286)[23]—Oothoon identifies as "the self enjoyings of self-denial," and adds,

> *Is it because acts are not lovely, that thou seekest solitude,*
> *Where the horrible darkness is impressed with reflections of desire.*
> (7.10–11)

The self-fancied virgin Oothoon, "fill'd with virgin fancies," knows that "the virgin / That pines for man; shall awaken her womb to enormous joys / In the secret shadows of her chamber" (7.3–5). The masturbatory overtones intensify as Oothoon proceeds to describe "the youth," who, "shut up from / The lustful joy. shall forget to generate.

---

23. Fuseli's loyalty to his wife, Sophia, perhaps lies behind Wollstonecraft's angry comment in the *Vindication*, "Who ever drew a more exalted female character than Rousseau? though in the lump he constantly endeavoured to degrade the sex. And why was he thus anxious? Truly to justify to himself the affection which weakness and virtue had made him cherish for that fool Theresa" (403).

& create an amorous image / In the shadows of his curtains" (7.5–7). These images may also allude to Mary Wollstonecraft, whose concern regarding youthful masturbation was mocked in the quick response to the *Vindication* that would have had personal interest for both Blake and Wollstonecraft, Thomas Taylor's *Vindication of the Rights of Brutes* (1792). Taylor's purpose is to discredit the theory of sexual and political equality, and he states early on that "Mrs Woolstonecraft . . . though a virgin, is the mother of this theory." (This public emphasis on her virginity helps to ground our association of Wollstonecraft and Persephone in the *Visions*.) As part of his attack, Taylor turns to the topic of masturbation, observing with mock concern that "every one knows how universally prevalent the practice of self-pollution is become amongst children." He then quotes verbatim the argument in Wollstonecraft's adaption of C. G. Salzmann's *Elements of Morality for Children* that "the most efficacious method to root out this dreadful evil, which poisons the source of human happiness, would be to speak to children of the organs of generation . . . and explain to them the noble use, which they were designed for, and how they may be injured" (47). Taylor was no doubt struck by the contradiction of such an uncompromising regard for "the source of human happiness" coming from such an ostensibly virginal and "pure" mind, and his response gives full rein to his Neoplatonic disgust:

> But however great and original this thought may be, yet it would certainly be very much improved, by committing the instruction of youth in this particular to dogs; for these sagacious animals, all of whom appear to be Cynic philosophers, would not only be very well calculated to explain the noble use for which the parts were designed, but would be very willing, at any time, and in any place, to give them the most delicate specimens of the operation of the parts in the natural way.
>
> (48)

This idle rhetoric receives its due rejoinder as Oothoon asks men, through her apostrophe to Urizen,

> *wilt thou take the ape*
> *For thy councellor? or the dog, for a schoolmaster to thy children?*[24]
>
> (5.8–9)

---

24. This association was first suggested in a cryptic note by Damon in his commentary on *Visions* (*Blake* 331); the fact that he refers only to "the obscene sixth chapter in Taylor's *Vindication*" perhaps accounts for the seemingly total neglect of a revealing allusion.

She then turns to the real issue of the "cold floods of abstraction" by which man has set up the system of sexual slavery.

Oothoon's indictment of loveless marriage includes some of the most powerful lines in the *Visions*—so powerful that they tend to be accepted without question as offering one of those rare moments of solid ground on which the hopeful critic can base a "reading." To be sure, Blake seems here to invoke some of Wollstonecraft's comments on "the slavery of marriage" (*Vindication* 232), but, having referred so extensively to an immediate context for the poem, we ought to note as well how neatly *Visions* functions as a book in the Lambeth "Bible of Hell." It presents, after all, one of the earliest references to Urizen. Oothoon wonders how the abstract institutions "where kings & priests may dwell" came into existence, and continues:

> *Till she who burns with youth. and knows no fixed lot; is bound*
> *In spells of law to one she loaths: and must she drag the chain*
> *Of life, in weary lust! must chilling murderous thoughts. obscure*
> *The clear heaven of her eternal spring? to bear the wintry rage*
> *Of a harsh terror driv'n to madness, bound to hold a rod*
> *Over her shrinking shoulders all the day; & all the night*
> *To turn the wheel of false desire: and longings that wake her womb*
> *To the abhorred birth of cherubs in the human form*
> *That live a pestilence & die a meteor & are no more.*
> *Till the child dwell with one he hates. and do the deed he loaths*
> *And the impure scourge force his seed into its unripe birth*
> *E're yet his eyelids can behold the arrows of the day.*
>
> (5.21–32)

The "incessant[ly] writhing" Oothoon describes a figure burning with youth who, like Orc, "incessant howls burning in the fires of Eternal Youth" (*M* 29.29) and who, like Orc, is soon "bound" with civil and religious laws and with "the chain of life," itself another form of "the Chain of Jealousy." In contrast to *Visions*, the optimistic end of *America* imagines that "the fires of Orc . . . in wreaths of fierce desire" finally force "the Priests" to flee, "leaving the females naked and glowing with the lusts of youth" (*Am* 15.22); the female spirits "pining in bonds of religion" are then free and feel again "desires of ancient times" (15.25). But the enchained "weary lust" of Oothoon's figure leads to chilling reflections that obscure her "heaven of generous love" (7.29)—like Oothoon's own "clear spring mudded with the feet of beasts." The "murderous thoughts," or unacted desires that stifle infant joys (following the famous Proverb of Hell), are the result, we read in *Jerusalem*, of "Jealousies" united into "a Religion of Chastity" (69.34).

The youthful female of Oothoon's imagination constantly reminds us of Oothoon's own experience—she is "to bear the wintry rage / Of a harsh terror driv'n to madness" like Oothoon, who is to bear (endure, bring to birth) "the child of Bromions rage." The reference to madness evokes again Bromios/Dionysos and his shattering effect on Pentheus and his mother Agave in the *Bacchae*. This male figure holding his "rod" also is "bound," so that, together with his mate "bound in spells of law," we have another image of the original couple "bound back to back in Bromions caves terror & meekness dwell" (along with its concern for "reflections," the *Visions* is fascinated with the concept of "dwelling," as over reflections). The terror is "bound to" because "bound with" meekness, which is "bound in." The whole system exists, then, in being bound through—the term seems needed—"enantiobiosis": differing expressions of bound energy that beget and live off of each other. This system continues "all the day; & all the night," and, via that repeated phrase, all through the poem as well.

While "the virgin / That pines for man; shall awaken her womb to enormous joys" (7.3–4), Oothoon's figure is limited to "longings that wake her womb / To the abhorred birth of cherubs in the human form / That live a pestilence." Oothoon adapts the language of "Albion's Angel" in *America*, who sees red Orc "writhing in pangs of abhorred birth" of revolution (9.17), and shows that she who falsely desires, like "he who desires but acts not, breeds pestilence" (*MHH* 7). "The child" she bears resembles, then, "the child Orc" (*BU* 20.6), who now recapitulates his mother's experience, dwelling with one he hates (his father and, later, his wife) and doing some mysterious loathed deed.[25] The bound system perpetuates itself—except in this poetry, where meanings proliferate to such an extent that we may read the line about the "impure scourge" as referring to the (possibly diseased) child masturbating, the (diseased) father with his "rod" forcing his son to an early, fruitless encounter with the institution of

25. According to Wollstonecraft, "Meek wives"—like those bound to "a harsh terror," perhaps—"are, in general, foolish mothers; wanting their children to love them best, and take their part, in secret, against the father, who is held up as a scarecrow" (346–47).

education or marriage, or the system of power itself. The "impure" scourge also raises the spectre of its double, a "pure" scourge—perhaps even Oothoon as she sees herself ("I am [i'm] pure"). But, hating or loathing, the child is still a son of his sire, one of "the swarthy children of the sun": "They are obedient, they resist not, they obey the scourge." The daughters of these children, to complete the cycle, "worship terrors." Since the child's "eyelids" should be "beamy," that is to say, "expansive as the morning" and "like the Sun" (*FZ* 73.37, 106.42), the fact that his seed is forced before his eyelids can behold the arrows (eros, arose [arising]) of day is equivalent to saying that the potential consciousness of the child (the force of Orc) is bound into the system before it can recognize itself. Hence, no delight for anyone.

But asserting, in effect, that she embodies purity and "Innocence! honest, open, seeking" and that, in particular, she is "open to virgin bliss," Oothoon turns to an analysis of modesty. Addressing herself through the personification of "Innocence," Oothoon asks,

> Who taught thee modesty, subtil modesty! child of night & sleep
> When thou awakest. wilt thou dissemble all thy secret joys
> Or wert thou not awake when all this mystery was disclos'd!
>
> (6.7–9)

The *Vindication* offers a discussion of "Modesty.—Comprehensively Considered, And Not as A Sexual Virtue," which begins with an apostrophe to "Modesty!" and the author's declaration that she will "presume to investigate thy Nature, and trace to its covert the mild charm" (273). Wollstonecraft's forceful conclusion is that "the modesty of women, characterized as such, will often be only the artful veil of wantonness instead of being the natural reflection of purity, till modesty be universally respected" (449). Oothoon sees that corrupted Innocence emerges as "a modest virgin knowing to dissemble / With nets found under thy night pillow, to catch the virgin joy" (6.10–11). Remarkably enough, after asking, despairingly, "And does my Theotormon seek this hypocrite modesty!" the virgin Oothoon dissemblingly imagines: "But silken nets and traps of adamant will Oothoon spread, / And catch for thee girls" (7.23–24). Considering Wollstonecraft's desire to join herself—nonsexually—to Fuseli and his dear wife, Oothoon's modest proposal to lie beside Theotormon, with its evasive syntax, is doubly pathetic:

Oothoon shall view his dear delight, nor e'er with jealous cloud
Come in the heavens of generous love; nor selfish blightings bring.
(7.28–29)

Why, one wonders, does she want to be present at all? Unless, perhaps, she doesn't. know. herself.

IV

But what of the eye behind *Visions*, the eye that "sees more than the heart knows"? The eye, as in *Julius Caesar*, that "sees not itself / But by reflection from other things?" For the *Visions* refers more to such a singular eye than any other of Blake's works and everywhere reflects an intensity of personal scrutiny. Even the title seems to go out of its way to break with the proper name format the other books of Blake's bible would lead us to expect—this work is of something seen.[26] There is, we can see, an eye outside the overt action of the poem, which yet inscribes itself within it, beginning with the frontispiece (fig. 10), where we look out through the cave/socket of one eye and (in most copies) see a dark sun peering angrily back, "like an eye / In the eastern cloud" (2.35–36). The nature of such perception from *hors de texte* emerges at the close of Theotormon's self-involved fantasy, as he addresses "O thought" rather than "Oothoon":

Where goest thou O thought? to what remote land is thy flight?
If thou returnest to the present moment of affliction
Wilt thou bring comforts on thy wings. and dews and honey and balm;
Or poison from the desart wilds, from the eyes of the envier.
(4.8–11)

"The envier" is within the "I" of Theotormon himself, as a local manifestation of the "Father of Jealousy" ("your eyes in"), living in "self-love that envies all! . . . / With lamplike eyes watching around the frozen marriage bed" (7.21–22). Bromion's response picks up with Theotormon's mention of "the eyes of the envier," thus showing itself to be

26. The oddity is emphasized by Catherine Blake's reference, after her husband's death, to *Visions* as "a work called Outhoun" (unless, of course, she is referring to a work of which we have no record; see Bentley, *Records* 363n.) One might also note that *Visions of the Daughters of Albion* has the same number of letters and the same order of subordination as *Vindication of the Rights of Woman*.

10.   *Visions of the Daughters of Albion*, frontispiece

as much directed at Theotormon as at Oothoon (the two men, or two aspects of a single man, discuss among themselves rather than deal with Oothoon): "Thou knowest that the ancient trees seen by thine eyes have fruit" (4.13). Oothoon, however, knows that "Love . . . / That clouds with jealousy his nights," will "spin a web of age around him . . . / Till his eyes sicken at the fruit that hangs before his sight" (7.17–20).

Oothoon believes that her clear eyes are "fix'd":

> Open to joy and to delight where ever beauty appears
> If in the morning sun I find it: there my eyes are fix'd
>
> In happy copulation
>
> (6.22–7.1)

The morning sun is also the mourning son on whom Oothoon is so fixated, though she would be satisfied "if Theotormon once would turn his loved eyes upon me" (3.15). Her eyes are so fixed, in ocular delight or scopophilia, that in promising to catch girls for Theotormon "& view their wanton play / In lovely copulation," Oothoon would become solar—for she says:

> Red as the rosy morning, lustful as the first born beam,
> Oothoon shall view his dear delight
>
> (7.27–28)

But as a "beam" she is simply a projection of sun (that "Jealous Globe" [M 10.19]), [27] so she becomes solus, soulless: a "darken'd . . . solitary shadow" enacting what she saw before, so that "instead of morn arises a bright shadow, like an eye." Oothoon's plight, finally, lies in our eyes. She asks:

> Does the sun walk in glorious raiment. on the secret floor
>
> Where the cold miser spreads his gold?
>
> (7.30–8.1)

"To the Eyes of a Miser a Guinea is more beautiful than the Sun," Blake writes in a letter, prefiguring the later parable that "the Suns

---

27. Ossian's Malvina is frequently described as a "lonely beam," "the beam of the east."

Light when he Unfolds it / Depends on the Organ that beholds it"
(*GP* frontispiece). Do we see light rays or "glorious raiment"? The two
obvious responses to Oothoon's conundrum are, "Yes, regardless of
what the miser sees, the glorious sun is still there," and, "No, if the
miser is secreted away and doesn't see the sun that way, then it
doesn't manifest itself that way." And yet, as soon as we see both possibilities, any decision is a heartless task, and we experience the eye
seeing more than the heart knows. We see, and we see our not seeing;
we know and know that we know only in part. The issue is not "ambiguity" or logical contradiction but the experience of various levels,
or "folds," of perception: contradictions in the logic of identity, in the
logic of this piece of writing. And Oothoon concludes entirely in this
mode, her question of whether the miser's eye beholds "the beam
that brings / Expansion to the eye of pity" reminding the reader further of Jesus' injunction to "first cast out the beam out of thine own
eye" (Matt. 7:5). As if to emphasize the multiple folds of perception,
even Oothoon's wailing finale, "Arise . . . Arise . . . ," is given in *The
Four Zoas* to Enitharmon, who sings the same words "in Rapturous
delusive trance" to revive Los to "delusive hopes":

> *Arise you little glancing wings & sing your infant joy*
> *Arise & drink your bliss*
> *For every thing that lives is holy. . . .*
>
> (34.78–80)

Oothoon's fear, that "beauty fades" from her so that she becomes
"a solitary shadow wailing on the margin of non-entity," is fully war-
ranted by the poem's conclusion:

> *Thus every morning wails Oothoon. but Theotormon sits*
> *Upon the margind ocean conversing with shadows dire.*
>
> *The Daughters of Albion hear her woes, & eccho back her sighs.*
>
> (8.11–13)

In Taylor, as we saw above, Blake encountered the Neoplatonic image
of "the dark sea of matter . . . the abyss of non-entity," and, more tell-
ingly, the explanation of the Narcissus myth given by Plotinus: "As
Narcissus, by catching at the shadow, merged himself with the
stream and disappeared, so he who is captivated by beautiful bodies,
and does not depart from their embrace, is precipitated, not with his

body, but with his soul, into a darkness profound and horrid to intellect, through which, becoming blind both here and in Hades, he con-
verses with nothing but Shadows" (Taylor, *Dissertation* 12–13; noted
by Raine 1:176). The "shadows dire" with which Theotormon con-
verses (Taylor elsewhere suggests the additional semantic possibility,
"mutual converse and copulation" [*Vindication* 46]) are the (literally)
atrophied forms of *desire*, the trajectory of which we have followed
from its engendering "moment" to its ever diminishing, increasingly
dire "reflections." The *Visions* thus illustrates the manifold applicability of the devil's contention that

> Those who restrain desire, do so because theirs is weak enough to be
> restrained; and the restrainer or reason usurps its place & governs the
> unwilling.
>   And being restrained it by degrees becomes passive till it is only the
> shadow of desire.
>
> (*MHH* 5)

Moreover, in suggesting that "conversing with shadows dire" represents Theotormon's involvement with his own narcissistic projections, the closing lines put forward the depressing possibility that *Oothoon herself is one of those projections*: herself, to repeat, "a solitary
shadow wailing on the margin of non-entity" (7.15). A creation of
Blake's vision of desire (like Thel, whose Greek echoes invoke want,
wish, and will) and desire for vision, Oothoon finally cannot connect
or develop because cut off by the impenetrability (or cunning) of history manifest in the psycho-cultural contradictions within Mary Wollstonecraft. She ends, then, as she began, a reflection:

> *Rend away this defiled bosom that I may reflect.*
>   (2.15)
>
> *Theotormon severely smiles. her soul reflects the smile;*
>   (2.18)
>
> *How can I be defild when I reflect thy image pure?*
>   (3.16)

A solitary shadow, she is the incarnation of the womb's "secret shadows," of the "amorous image" created by the youth "in the shadows
of his curtain," the embodiment of "solitude, / Where the horrible
darkness is impressed with reflections of desire" (7.10–11). As an un-

11. *Visions of the Daughters of Albion*, pl. 8

connected projection/reflection of desire, "she" can have no one identity, and any discussion that pretends to discuss what "Oothoon"
thinks or means or feels merely repeats (as we have here) the movement of the poem and impresses its own reflections of desire, "making" a subject out of an energy. "She" is a figure (a figuration) of the
text and, as such, searching for (her own) soul—and the sol or sun,
principle of self-generated energy that beams it forth—and searching
for an "I"—and the eye to hold it in view. But in the closing illustra-

tion (fig. 11) we see the image of her body on a verso page (in copy J, for example) drawn so that it appears to extend back through the pages, into the body of the book we are finishing, the book we complete: her case is in our hands and in our eyes (it certainly does not rest with the Daughters, Echoes to Theotormon's Narcissus!). So we might go further and say that "she" is the text, the other that lives in a desire not to master but to know, even in our hearts, "how much risk there is in a text, how much nonidentity, nonauthenticity, impossibility, and corrosiveness it holds for those who chose to see themselves within it" (Kristeva, *Desire* 163).

5

Re-Visioning *The Four Zoas*

DONALD AULT

GENERAL PRELUDIUM: UNBINDING NEWTONIAN NARRATIVE

Without giving full weight to the narratological implications of Blake's well-known visionary dictum that "the Eye altering alters all,"[1] it is difficult, if not impossible, to realize how the disruptive complexities that beset Blake's composition and revision of the verbal text of *The Four Zoas* constitute not a confusion of purpose or lack of fit between philosophy and poetic method but the emergence of a radical poetic ontology that fundamentally revises the meaning of "narrative," of "text," and of "reader." Taking Blake's "Eye altering" dictum seriously, however, puts us immediately at odds with a powerful assumption without which most scientific and technological progress prior to the twentieth century would not have been possible: that behind the complex world of external appearances lies one single, unified world toward which all true explanation must point.[2] This world view presupposes that subjective experience partially grasps and partially distorts features of the hidden unified field that allows "external objects" to appear; in this metaphysics, such external objects acquire the authority to pass judgment on the validity and completeness of subjective experience. In this world view it seems inconceivable that the way something is perceived constitutes its being or reality; indeed

---

1. From "The Mental Traveller" (line 62, E485). Like most lines in Blake, this one enacts in the reader (the "Eye" or "I") the event or principle it expresses or invokes.

2. For detailed historical and conceptual elaboration of this point, see my "Incommensurability," which exploits Paul Feyerabend's subversive speculations in *Against Method*.

such a constitution would seem to imply an idealism profoundly more problematic than Bishop Berkeley's "*esse* is *percipi*."[3] Blake, however, labeled this pervasive world view "Single vision & Newtons sleep" (E722), insisting that the surface dualism in, for example, such guises as Locke's primary and secondary qualities and powers betrays a yearning to penetrate and merge with the mysterious underlying unified world, a nostalgic desire for final rest and complete certainty in a state of metaphysical incest.[4]

Throughout his career Blake waged uncompromising war against "Single vision," which he perceived as infiltrating the most crucial fields of existence, binding down and artificially limiting social organization, individual fulfillment, narrative possibility, and language itself. Especially in his extended struggle to compose and revise *The Four Zoas* Blake experimented with developing narrative structures that could function therapeutically to rehabilitate imaginations damaged by "Single vision." This experiment is by no means restricted to *The Four Zoas*, although the manuscript state of the text of the *Zoas* affords peculiar insight into Blake's process of narrative composition. *Milton* and *Jerusalem* are saturated with the strategies he developed in the *Zoas* to combat and subvert the form of explanatory storytelling that can be labeled generically as "Newtonian narrative."[5]

"Newtonian narrative" presupposes that behind the text lies a single unified field (*ur*-narrative, privileged originating event, state of consciousness, and so on) whose essential features do not irreconcilably and incommensurably conflict with one another but can (in theory at least) be fully captured through systematic analytic explanation. In such a view, discrepancies between textual details merely reflect errors of perception or memory in characters or in the narrator. Both "Single vision" and "Newtonian narrative" aim toward realizing the coherence and completeness of a narrative world or text (which, in this view, contains a narrative world in potential form) and toward realizing a preordained "end" or closure that resolves conflicts into a

---

3. For a discussion of Blake's response to dualism in Locke, Berkeley, and Hume in a context somewhat different from the present essay, see my "Blake and Newton."

4. For an extended discussion of these matters, see my *Visionary Physics* 58–68.

5. In its generic sense, "Newtonian narrative" underlies most conventional narrative forms; in its specific sense—narratives produced by the "historical" Newton—"Newtonian narrative" is an extreme case of the generic drives toward unity, repression, closure, and so on. See note 6 below.

unified whole.[6] The implicit goal of Newtonian narrative is imaginative death through positive affirmation; the explicit goal of Blake's narrative is an intense awakening, through negative dialectic, to hitherto buried possibilities of the human imagination.

The conflict between, on the one hand, Blake's desire to renovate his reader's perception by relentlessly subverting "Single vision," and, on the other, the powerful temptations of Newtonian narrative itself is played out in the radical process of revising that *The Four Zoas* underwent. At times, Blake's disruptive revisions seem almost an overreaction against his own Newtonian impulses, resulting in alien poetic strategies and narrative complexities that easily could be (and have been) taken as demonstrating incoherence or a loss of control and purpose.[7] How the poem was transformed from its *Vala* state into *The Four Zoas* suggests that revision takes on a double significance: it is both something that Blake did to the text and something that the text does, through the agency of narrative, not only to the reader but to itself. Indeed, Blake's whole enterprise constitutes the irreducible presence of multiple interfering and incommensurable structures that operate (1) to rule out a pre-existent underlying world that surface events (i.e., those narrated by the linear text) partially rearrange and

6. What I am calling *generic* "Newtonian narrative" fulfills almost exactly the conditions Peter Brooks sets forth for all narrative in general in his excellent psychoanalytic essay, "Freud's Masterplot," which I encountered only after I had completed this present essay. In discussing the drive toward narrative closure as the death impulse, for example, Brooks says: "The very possibility of meaning plotted through time depends on the anticipated structuring force of the ending; the interminable would be the meaningless" (283). Again: "Textual energy, all that is aroused into expectancy and possibility in a text . . . can become usable by plot only when it has been bound or formalized. . . . To speak of 'binding' in a literary text is thus to speak of any formalizations (which, like binding, may be painful, retarding) that force us to recognize sameness within difference" (290). Blake's *Four Zoas* narrative subverts these conditions systematically, even in its persistent emphasis on difference within sameness. In terms of *specific* "Newtonian narrative," these concerns are part and parcel of the mathematical and experimental-scientific texts Newton composed; these issues are perhaps even clearer, however, in his nonscientific work—especially in his published *Chronology of Ancient Kingdoms Amended* (which lays the foundation for tracing a single, linear course of events from creation to apocalypse), and in his unpublished commentaries on "The Book of Revelation," in which the symbols of the apocalypse, as the closing event of our world, can be interpreted only by means of Newton's own exegetical algebra (Ault, "Incommensurability" 294–96, and Manuel).

7. For example, Bentley claims that "as time went on Blake tended more and more to let the thought determine the form of his poetry, and the thought was becoming more amorphous. . . . His absorbing interest in the growing myth obscured or somehow denied his sense of poetic form" (*Vala* 186).

partially distort, and (2) to generate a narrative field in which the past is not closed and complete but open—unfinished and revisable. That is, instead of a prefabricated underlying single world or *ur*-narrative (whether it be an ideal substratum of the text or *Vala* itself) that supports the details of the surface narrative and is signified by them, Blake substitutes a deep structure that is a transformational process at the service of (and brought into existence by) the temporally unfolding surface narrative. In this sense, the surface narrative is primary, and the deep structure is an evolving secondary by-product of the operations of the poem's narrative surface. By incorporating into *The Four Zoas* subversive narrative processes (perspective transformation and aspectual interconnection) and textual features (text as flight and text as woven pattern), Blake achieves what otherwise might seem virtually impossible—a narrative field with an open past such that past narrative facts can be altered and revised by present ones, thereby allowing present events to resist being absorbed passively into a static, dead, and unrevisable underlying world. In this sense, *The Four Zoas* embodies a vision of the process of linear re-visioning. The narrative ontology that thus emerges from the poem necessarily resists being completed into a closed, reified object that permits no further revision.

Although the conflict between closure and revision indirectly parallels the struggle between Newtonian and anti-Newtonian composition, it is possible (though unlikely) that Blake was unaware of this aspect of the conflict and thus may have been tempted (by the lures of Newtonian narrative) to "complete" the poem even though it progressively assumed a form he did not intend. Presuming to delineate authoritatively what Blake's conscious "intentions" were in the face of the manuscript's textual tangles, which evolved over many years, would necessarily be misguided and misleading. Since our purpose is to describe and demonstrate the operation of narrative processes and textual features that are manifest in the poem itself, it is possible to defer or bracket the question of intention in favor of the analysis of the poem's narrative field (including the features that the revisions brought into existence). It must be said, however, that Blake's tendency to subvert the idea of a "definitive" text—by altering details in different copies and subsequent printings of poems and by allowing narrative segments, under revision, to migrate from one poem to an-

other, with the effect of de-entifying the meaning of those segments—suggests that he was well aware of the threat that closure
posed to his transformational narrative ontology.

It is inevitable that, in assaulting his reader so aggressively with
presuppositions and techniques that fundamentally conflict with
Newtonian narrative and thus with habitual thought processes and
conventional narrative procedures, Blake risked losing most of the
audience that he intended for the poem (readers caught up in "Single
vision"). Moreover, in order to square his philosophical principles
with the narrative strategies they demand—which include a continual teaching of subversive narrative rules and a subsequent testing of
the reader's imaginative judgment in terms of those rules, a continual
laying of traps to ensnare, especially, the Newtonian reader—he
risked, almost invited, a total misunderstanding of the poem even by
those readers more sympathetic to his poetic program.[8]

Blake's risky challenge to normal reading procedures demands a
revision of those Newtonian notions of text, of narrative, and of
reader that cling to a rigid subject-object division. Specifically, the assumptions that the text is purely "objective," an unchangeable, inert,
pre-existent given; that the reader is purely "subjective," a self-iden-
tical, centralized, unified consciousness whose function is merely to
respond to and interpret the given text; and that the narrative world
exists potentially complete within the text and is progressively realized through the interaction between subjective reader and objective
text—all these are ruthlessly undermined by *The Four Zoas*. In the
poem Blake experiments with creating a text that cannot sustain its
authentic existence independent of and prior to the narrative world in
the process of being constituted through sequential acts of reading,
thereby creating a reader whose perception is able to alter the very
being of the text's supposedly fixed facts and devising a narrative
world that, although it comes into existence temporally through the
mutual interconstitution of reader and text, functions as the primary
agent by which the reader and text are able to transform one another
mutually.

---

8. It is interesting to note that Newton's own personal strategy was exactly the opposite: he suppressed public acknowledgment of any doctrine he felt might "prejudice"
his readers against him or make them think he was an "extravagant freak" (Ault, "Incommensurability" 289; see also McGuire 165).

NARRATIVE PROCESSES AND
TEXTUAL FEATURES

Because of its subversive poetic program, *The Four Zoas* resists penetration by traditional critical tools. It is therefore necessary to make a
sudden break into the explanatory circle of text, narrative, and reader,
much like the rupture near the poem's opening where Blake inter-
rupts the unfolding pseudo-invocation with the manifesto, "Begin
with Tharmas Parent power" (*FZ* 4.6, E301). One episode that can be
isolated from its context with little damage to the poem's complex dialectics and which, at the same time, clearly exhibits the narrative and
textual features that are the building blocks of *The Four Zoas* occurs in
the cryptic events surrounding the appearance of the "Circle of Destiny" (whose minute details are understandably often disregarded),
near the beginning of Night 1. In this episode, following an elliptical
conversation with his female counterpart Enion, "Tharmas Parent
power," the ostensible narrative nucleus out of which the poem generates, turns "round" the Circle of Destiny and then sinks into the
sea. As he descends, Tharmas exudes bodily "fibres" that Enion
weaves into a "perverse" form with "a will / Of its own" that then becomes (or brings into existence) the Circle of Destiny itself.[9]

---

9. In presenting this reductive summary of the episode in order to bring the causal
paradox more clearly into view, I have omitted numerous important details, which actually intensify the argument here. In resorting to a brief description of how some of
these details function, I warn the reader that much of this will probably make more
sense if read after the discussion of narrative principles in the text proper. Blake indicates the parallelism between the departures of Tharmas and Enion by marking their
departures with brief, repeated utterances: "So saying—From her bosom weaving" (*FZ*
5.6, E302) and "So saying he sunk down" (*FZ* 5.13, E302). When Blake uses the phrase
"*So* saying" it usually means that the saying is a version of the doing (bodily action). In
this case, Enion had said she would "die" and "hide from [Tharmas'] searching
eyes"(*FZ* 5.5, E302)—reversing Tharmas' earlier accusation toward her (and thus anatomizing her)—hence her ability to weave from the fibers of her own "bosom." Yet it is
Tharmas who hides and dies by sinking beneath the sea in the form of a "pale white
corse" (*FZ* 5.13, E302). Signaled by the repeated "So saying," these two speech/bodily
acts interconstitute each other in such a way that the "Sinewy threads" from her bosom
(*FZ* 5.6, E302) reappear as the fibers she draws from the descending Tharmas: "In
gnawing pain drawn out by her lovd fingers every nerve / She counted. every vein &
lacteal threading them among / Her woof of terror" (*FZ* 5.16–18, E302). Though she
begins weaving in the text *prior to* Tharmas' turning around the Circle of Destiny, the
fibers do not become explicitly the residue of Tharmas until *after* (in the surface of
the text) he has turned around the Circle of Destiny and sunk down into the sea. In
any case the causal series is irreducibly circular. Features of Blake's text (such as the
interpenetration of and counterpoint between narrative and spoken information)
are packed into this short sequence as well.

NARRATIVE IMPLICATIONS OF THE
CIRCLE OF DESTINY EPISODE

Perspective Transformation. This sequence exemplifies perspective transformation (specifically retroactive transformation) under the guise of a causal loop or circle on the surface of the text: if the Circle existed *before* Tharmas sank down into the sea, how can it come into existence as a *result* of his sinking down? By means of this causal paradox in the narrative surface, Blake invites the reader to undergo a retroactive perspective transformation, a process that always requires a conflict (or discrepancy) between two very different but closely related reader events. In this case the Circle first appears as if it does not need explanation, as if it were a given, pre-existent feature of the poem's underlying or presupposed world. But the Circle's second appearance retroactively corrects the reader's natural assumption that the Circle must have existed prior to the action of the poem or it could not have been referred to. Now, in the Circle's second appearance, its origin requires elucidation in terms of the most specific details of the emerging plot (Tharmas' sinking down, his bodily fibers, the weaving of the Circle). The second appearance interferes with the first, nearly but not quite canceling it out. This retroactive transformation is anything but unique; the process occurs relentlessly throughout the poem, often in cases more radical.

Aspectual Interconnection. As noted above, the appearances of the Circle are situated in the poem following an elliptical conversation between Tharmas and Enion in which he accuses her of a kind of questioning or examining that extracts fibers from his soul. When these fibers are transferred from Tharmas' speech into the narrative proper (events uttered by the narrator), they become bodily fibers, the material out of which Enion weaves the Circle of Destiny. This aspectual interconnection, by which details can migrate from inside a speech into the narrative proper (and vice versa), reveals how the narrator, the characters, and the landscape interconstitute one another. While information seems to be divided between two discrete sources (the narrator proper and the speeches, questions, visions, and so on, of characters) with ostensibly minimal overlapping of the two sets of events, these two streams of information are in reality aspects of one another and transformations of each other. The possibility of such a process of interconnection presupposes that continually originating and transforming relationships constitute the primary identity of characters, of the narrator, and of the events. When relationships between narrative details crystalize in such a way that they can acquire names, they begin to act as if they were independent beings with lives of their own (much as, in Night 1, the alternate version of the form that emerges from Tharmas' woven fibers is actually a separate character, the Spectre of Tharmas). At any time, however, independent characters can dissolve back into the landscape or into the narrator's voice. Events, characters, and perspectives are completely interconnected, but only by implication. Since the characters suppress (or are unaware of) their mutual interconnection and treat themselves as isolated entities or egos, even the narrator cannot make connections for the reader, because the narrator takes on the aspects of the characters and events he is narrating.

TEXTUAL IMPLICATIONS OF THE
CIRCLE OF DESTINY EPISODE

The Circle of Destiny episode involves two actions, Tharmas' withdrawal beneath the surface of the sea and Enion's weaving. These actions constitute two opposing aspects of Blake's *Four Zoas* text. The word *text* has etymological roots in the process of weaving, and the aspect of Blake's text that interweaves minute details into complex and interfering ("perverse") patterns is dialectically opposed to the aspect of Blake's text that conceals, represses, and evades, in flight, withdrawal, and hiding; this flight manifests itself as discrepancies, inconsistencies, gaps, and discontinuities in the text. *Text as flight* makes mandatory the reader's microscopic scrutiny of syntax and diction, an anatomizing attention that constitutes the discrete acts of perception through which the continuously unfolding and originating narrative field is shattered and reconstituted; *text as interwoven pattern* is the ground for extrapolating visual graphic schemas that express (through arbitrary signifiers) those (signified) structural strategies, narrative switchpoints, and so on, that are inherently inaccessible to direct temporal experience of the poem but that in part govern the organization of narrative details and discrepancies (see below, figs. 13–17, for some examples of these textual possibilities). Taken by itself, text as flight gives rise to the impression of arbitrariness and incompleteness; text as interwoven pattern, taken by itself, divides the narrative into finite, reified, closed structures. These schematic patterns are second-order phenomena, generated by the primary surface narrative, which acts inexhaustibly to revise, subvert, and desubstantialize the very perceptual structures that allow the temporal narrative to exist.

The narrative aspects of Blake's *Four Zoas* (perspective transformation and the aspectual interconnections between the narrator's voice and other narrative voices) and the dialectical conflict between flight and weaving of the text itself produce the tight, dense network of transformations that is the primary reality of Blake's *Four Zoas*, apart from which there are no events in the poem. These narrative and textual aspects, taken together, guarantee that there is no pre-existent substructure of specifiable events that is partially distorted or partially interpreted by surface perspectives. The narrative principles reflect or mirror the workings of the text itself, because each of these features is an aspect of the others: they invade and interconstitute one another in an incestuous or narcissistic way, so that any language that attempts to describe them must fold back on itself, and so that any attempt to isolate them analytically from one another must rupture their field of mutual interrelations. Nevertheless, because Blake was unwilling to compromise the difficulty of realizing his goal—a fundamental restructuring of his reader's consciousness—it is necessary not to recoil from Blake's challenge but to respond to it directly, no matter to what alien territory such an investigation may lead. Thus, in order to move forward, it is necessary to back up and examine these narrative and textual features in more detail.

NARRATIVE AND TEXT
RECONSIDERED

The Narrative Field

Perspective Transformation. An implication of the apparent causal loop at the center of the Circle of Destiny episode is that the very possibility of an event's occurrence (Tharmas' turning around the Circle) is nearly canceled out at the exact moment its preconditions come into existence in a posterior event (the emergence of the Circle itself from Tharmas' woven fibers). A natural Newtonian reflex in the face of this causal paradox might be to posit an underlying event, object, or structure—the *ur*-Circle of Destiny—then assign subscripts to the two narrated events in the order of their appearance (i.e., $Circle_1$ and $Circle_2$), and treat each of these as surface transformations or aspects of the primordial underlying Circle of Destiny event. This gesture defeats the purpose for which it was made, however; it cannot account for causal discrepancies because such a primordial event must be constituted—as must all such substantialist abstractions—by features that the two surface events have in common.[10] Beyond the words of the text, however, the two narrative Circles have little in common.

A more productive strategy would be to treat $Circle_2$ as a transformation of $Circle_1$, and indeed this approach finds some support in the minute verbal differences between the two events.[11] Although this tactic avoids the distracting and unexplanatory assumption of a completed underlying world, it does not go far enough; it does not account for the way $Circle_2$ actually subverts the possibility of $Circle_1$. While it acknowledges that relationships between elements in a narrative series can significantly be constituted by differences rather than

10. Techniques of isolating and extracting common elements from objects, events, and other sundry particulars in order to reify ideal forms (naive Platonism), substantial forms (Aristotelianism), conceptual fictions (Lockean empiricism), and so on, in order to account for the metaphysical mystery of language, are so well known as to need little elaboration here. A critique of this process that accords well with our present enterprise, however, appears in Ernst Cassirer's early *Substance and Function* (3–26). Abstraction by resemblance stands in contrast to structural, differential, and transformational techniques.

11. I am thinking primarily of details such as these: (1) The "circle" appears with lower-case *c* (i.e., "circle of Destiny") in *FZ* 5.11, E302, while it appears upper case in *FZ* 5.24, E302; (2) the second appearance of the Circle is followed by the word "Complete," giving rise to the possibility that it is a later or more definitive (closed) form of the Circle than the previous occurrence—perhaps even that the second is three-dimensional ("a watry Globe") (*FZ* 5.25, E302), while the first might have been only two-dimensional; and (3) the syntax that surrounds the second is, unlike the first, ambiguous, indeed, almost *in*complete—"on the tenth trembling morn the Circle of Destiny Complete / Round rolld the Sea Englobing in a watry Globe" (*FZ* 5.24–25, E302). These differences (which could be dismissed as flaws of an unfinished manuscript) do not in any way dilute the causal/temporal paradox at the heart of the episode. The strongest evidence of a linear, causal relation between the two occurrences of the phrase ("Circle of Destiny") lies in the possibility that $Circle_1$ is somehow incomplete or two-dimensional—yet the narrator gives no hint of this as a possibility, nor does Tharmas act as if there were anything other than a pre-existent structure with no need for further articulation, which he can "turn round" prior to his descent. Thus, the additional information the narrator gives about $Circle_2$ acts as a lure to the reader to try to explain away the discrepancy in more naturalistic terms, but Blake refuses to give enough evidence about $Circle_1$ to make that easy retreat possible.

similarities, it stops short of seeing that what primarily connects the two events is a radical narrative principle: that the past itself is not fixed and stable but can undergo transformation or revision.

Such retroactive transformations appear at almost every juncture, sometimes in cases much less noticeable than in the Circle of Destiny, but often in cases even more radical. The process is always the same: details that are the consequences of a linear narrative chain turn out not only to establish the preconditions of a prior event in the chain but actually to subvert the prior event per se: the posterior event seems to cause and nearly rule out the prior event at the same time. Retroactive transformations must alter significantly the reader's perception, not only of the transforming past but of the *future* as well. The text evokes a kind of free-floating anxiety (which in any given narrative situation is nevertheless quite precise) concerning how the future of the text will make possible or cancel out the contours of the present narrative event.

This process cannot be explained away by the Newtonian assumption that the "events" in question occur only in the "reader" and not in the "text" itself. Retroactive perspective transformation is, we must recall, an aspect of the narrative, and the narrative is the primary agent by which the reader is able to cause the text to alter or revise itself. Retroactive transformation must, of course, occur in the reader, or it cannot occur in the text; but it must be perceived by the reader (through the agency of the narrative) as occurring in the text itself (and not just in the reader). If the reader does not experience the text as transforming itself, the reader will simply perceive the discrepancy between the two textual facts and interpret it as a subjective error on the part of the reader or the narrator. In this latter case, the radical *Four Zoas* narrative fails to come into existence at all, and the text exists as an inert nest of paradoxes, mistakes, and non sequiturs. Any reader who is able to perceive the text as though it were itself undergoing transformations, dissolving fixed facts in the receding narrative and allowing the past to be reenacted and revised, has already been initiated into Blake's perspective drama. The reader who resists Blake's text and anxiously clings to the security of one of the fundamental elements of a pre-existent underlying world—a privileged originating event, a primal rupture, or "Fall"—refuses to acknowledge that the "Fall" or rupture actually comes into existence through the reader's failed imaginative judgment in the face of radical discrepancies and does not lie before or beneath the text (see below).

Because it rules out the existence of a prefabricated world that acts as a mysterious substratum of the text (akin to the "I know not what" of Locke and Berkeley), perspective transformation argues that whatever underlying world or deep structure the poem exhibits must come into existence in the process of being narrated. The operation of this generative process imposes on Blake's narrative field a severe restriction—the primacy of narrative sequential order—that dictates that the *order* in which characters appear and events occur is a primary feature of their reality. This narrative requirement in part accounts for the intensity of Blake's obsession with rearranging, inserting, and deleting segments of *The Four Zoas*.[12]

Aspectual Interconnection: The "Fall" as Privileged Event and Pretext. Throughout the poem Blake distinguishes between two sources of information: the constantly modulating voice of the narrator and the spoken words—questions, interpolated visions, remembrances, and so on—of characters who appear in the narrative proper. Initially it seems as if there are two distinct and contrapuntal streams of information alternating with each other: spoken visions, memories, and so on that seem to refer compulsively to a privileged originating event

---

12. This restriction acquires ontological priority because (1) order (and mode) of entry and occurrence absolutely determine *how* a subsequent event can take into account and modify a prior event; and (2) the experiential significance of an event is determined by its location (radically altered by its relocation) in the temporal series, since there is no ontologically prior underlying sequence of events that could renarrate the surface events in their "proper" order (that is, the surface order is the narrative proper). "Simultaneity," in its popular sense of two events happening at the same time, is ruled out because the absolute authority of the temporal series in generating the narrative field forces all the reader/text events to be realized under a lapse of time. Although a present event can (and usually does) enact several narrative functions "simultaneously," there is no rigorous sense in which two events (say, A and B), separated in the narrative sequence, occur "at the same time" in the world of the narrative itself (since that world is bound to the unfolding temporal sequence). It is more accurate to say that such events (which share features such as phrase repetition) are *aspectually* related (A is an aspect of B) or *intersectionally* related (the features of A intersect the features of B in such-and-such a precise way). Retroactive transformation, however, reintroduces a more subversive "simultaneity" by allowing a prior event to come back to life, literally to be resurrected, as it is gathered into (constituted/canceled out by) the present event that reincarnates it.

(the primal "Fall" of "Man") and the narrative proper (whose events seem to be happening *after* the events in the spoken accounts). Since the characters (and even the narrator) rarely talk about, remember, or directly refer to what has been happening in the unfolding narrative proper, its events seem to be constantly disappearing. Characters' speech gestures often act as decoys to draw attention away from the actions they are engaged in and which are disguised (though sometimes obliquely enacted) by their speech gestures. Despite the fact that in these interpolated visions the characters claim to be referring to another state of being altogether, the poem invites the reader to interpret these visions as the characters' own fictional transformation of relationships between already present characters and events.

Though nothing less than a vast accumulation of instances could be fully persuasive here, perhaps a simple example will suffice. In Night 4, the "Spectre of Urthona" enters the narrative proper at the moment Tharmas separates Los from Enitharmon, but the Spectre retells this event as if it had not just occurred but had happened in the distant past, at the original "Fall," associated with an utterly different causal background. Significantly, he has no memory of, or makes no reference to, his immediate separation in the narrative proper. In general, the characters behave as if they were referring to (rather than fantasizing or fictionalizing) a world other than (temporally prior to, spatially beyond) the world of the narrative proper. In fact, the near absence of references (by characters) to events in the narrative proper cumulatively creates the possibility that the retroactively dissolving events in the narrative proper are themselves the fantasy and not the common world that the characters mutually inhabit.

Within this framework of a fundamental, though undermined, distinction between narrated events and visions, songs, soliloquies, and so on, the reader is constantly caught between the narrator's version and various characters' versions of "events": it is in this moment of suspension that the reader's (Newtonian) reflex yearning to grasp the primordial event (the "Fall") itself enacts in the reader the breach that the reader is attempting to locate before or beneath the text. In terms of Blake's anti-Newtonian strategy, narrative events do not occur *after* a primal "Fall" beyond the text, nor do interpolated visions refer to a primal "Fall" in the dim past. The "Fall" is a narrative pretext, occasioning a breach in the reader who refuses to recognize that the opposition between narrative and interpolated information is only apparent, and who thereby reenacts the speakers' evasive directing of their speech gestures away from the present narrative context, fictionalizing that context in parables involving other names, times, and places in order to deny the living reality of their present situation.

Blake's narrative thus intermittently teases the reader into believing that the poem's events are linearly unfolding reenactments of a single unapproachable, pre-existent moment, all the while undermining the possibility of such a privileged primordial moment. In addition, beginning especially in Night 7(a), the narrative begins to hold out the hope that the knotted complexities and paradoxes of that precipitating event, which always seems outside the text, will be revealed, reversed, and resolved within the text itself in Night 9. The asymmetry is obvious: in this reading, the precipitating event cannot be directly dramatized but the resolving event can be. There is, however, strong evidence that the precipitating event (the "Fall") finally materializes in the text itself at the moment the apocalyptic reunion of Tharmas and Enion takes place—in which case it is the most radical case of retroactive constitution/canceling out in the poem.

The Dialectic of the Text

Text as Flight. The subversive microscopic surface of the poem's narrative is the aspect we have identified with Tharmas' withdrawal beneath the oceanic surface in the Circle of Destiny episode. Indeed, this is no unique act by Tharmas: he is constantly perceived as fleeing from confrontations, leaving in his wake perceptual "vortexes" and voids. His compulsive fleeing reappears as an aspect of the text under the guise of discrepancies, gaps, and discontinuities. Perhaps the most problematic point at which to enter the text under the aspect of flight is one of the points that caused Blake the greatest difficulty (as evidenced by massive deletions and revisions)—the opening lines of the poem itself. In the first eight lines of the poem proper, the narrative voice divides into a sequential dialogue or dialectic whose physical, spatial layout on the page possesses significance in itself. The first three lines focus on the "Song of the Aged Mother"; the next three lines emphasize the "Universal Brotherhood"; and from the last two lines of this sequence the "Heavenly Father" emerges. (This family constellation is further completed when the "Daughter of Beulah" ap-

pears six lines later.) The physical relationship of these three segments to one another on the space of the page sandwiches the Brotherhood between the Mother (on top) and Father (below). In so doing
these lines embody a fundamental discrepancy ideographically: is it
significant that the Brotherhood has come spatially *between* the Aged
Mother and Heavenly Father? And why does the physical arrangement of the lines of the text seem to invert the traditional spatial arrangement (by analogy with nature) in which the "Heavenly Father"
is a sky god above and the "Aged Mother" is the earth below? If we
read this spatial descent down the page as signifying a temporal order, it is possible that the sequence of the lines embodies a narrative
sequence in which the Aged Mother's matriarchy precedes the seizure of power by the sons, and the Father appears as a reflex of the
sons' achievement of Brotherhood, from which females (such as the
Daughters of Beulah) are excluded.

These observations concerning the spatial layout of the text do not,
of course, fully take into account the microscopic detail of the poem's
surface at this point. David Erdman points out that Blake made several tries at a six-line introductory stanza, "with erasure on erasure"
(E819). The original versions of these lines clarify the syntactic tension
in a way that (for whatever reasons) did not satisfy Blake. As they
stand in Erdman's edition in the state beyond which Blake revised no
further (usually attributed to his giving up), these lines read:

> *The Song of the Aged Mother which shook the heavens with wrath*
> *Hearing the march of long resounding strong heroic Verse*
> *Marshalld in order for the day of Intellectual Battle*
> (FZ 3:1–3, E300)

The earliest layer of the text Erdman could recover made explicit the
relation of the "Song" to the poem we are reading, and the relation of
both the song and the poem to the individual reader of the poem:

> *This is the* [Dirge] *(Song) of* [Eno] *(Enitharmon) which shook the heavens*
> *with wrath*
> *And thus beginneth the Book of Vala which Whosoever reads*
> *If with his Intellect he comprehend the terrible Sentence*
> *The heavens* [shall] *quake: the earth* [shall move] [moves] *(was moved) &*
> *[shudder] [shudders] (shudderd) & the mountains*
> *With all their woods, the streams & valleys:* [wail] *(waild) in dismal fear*

[To hear] *(Hearing)* the [Sound] *(march) of Long resounding strong heroic verse*
Marshalld in order for the day of intellectual battle

[E819]

The fact that Blake at some time numbered the lines 1, 2, 3, 6, 7, 4, 5 [E819], a revision that dictated some of the verb-phrase alterations, does not remove the fundamental gap between the three-line introduction (which Blake revised no further) and the earlier, longer, deleted version(s). In the original version(s) the opening lines express the analogy between the shaking of the heavens in *wrath* against the Song (which *begins* the poem we are reading, the "Book of Vala") and the shaking of the heavens in *fear* at the comprehension by any individual of the "terrible Sentence" of the Song/Book. In the final version, it is quite unclear who or what is doing the "hearing": it is possible that the "heavens" are hearing the song composed of "strong heroic verse" and are shaking in wrath against it; it is also possible that the Aged Mother is doing the hearing and that her "Song" is a wrathful response to Blake's own strong heroic verse that composes *The Four Zoas*.

As Blake left it, the revised version of these lines decisively compresses the reader into the ambiguity of the syntax, deletes the "Book of Vala," and thereby complicates the relation of the "Song" to the poem we are reading. Equally significant is Blake's deletion of acknowledgment that the poem potentially has the power to pronounce a "Sentence" so "terrible" that its comprehension will issue in immediate and catastrophic apocalyptic consequences in the reader Blake hopes to create through the process of reading *The Four Zoas*. This strategy of deletion deflects the Newtonian reader from awareness of the immediate urgency of the poem's radical theme—the opening up of terrifying ontological options through the act of reading the poem's "Sentence," in all its polysemous suggestiveness. By withholding this information Blake refuses to call attention to the poem's frightening urgency and thus refuses to set in motion self-conscious ego-gratifying expectations and anxieties directed toward a goal—either achieving or fleeing from the judgment of the "terrible Sentence" that the deleted segment hides from the reader and yet (by virtue of the gaping hole left by its exclusion) simultaneously thrusts upon the reader.

Thus in these three lines, there is an urgent feeling that something is missing or lost—in this case both the vanished elements that would complete the syntax and the explicit reference to the reader and the basic underlying narrative pretext (hidden from the reader), the "Book of Vala," whose only trace is the word "Vala" suspended over the page. It is no accident that such a gap or discrepancy stands at the very threshold of the poem. It seems likely that Blake tried to undercut the clear causal relations the original version provided, first by altering line order with attendant changes in verb tenses and then by completely striking the lines that fill in the causal gaps. The original version adheres strictly to subject-predicate syntax ("This is . . . ," "Thus beginneth . . ."). The revised lines eliminate the predicate per se but still imply that there has been a radical grammatical transformation that has deleted and/or suppressed the predicate. The earlier version is neatly divisible into causally connected phrases. The revised version complicates even the subordinate clause ("which shook . . .") by juxtaposing it with the participial form "Hearing," which is ambiguous in temporal and spatial reference. As they stand, apparently incomplete and incompletable, the revisions do not move toward a visual surface text that simplifies, reduces problems, unpacks syntax, and clarifies the reader's response. Blake's vision moves toward compression and complication simultaneously.

In the next three lines, two periods occur that function to make more explicit the subversive nature of the statements they punctuate. The narrative voice shifts from the initial pseudo-epic diction, saturated with imagery that hints at violent conflict, to a propositional form:

> *Four Mighty Ones are in every Man; a Perfect Unity*
> *Cannot Exist. but from the Universal Brotherhood of Eden*
> *The Universal Man. To Whom be Glory Evermore Amen*
> [FZ 3.4–6, E300–301]

The spatial layout of these lines requires constant reinterpretation and redirection of expectation as the words are read. The first line taken alone asserts and visualizes the perfect unity of the Four. The next line begins by denying that unity—it "Cannot Exist." Nor does the syntax that follows completely relieve the tension. The crux of the line is "but from," following the intrusive period. Even if the problematic period after "Cannot Exist" were not there, these two words would, in themselves, disruptively revise the settled, completed, unified world/utterance of the previous line. Blake holds in balance the discontinuous shock of denying the perfect unity and the continuous syntax that proceeds to assert the conditions under which that unity is possible, however tenuous they may be: "but from" may signify that unity can exist only as derived from the Universal Brotherhood— a reading that simultaneously neutralizes the shock effect of Blake's spatial grammar (and punctuation) and readily conforms to the traditional paradigms of Newtonian narrative.

In order to move beyond such Newtonian reflexes and get a glimpse of why Blake had so much trouble with the opening, whose revisions move in the direction of making outrageous demands on the reader, it is necessary to recognize that this disjunctive period opens up the disturbing possibility that perhaps only apart from, that is, outside the context or beyond the influence of the Universal Brotherhood, can Perfect Unity exist—that is, the Brotherhood is somehow at odds with unity. This second reading is complicated by the fact that, as we have seen, "unity" is not always unambiguously valorized by Blake, since it is easily a characteristic of "Single vision."[13] The previous Newtonian reading neatly collapses the object and seeker of de-

---

13. Because "unity" is as close to the forces of analytical reduction as it is to the forces of imaginative integration, Blake's use of the term in any particular situation must be carefully considered in its dialectic context: any kind of "unity" that irreducibly involves closure must, in general, be suspect. For example, unity or oneness infects Urizen's entire project: his "Laws of peace, of love, of unity" (*BU* 4.34, E72) rapidly degenerate into a mere reflex single vision, absorbing peace into "King," love into "God," and unity into "Law" in constituting a totally reductive unified world—"One King, one God, one Law" (*BU* 4.40, E72). Some unions in Blake's poems are delusions, some are misdirected, some are treacherous, and some (perhaps fewer than we might like to think) are positive. In his short critical commentary ON HOMERS POETRY (E269–70), Blake plays out a minor, though informative, dialectical exercise on the term "unity." When he begins, apparently unambiguously, "Every Poem must necessarily be a perfect Unity," Blake does not define the term, as if the meaning it signifies were already given, or as if it were to be constituted in the process of his commentary. As he proceeds, Blake progressively narrows and complicates the role of "Unity" without disturbing its undefined state: "But when a Work has Unity it is as much in a Part as in the Whole." In this progression, "Unity" has shifted from being something a work *is* (its ontological ground) to something it *has* (an external attribute). "Unity" is progressively demoted—first to the status of a "cloke of folly," then to the level of a "secondary consideration," then to a complicity in the Fall ("eating of the tree of good & evil"), and finally to a "Classical" force that now "Desolate[s] Europe with Wars." In the shifting logic of his discourse, Blake drastically locates present political conditions (in part at least) in the classical drive for unity—and probably its counterparts in forces such as nationalism—with which his commentary began so innocently and unambiguously.

sire: the Brotherhood equals "Perfect Unity," whereas the radicalized text opens gaps precisely at the points of ostensible unity. These three lines abruptly end with an incantation and prayer, which modify the seriousness of the matter at hand (even though we know from the opening epigraph that issues of great import are in play). Either this line is a parody of a prayer, as its perfunctoriness and second intrusive period (which divides the prayer from the being about whom it is uttered) suggest, or it literally is one.[14] The optical illusoriness of the preceding lines creates an environment of instability that subverts the possibility that only one of several mutually conflicting readings must hold.

The next two revised (possibly incomplete) lines are uttered as a question-and-answer dialogue (which holds true regardless of possible deletions) that could well end the poem, or at least its relevance to the individual reader:

> [What] *are the Natures of those Living Creatures the Heavenly Father only*
> [Knoweth] *no Individual* [Knoweth nor] *Can know in all Eternity*
>
> [FZ 3.7–8, E301]

What is the purpose of going any further? Individuals are barred "in all Eternity" from knowing the "Natures" of (supposedly) the "Four." In the first three lines of the poem Blake deleted reference to the reader's comprehension; here we have an implicit reintroduction of the reader as an individual spectator to a drama that the reader, as an individual, will be unable to comprehend. Since the poem immediately continues with the line "Los was the fourth immortal starry one" and seemingly proceeds to delineate his nature, either the previous statement is irrelevant to the individual reader of the poem, or the narrative voice has, once again, undergone an internal transformation.

In these opening lines Blake calls direct attention to the act of reading, and the revisions compress or suppress information that subsequently (inadvertently or intentionally) turns up in transformed or disguised form, as happened in the case of the initially deleted reader. Another feature of these opening lines is the submergence of causal connections under incomplete syntax (as in the exclusion of

---

14. Helen T. McNeil succinctly acknowledges points such as these (which remain embarrassing to traditional readings) and thereby opens up new reading possibilities.

subject-predicate forms as if under grammatical transformation) and the structural overlapping of discrete pieces of information (as in the case of the emerging family constellation in which the Mother and Father are spatially separated by the "Brotherhood").

Text as Woven Pattern or Schema. The aspect of the text that weaves minute details into large, abstract tapestries or schematic patterns lies at the opposite extreme from the frustrating gaps in the text that enact Tharmas' flight. Moreover, Enion's weaving of the Circle of Destiny, which serves as a model for this most complex sense of Blake's text, connects the process of perspective transformation to the sequential discrepancies of the text as flight. As Enion weaves the Circle out of elements of the conversation she just had with Tharmas, her weaving takes on a will of its own, "perverse & wayward." Similarly, the schematic patterns of *The Four Zoas* mutually interfere with, as well as mutually constitute, each other.

The narrative of each Night of *The Four Zoas* has its own perspective or perceptual grammar whose features are marked by minute details of the text. These patterns are no more primordial than the temporal surface details: in a sense they have less claim to *textual* reality because they can be experienced by the reader only indirectly. These textual structures work to subvert normal patterns of processing and grouping perceptual and conceptual information and to open up new ways of structuring consciousness. Among the comprehensive textual models or patterns for perspective transformation that Blake invokes throughout the poem, the following are most prevalent: (1) perspective analysis and linearly embedded structures; (2) hierarchical displacement; (3) fictions of causal sequence; (4) overlapping of "events" by repetition; (5) involution of events by causal circularity and information loops; (6) disjunctive jumps (within a nexus of events) between discrete information bits; and (7) continuous deformation of perspective. There are many others, but these are the primary organizing/disorganizing textual patterns.

Night 8, for example, makes maximum use of technique 6, while Night 2 seizes on technique 2; Nights 1, 3, 7(a), and 9 are strongly influenced by technique 1; and so on. But these types are never simply dormant while others operate: each can occur at any moment the narrative permits, and each structure is struggling to be dominant at each point in the narrative. Night 2, for example, though initially controlled by spatial imagery and by a spatialization of the narrative structure, is finally overwhelmed by the emerging embedded structure of which Los and Enitharmon are the bearers. In addition to these supervening structures, without exception the narrative of each Night of *The Four Zoas* shifts perspective and/or plot focus approximately one-half to two-thirds of the way through, though in each case the significance of such a shift is unique.

Switchpoints at which one phase of structure transforms into another are often marked either by the most radical discrepancies and gaps or by quite explicit forms of repetition. Though there are always markers for dividing the text into definite perspective patterns, these markers often get buried, overwhelmed by other details. By continual use of excessive repetitions and discrepancies, Blake juggles the linear surface of the poem in such a way that there are several legitimate ways of dividing the text, and, since a serious shift of the boundaries within which perspectival structures are deployed totally reorganizes the narrative field, such a transposition of pattern markers at a critical point in the narrative could completely invert the perspectival significance of an event.

If a reader loses track of which details are perspective switchpoints in the narrative and which are elements within a perspective structure, or misses a key transformational signal planted strategically in a particular Night, or disregards textual perspective markers altogether, the reader might well be completely baffled by the apparently random flowing of events. In such a state, the reader becomes vulnerable to intrusive appearances in the text of conventionally providential figures (like the Lamb of God or Jesus): these flashes or fragments of Eternity tempt the reader to believe that the poem's complexities will be satisfactorily resolved by the intervention of such redemptive agents. The interference between variable perspective boundaries and the possibility of redemption being represented in the text itself becomes most urgent in Night the Ninth, which nearly unhinges Blake's text and passes harsh judgment on any analytical method which tries to penetrate it.

The most powerful way Blake incorporates perspective structure into the dialectic between character-originated and narrated information is in the formation of "perspective analyses" of events—a process that reveals how fully narrative processes and textual features constitute one another. A perspective analysis of a prior event reenacts the

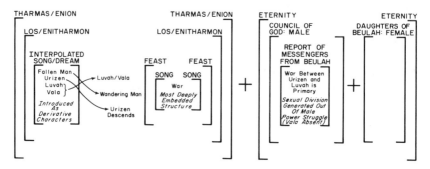

12.   Abstract Bracketed Structures for *The Four Zoas*, Night 1

earlier event within the *same* fictional framework—as when the key
Tharmas/Enion conversation in Night 1 is twice reenacted, once in
the metaphoric action of weaving and once in the metaphor of sexual
union. Blake overlaps contexts by careful repetition of syntax and diction to subvert linear causal order and make the two narratively posterior actions function as retroactive transformations of the prior conversations. As discussed earlier under the category of narrative, these
successive analyses further make the initial event possible by establishing in the posterior event the conditions for the narratively prior
event, often at the same instant they cancel the possibility of the earlier event.

The most complex mode of perspective analysis "embeds" subsequent events in prior plots. In an embedded plot previous narrative
events are reenacted within a new fictional framework; new characters reenact prior events under a transformed perspective, thereby revealing (bringing into explicit narrative existence) information that
retroactively seems to have been repressed within the previous fictional framework. This narrative process of embedding can be visualized by bracketing textual details into groups within which subgroups
of details are embedded. The Tharmas/Enion plot constitutes the *first
primary bracket* of Night 1, and the Los/Enitharmon plot functions as
the first embedded structure of the Tharmas/Enion plot: as narratively derivative characters, Los and Enitharmon act out in great detail the actions of the Tharmas/Enion plot and generate other characters (the Fallen/Wandering Man, Urizen, Luvah, and Vala) through
interpolated visions. The most deeply embedded structure of the
Tharmas/Enion bracket is the "Song" at the Feast of Los/Enitharmon:
in it the maximum information surfaces, and the prior narrative ele-

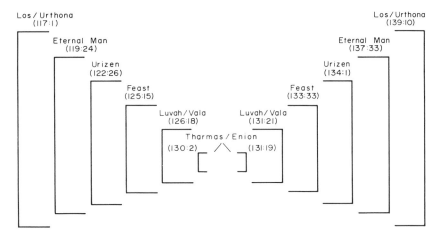

13. Abstract Bracketed Embedded Structures in *The Four Zoas*, Night 9

ments are most radically revised and redistributed. The *second primary bracket* of Night 1, which competes ontologically with the Tharmas/Enion plot, is the "Eternity" plot, which generates characters in the opposite order from that of the first primary bracket. The massive "war" that surfaces in the "Song" at the Feast is narratively *generated out of* the primary Tharmas/Enion sexual division; in the "Eternity" plot, however, war is the *generative nucleus* that forces to the surface the sexual division of Tharmas and Enion as a secondary by-product of the war.

The interesting discontinuities and repetitions on the level of syntax and diction (text as flight) thus mark boundaries and reveal organizing principles of the perspectives constituted through them, along with the elements that enter into and are constituted by the perspective. When seen from a Newtonian perspective, the sequence of events of Night 1 appears to be random; when taken as a narrative process of perspective and embedded analysis, this sequence can be mapped as a complex symmetrical pattern (fig. 12).

Night 9 exhibits an even more narcissistically nested set of bracketed structures. The complex embedded structures of Night 9 strongly suggest that the "Last Judgment" is an act of consciousness Blake challenges the reader to make in relation to the unsatisfactory "End" of Night 9. The text of Night 9 inverts and superimposes the two halves of Night 1. In Night 9 the Tharmas/Enion bracket is the innermost narrative structure, being enclosed within the Urizen/Eter-

nal Man plot, which is itself contained by a fusion of the Los/Enithar-
mon sexual plot with the imagery of war. Tharmas and Enion assume
the role of children as Los and Enitharmon did in Night 1, and the
"Eternals" eventually interact with the main characters of the narrative at a great "Feast," not as in Night 1 where the Eternal and first
primary narrative perspectives are askew (fig. 13).

The neatness and symmetry of these embedded structures indirectly give rise to the ominous feeling that something sinister is happening offstage, that the narrative surface is, even more than usual,
pervaded by delusional traps. The embedded structures of Night 9
thus throw into relief and complexly refocus the sequence of events
that seems to override the embedded structures—the sequential
unions of the Zoas with their female counterparts. Even at the level of
the unfolding narrative surface, the accumulating frustration of the
reader's desire that (finally) complete joy will characterize these
unions points to a more hidden and opposite movement (fore-
grounded by the embedded structures) in 9—the eventual *separation*
of the "female form" from the Eternal Men themselves, as a direct response to the *reunion* of Tharmas and Enion, the first sexually divided
pair in the poem. Seen from the perspectives of Night 9's embedded
structures, this separation of the female form finally enacts the "Fall"
in the text itself, but as the outcome or result of the vast prior narrative chains and not as it seemed to be to the Newtonian reader—a primordial reality prior to the text, its originating privileged event.

REFLECTIONS ON THE ONTOLOGY
OF READING *THE FOUR ZOAS*

As we have just seen, the crisis of "Last Judgment" in Night 9 raises
most urgently, indeed makes unavoidable, the question of what happens to the narrative and the text of the poem when they are perceived by a reader in a state of failed imaginative judgment.[15] Since

---

15. These speculations are in part a response to interesting questions raised by Nelson Hilton, Paul Mann, Hazard Adams, Geoffrey Hartman, and Thomas Vogler in the
discussion period following this paper at the Santa Cruz "Blake and Criticism" conference. Will Tomlinson, Mark Bracher, and Fred Dortort have been patient sounding
boards for these ideas. Thanks also go to Donna Halliburton, who rendered the final
form of my graphic designs in figs. 12–16.

narrative, text, and reader interconstitute one another ontologically, whenever the reader encounters the text through a sequence of failed acts of judgment, the narrative in the radical sense of *The Four Zoas*— a perceptual agent enacting perspective transformations and aspectual interconnections—simply does not come into existence. Rather, the text is constituted by such a reader as if it were given, fixed, unalterable, purely objective—that is, as if it were not being constituted by the reader at all but actually existed prior to the act of reading. In this state the reader's eye (I) constitutes itself as a tyrannical, centralized, unified consciousness, inert and inflexible, incapable of altering or being altered by the apparently objective Newtonian beings it encounters in the fixed text. Thus the only narrative that can emerge from the encounter between inertial reader and text is a Newtonian narrative that seems to be (and thus, to this state of consciousness, is) potentially already contained in the inert text itself—the core event, the presupposed world, and so on—a narrative that is not at all a transformative agent through which reader and text mutually alter and revise one another but merely an interpretation by the reader that attempts to construe a coherent, unified world (analogous to the reader's own singular consciousness) from the multiple details of the text.[16]

Though the actual individual reader is absolutely indispensable to the existence of the *Four Zoas* narrative and text, the narrative, not the reader, is the primary agent of transformation, and the text equally participates with the reader in their acts of mutual constitution and revision. It would thus be as much a misappropriation of terms to say that the *Four Zoas* text or narrative already contains the reader's re-

---

16. In my *Narrative Unbound* this discussion of reader orientation is expanded in the context of three kinds of perspective ontology: *primary perspective*, which has the power to constitute the rules that govern the fields (narrative, chemical, physical, anthropological, and so on) it generates; and *secondary* and *tertiary* perspectives, which operate *within* a primary perspective to maintain its structural features. Secondary perspective guides (by degrees of inclusion and exclusion) the incorporation of residues of prior events in present emerging events: it operates within a narrative field like *The Four Zoas* to assure the authority of sequential priority and to guarantee that, once narrated, no event can ever vanish or be totally repressed or lost. Tertiary perspective operates in a field akin to Newtonian narrative and strives to make unwanted information vanish: it thrives on a fundamental gap between signifier and signified and presupposes and yearns for a primordial originating event (the creation, the fall, and so on) and its corollary, a predetermined, definitive sequence with preordained closure.

sponse (even potentially), or that the text and reader already contain the narrative, as it would be to say that the narrative and the reader already contain the text. From the perspective of the reader's response, however, the *Four Zoas* narrative and text either come into existence or fail to come into existence only through the reader's imaginative acts and decisions. Once the reader makes a crucial decision (which may be unconscious) concerning a textual feature—say, a disturbing discrepancy of the text as flight—this decision either allows the text to revise itself through the agency of a narrative process such as perspective transformation, or it merely interprets that textual detail as a feature of Newtonian narrative, such as error, inconsistency, or incoherence, generally to be repressed or condemned. Likewise, the reader's decision in the face of the excessive repetition of diction or syntax, which often marks the boundaries of the text as woven pattern, either allows the text to revise itself through the agency of a narrative process such as aspectual interconnection, or the decision interprets that textual detail as a Newtonian rhetorical or decorative trope to be admired on the basis of its appropriateness or rejected on the basis of its obsessiveness.

Unlike the individual reader, who to Newtonian consciousness seems to exist as an individual human being, able to be pointed to independent of and prior to the act of reading, and unlike the text whose palpable physical, visible features (words, spaces, punctuation, and so on) and even structural features (not directly observable but inferable; hypothetical but verifiable in terms of lines of the poem) can likewise be pointed to arbitrarily apart from any particular act of reading (witness the schematic charts in this essay), the *Four Zoas* narrative is a purely relational process that has no existence (cannot be pointed to) in any form except through the act of reading. But instead of simply coming into existence as a dialectical product of the interaction between reader and text, the narrative actually brings the reader and text into mutual existence. This radically relational narrative process undermines Newtonian narrative ontology (through retroactive transformation, aspectual interconnection, and so on): it invades and desubstantializes the independently existing Newtonian reader and text, reconstituting them relationally as the primary conditions of the coming-into-existence of the narrative. The *Four Zoas* narrative can come into existence only if reader and text are freed from existing independently of reading, but this liberation can be performed only by the narrative itself: reader, text, and narrative are thus mutually pre-conditions for one another's existence. The explanatory circle of reader, text, and narrative closes once again, only to open up as yet unforeseen possibilities of reading *The Four Zoas*.

CODA: ON THE EMBEDDING OF
NIGHT 7(B) IN 7(A)

> If termini did vary with the paths traversed to reach them, space would lose its coherence and thereby be annihilated.
> Jean Piaget 20

In the otherwise generally admirable new Erdman edition of Blake's poetry and prose, one glaring and uncharacteristically speculative de-cision (which reflects several smaller ones, especially in Night 1) di-rectly addresses the issues of this essay—I refer, of course, to Erd-man's decision, suggested by Mark Lefebvre, to embed the rearranged version of Night 7(b) in the middle of 7(a). Erdman gave serious consideration to at least three different proposals for conflat-ing the two Nights—including Andrew Lincoln's hypothesis of embedding 7(a) in the middle of rearranged 7(b), and John Kilgore's recommendation that 7(b) (in its original order) be embedded in 7(a) (E836). Erdman's willingness to entertain these possibilities (with lit-tle encouragement from Blake) reflects his deep concern for what he repeatedly calls "fit" between the two Nights—an odd concern, it might seem, in a poet who refused to accept even the "fit" between world and mind: "You shall not bring me down to believe such fitting & fitted I know better" (Annotations to Wordsworth, E667).

Erdman's concern is real and justifiable, however. The existence of two Night 7's poses a serious challenge to the principle of the primacy of narrative sequential order: if the two Nights are separate, to be read sequentially, then the order in which they are read is a funda-mental aspect of the being of their respective narratives; if they are to be somehow combined, how does this new sequencing affect not only the temporal narrative order but the underlying textual patterns as well? Given the intense tendency of the narrative toward temporality and that of the woven textual patterns toward spatiality, it seems un-avoidable that, although embedding 7(b) in 7(a) must radically alter

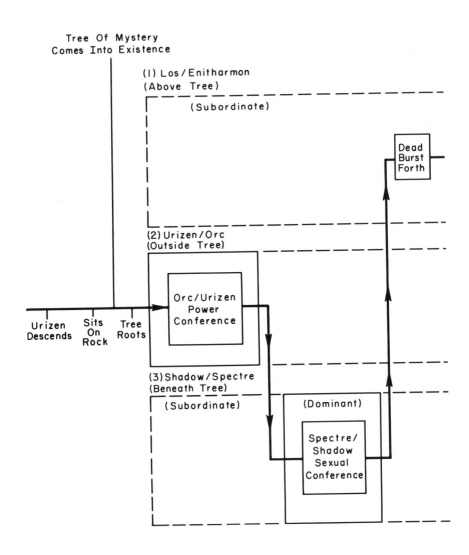

Tree Of Mystery
Comes Into Existence

(I) Los / Enitharmon
(Above Tree)

(Subordinate)

Dead
Burst
Forth

(2) Urizen / Orc
(Outside Tree)

Orc/Urizen
Power
Conference

Urizen   Sits   Tree
Descends   On   Roots
          Rock

(3) Shadow / Spectre
(Beneath Tree)

(Subordinate)   (Dominant)

Spectre/
Shadow
Sexual
Conference

Three Verbal / Bodily Conferences
(Three Branches Of The Narrative And The Tree Of Mystery)

14.   Abstract of *The Four Zoas,* Night 7(a)

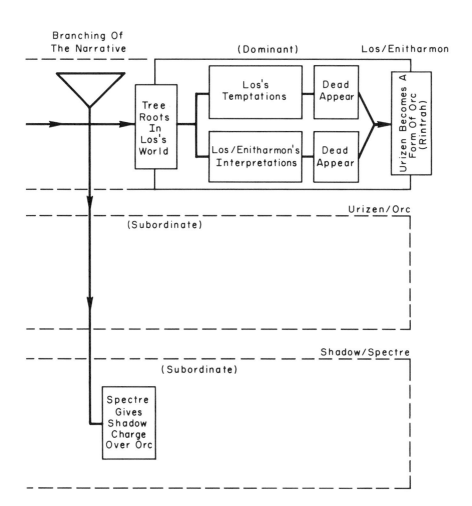

Branching Of
The Narrative

(Dominant)   Los/Enitharmon

Tree Roots In Los's World

Los's Temptations

Dead Appear

Los/Enitharmon's Interpretations

Dead Appear

Urizen Becomes A Form Of Orc (Rintrah)

Urizen/Orc

(Subordinate)

Shadow/Spectre

(Subordinate)

Spectre Gives Shadow Charge Over Orc

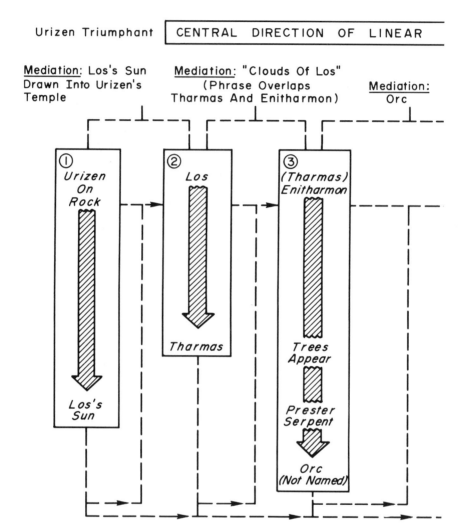

Urizen Triumphant | CENTRAL DIRECTION OF LINEAR

Mediation: Los's Sun Drawn Into Urizen's Temple

Mediation: "Clouds Of Los" (Phrase Overlaps Tharmas And Enitharmon)

Mediation: Orc

① Urizen On Rock

Los's Sun

② Los

Tharmas

③ (Tharmas) Enitharmon

Trees Appear

Prester Serpent

Orc (Not Named)

Continuous Mediation (Deformation Of Perspective) Through Parallel Actions

15.   Abstract of *The Four Zoas*, Night 7(b)

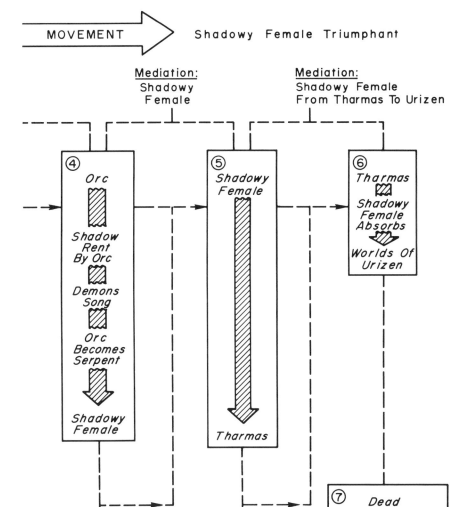

MOVEMENT ➡ Shadowy Female Triumphant

Mediation:
Shadowy
Female

Mediation:
Shadowy Female
From Tharmas To Urizen

④ Orc

Shadow
Rent
By Orc

Demons
Song

Orc
Becomes
Serpent

Shadowy
Female

⑤ Shadowy
Female

Tharmas

⑥ Tharmas

Shadowy
Female
Absorbs

Worlds Of
Urizen

⑦ Dead
Burst
Forth

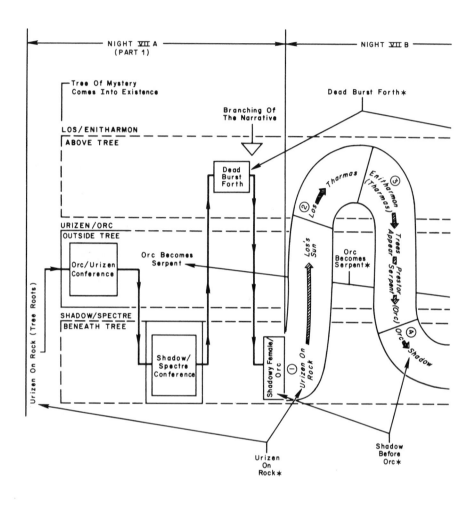

16. Abstract of Night 7(b) Embedded in Night 7(a)

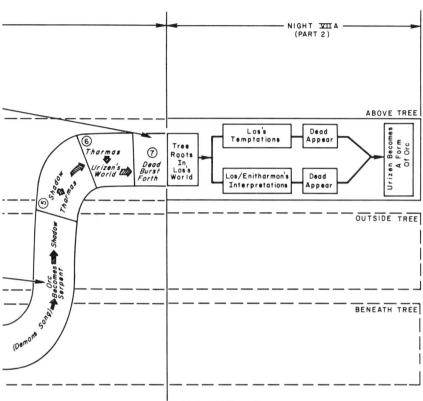

NIGHT Ⅶ A
(PART 2)

ABOVE TREE

⑥ *Tharmas*
Urizen's World

⑦ *Dead Burst Forth*

Tree Roots In, Los's World

Los's Temptations → Dead Appear

Los/Enitharmon's Interpretations → Dead Appear

Urizen Becomes A Form Of Orc

⑤ *Shadow* *Tharmas*

OUTSIDE TREE

Orc Becomes Serpent *Shadow*

(Demons Song)

BENEATH TREE

*Points Of Direct Intersection Between Ⅶ A And Ⅶ B

both the narrative and the textual fields, the impact of that embedding should be most directly and dramatically evident in the transformation of spatial/textual structure of 7(b) when it enters the field of 7(a).

Considered as independent structural patterns, the two Night 7's constitute a narrative branching by means of which radically alternate paths or world-lines both converge and diverge, make possible and undermine, issue in and cancel out, a finite set of narrative happenings. That is, these two Nights are not different versions of how the same events occur but are two different ways they actually *do* occur—a branching of the narrative that allows Blake to explore the implications of alternative fictional possibilities, each Night repressing key aspects emphasized by the other Night 7 while directly intersecting other critical points. Mapped independently of one another's controlling structural patterns, Nights 7(a) and 7(b) each reveal strongly defined but orthogonally opposed spatial properties. Night 7(a) is massively dominated by the controlling image of the Tree of Mystery: Blake carefully coordinates every key event spatially by reference to it. The events of 7(a) are organized tightly within three horizontal tiers, marked off along the vertical axis, and defined by the spaces above, outside, and beneath the Tree. Figure 14 schematizes Night 7(a). In Night 7(b), however, the Tree of Mystery is virtually absent except for two quite important direct references. It is as if in Night 7(b) the Tree has absorbed the characters and mystified the narrator so completely that they are almost unaware of its presence and power. In the absence of the presiding image of the Tree—indeed of any single controlling spatial image—Night 7(b) is organized, in direct opposition to 7(a), through a series of discontinuous (though implicitly overlapping) parallel temporal segments, deployed along the horizontal axis as parallel, vertical, self-contained fragments whose details nevertheless feed from one segment to the next by means of shifting gaze and speech direction of characters. Night 7(b) is schematized in figure 15.

When this sequence of discrete vertical segments of Night 7(b) is embedded—as Erdman has done—in 7(a), which is dominated by its horizontal tiers, Night 7(b)'s segments become subject to the structural laws of 7(a), and the events and characters that before functioned independently must now be plotted in relation to 7(a)'s grid. Events in 7(b) involving Los, for instance, must now be plotted to intersect the upper world (above the Tree) where Los functions in 7(a); Orc before the Shadow in 7(b) must be mapped into the space beneath the Tree (in accordance with 7[a]); Orc's becoming a serpent must be projected into the middle tier (outside the Tree); and so on. What emerges from this mapping of the events of 7(b) in terms of the 7(a) grid is a curved graph in which the discontinuous segments of 7(b) are transformed into a continuous serpentine movement (already latent, it is true, in the "continuous deformation of perspective" that pervades the discontinuous structure of 7(b) considered as an independent Night). Mapped according to these principles, the composite structure of Night 7(b) embedded in 7(a) takes the form of figure 16. Visualized in this way, the embedded textual pattern of 7(b) itself becomes the serpentine form wrapped around the (almost invisible) Tree of Mystery. This radical transformation of 7(b) when it is embedded in 7(a) is a dramatic and surprising example of the ontological principles outlined in this essay and thus carries with it a transformation of the narrative far too complex to assess here.

It is perhaps significant that, while the embedding of 7(b) in 7(a) in the above fashion yields interesting structural results by revealing how 7(a) accommodates 7(b), attempting to embed the spatially rigid pattern of 7(a) in 7(b) radically disrupts the chain of shifting gaze and speech act (Urizen to Los to Tharmas to Enitharmon to Orc to Shadowy Female to Tharmas to Urizen's spatial worlds to the dead bursting forth) that served as the ground for simultaneously dividing 7(b) into parallel segments and connecting those segments in an unalterable order. The disruption of the textual pattern of 7(b) that the insertion of 7(a) immediately produces could well serve to emphasize the incompatibility of the textual programs of 7(a) and 7(b) and thereby to argue that they be kept as separate and distinct Nights. This disruption could also be an indication that a new rule of organization for 7(b) would have to be discovered that could accommodate 7(a), a rule that would probably redefine the structural patterns of both Nights. For the time being, however, it seems fair to say that if one is determined to force 7(a) and 7(b) into one textual unit, the way Erdman has done it is not only probably the best but inadvertently produces interesting structural by-products. Nevertheless, it seems completely unwarranted to pursue the seamless fitting together of the elements of a text as radical as Blake's *Four Zoas*.

17. *MIL/TON*, title page

6

Re: Naming *MIL/TON*

THOMAS A. VOGLER

O quam te memorem virgo. . . .
(Vergil)

I am become a name. . . .
(Tennyson)

When a Blake poem "rouzes the faculties to act" there is an inevitable danger that the faculty most roused will be in the service of our interpretive urge for closure and univocal meaning—an urge that marks every aspect of the production and interpretation of texts. This urge is thematized in *MIL/TON*, where the inevitable Urizenic impulse that informs the production of meaning is a force at work in the poem, struggling for control over the text and its possible readings, capable at any moment of leading both poem and readings to exemplify the loss of "Living Form," hardening it into marble unless the "furrows of many years" are constantly filled in with the red clay that creates "new flesh on the Demon cold" (23.54, 59; 21.9–10). The poem seeks to open itself to a different mode of engagement:

> *Seest thou the little winged fly, smaller than a grain of sand?*
> *It has a heart like thee; a brain open to heaven & hell,*
> *Withinside wondrous & expansive; its gates are not clos'd,*
> *I hope thine are not*
>
> (20.27–30)

> *And he whose Gates are opend in those Regions of his Body*
> *Can from those Gates view all these wondrous Imaginations*
> (34.17–18)

In what follows I shall try to suggest some challenges the poem offers to the reader who would meet it with comparable openness in sensibility and expectations.

I

I write Blake's title in the form *MIL/TON* in order to approach a little more closely the emphatically chirographic splitting represented on the title-plate (fig. 17), as Milton's (?) own hand is shown reaching *through* and "breaching" the name, thereby creating the "Breach of Miltons descent" (34.42). This act is further emphasized by the ninety-degree turn in the letters, which give the weighty *TON* a descending trajectory. Milton's attempts to justify the ways of God to man had taken the form of *Paradise Lost. A Poem Written in Ten Books* (1667), *Paradise Lost. A Poem in Twelve Books* (1674), and *Paradise Regained. A Poem in IV Books* (1671). Blake's titular onomastics ("a Poem / in [1]2 Books") echoes the sameness of these variations, with the added emphasis of including a name *in* the name, a fractured name, anticipating a complex act of un/re-naming.[1] At the threshold of the work we thus encounter an emblem of a heightened self-consciousness about names and titles (*titulus*, "inscription, label, a signifying mark"), which identifies and prefigures the basic issues of the poem. Milton's "track" in the poem is the track or trace of the signifying power of the name "Milton," and of the power and the limitations of patriarchal discourse that inform the poem's basic struggle. As the Name-of-the-Father, it implies the existence and power of what Jacques Lacan has called the "Symbolic Order," and it should remind us of the power and function of the act of naming within that order.

In Genesis 1 God announces that in his new creation man shall have "dominion . . . over every living thing that moveth upon the earth." In Genesis 2 the initiating act of dominion is Adam's naming of each creature in turn as it is brought before him: "And whatsoever Adam called every living creature, that was the name thereof." In Genesis 3 Adam's spouse is "the woman" until the fall and Adam's decision to call "his wife's name Eve; because she was the mother of all living." The full import of these initiating gestures is spelled out by Freud in his analysis of the Mosaic religion in *Moses and Monotheism*, where he links the discovery of language and "the movement of air that provided the image of spirituality" with the dematerialization of

1. Milton's *Paradise Regained* has a total of 2,070 lines. Blake's *MIL/TON* in copy D (without the "Preface") has 1,963 lines. In the edited composite form in which most readers encounter it there are 2,006 lines.

God in the prohibition against images. The "inclination towards spiritual interests" of the Jews is further evidenced by their privileging of writing and written records at this time, and by the "revolution in the existing state of the law" that accompanied the shift from a matriarchal to a patriarchal structure of society.

> This turning from the mother to the father, however, signifies above all a victory of spirituality over the senses—that is to say, a step forward in culture, since maternity is proved by the senses whereas paternity is a surmise based on a deduction and a premise. . . . The progress in spirituality consists in deciding against the direct sense perception in favor of the so-called higher intellectual processes. . . . An example of this would be the decision that paternity is more important than maternity, although the former cannot be proved by the senses as the latter can. This is why the child has to have the father's name and inherit after him. . . . We are therefore confronted with the phenomenon that during the development of mankind the world of the senses becomes gradually mastered by spirituality, and that man feels proud and uplifted by each step in the progress.
>
> (144–51)

For Freud this phylogeny was recapitulated in the ontogeny of the individual human subject as it became capable of perceiving the sexual distinctions that register the subject's place in an external world, giving the subject a distinct identity in contrast to the primary merging with the mother and mediating all relationships with the consciousness-structuring effects of language. Since the identity achieved in this process is marked in our society by the subject's taking the Name of the Father, Lacan's phrase has proven a convenient way to indicate the third term or mediating concept (law, prohibition, denial of instinctual desire; *nom/non*), which is necessary to establish the triangular structure of the Symbolic Order in its patriarchal-Oedipal form.[2]

One does not need the whole apparatus of Lacanian psychoanalysis to grasp the most immediate potency of naming, where "giving the right name to an object not only helps to control it, but establishes ties of love and hate" (Ehrenzweig 284) and where "anything which

---

2. The most convenient introduction to Lacan's development of Freud's thought is still "Fonction et champ de la parole et du langage en psychanalyse." Jameson, "Imaginary," is also very useful. Blake's most extensive and explicit treatment of "Patriarchal pride" is in *Jerusalem*, chapter 2, with its less obvious consequences spelled out in chapter 3.

one names is no longer the same; it has lost its innocence" (Sartre 22). Nietzsche claimed that "the lordly right of bestowing names is such that one would almost be justified in seeing the origin of language itself as an expression of the rulers' power. . . . they seal off each thing and action with a sound and thereby take symbolic possession of it" (*Genealogy* 160). The Judaic God's name was to be "unutterable" by man, so that with the prohibition of representation God became the unnamed and unnameable power that authorizes the Symbolic Order inscribed under the Name-of-the-Father. There is in Blake another modality of the unnameable, one that plays a key part in the dynamics of *MIL/TON*. The "nameless Shadowy Mother" of Beulah suggests something that has escaped complete inscription in the Symbolic Order, a gap or rupture within the order itself. Julia Kristeva has attempted to describe what she calls "the *unnameable*" as "that which is necessarily enclosed in every questionable, interpretable, enigmatic object," and is that part of the object that resists the interpretive "delirium, in its phallic ambition . . . in the belief that light can rule everywhere, without a shadow." Her imagery is doubly suggestive here, since it is materiality itself that resists the dominance of interpretive light and causes shadowy voids and spaces in its reign, at the same time both resisting interpretation and making it possible.

> As origin and condition of the interpretable, the unnameable is, perhaps, the primordial phantasm. What analysis reveals is that the human being does not speak and that, a fortiori, he does not interpret *without* the phantasm of a return to the origin, without the hypothesis of an unnameable, of a *Sachverhalt*. Furthermore, analysis reveals that interpretive speech, like all speech which is concerned with an object, is acted upon by the desire to return to the archaic mother who is resistant to meaning.
>
> ("Psychoanalysis" 84)

Kristeva here offers an example of the feminizing anthropomorphization that tends to mark almost all discussions that try to identify the tension between the Symbolic Order and that which resists inscription within it. The archaeology of naming imagines the unamed as characterizing a mode of existence *before* it is organized into the Symbolic Order under the Name-of-the-Father. For Kristeva this modality is governed by a feminine principle that she calls "the semiotic," with its origin in the preverbal situation of the pre-Oedipal mother-infant

dyad, when the child's physical symbiosis with the mother still pre-
vails. The semiotic is the phase of rhythmic babble that precedes the
acquisition of linguistically structured speech, and which remains—
though for the most part repressed—in a rupturing potential for in-
trusion into the Symbolic Order of the patriarchal discourse.

> It is chronologically anterior . . . to the sign, syntax, denotation, and
> signification. . . . The semiotic is a distinctive, non-expressive articula-
> tion; neither amorphous substance nor meaningful numbering. We
> imagine it in the cries, the vocalizing, the gestures of infants; it func-
> tions, in fact, in adult discourse as rhythm, prosody, plays on words,
> the non-sense of sense, laughter.
>
> (*Polylogue* 14)

She sees semiotic discourse (in the language of "modernism" sought
by writers like Artaud, or in the *écriture féminine* attempted by a number of French feminists) as an assertion of the writer's still active and
available relation to the pleasures associated with the preverbal maternal symbiosis, and with a refusal to identify with, or take identity
from, the articulate linguistic logic of patriarchal discourse.

> Any attentiveness to "infantile language" . . . seems to be located at
> that ambiguous point where psychoanalysis opens up the limits of phe-
> nomenological meaning by indicating its conditions of production . . .
> the question that the infant-analyst puts to maternal attentiveness be-
> fore any language begins to encode his "idealities": what about the par-
> adoxical *semiosis* of the newborn's body, what about the "semiotic
> *chora*," what about this "space" prior to the sign, this archaic disposition
> of primary narcissism that a poet brings to light in order to challenge
> the closure of meaning. . . . Neither request nor desire, it is an invoca-
> tion, an anaclisis. Memories of bodily contact, warmth, and nourish-
> ment: these underlie the breath of the newborn body as it appeals to a
> source of support, a fulfillment of care. . . . Vocal and muscular con-
> tractions, spasms of the glottis and motor system—all make up for the
> absence of intrauterine life components. Voice is the vehicle of that
> call. . . .
>
> (*Desire* 281–83)

For the poet as well as for the analyst the *quality* of that imagined
state and the *meaning* of the call, invocation, or cry, will be a question
of how we hear what Blake calls "Infant noise" (*infans*, "unable to
speak") in the *Songs of Innocence*. The striking emphasis on attentive-
ness to the sounds of the Nightingale and Lark on plate 31, reinforced

by the anagrammatic emphasis of the repeated phrase "listens silent," calls our attention to the issue of hearing in *MIL/TON* and to what is at stake in how we hear the Lark's "trill, trill, trill, trill" when in Book II the "high ton'd Song" of the "loud voic'd Bard" gives way to "this little Bird," whose trill, though not "words," may concern our "eternal salvation."

The Bard's song for the most part operates within the Symbolic Order, with its thetic function of naming (from outside) that establishes meaning and signification comparable to that which the paternal function represents within reproductive relationships in society. Although he may well be inspired, as he claims, the Bard's emphasis on his song as "words" reflects its operation within the Symbolic Order where language governs as nomination, sign, and syntax. The *Bard's* song "produces" *mourning*; the *bird's* song "produces" *morning*. The name "Ololon" and her identification with a place, Beulah—which is comparable to that prelinguistic, semiotic *chora* of anaclitic facilitations described by Kristeva ("As the beloved infant in his mothers bosom round incircled / With arms of love & pity & sweet compassion")—establishes it/her/them not as a "named" object or entity but as a modality; not a change in *name* (as from Saul to Paul) but a change in *naming*. Like the infant in "Infant Joy" who says, "I have no name / I am but two days old," Ololon's is an emanation-name, a name-as-emanation or emanation-as-name; it flows out of her; it is a flowing; it is her flowing; it is her, flowing. To call it/her/them "Ololon" is like calling a dog a "bow-wow" because that is the sound it makes and in making names itself:

> For a LION roars HIMSELF compleat from head to tail
>
> For a man speaks HIMSELF from the crown of his head to the sole of his feet
>
> For the VOICE is from the body and the spirit—and is a body and a spirit
>
> (Smart 51, 50, 52)

To hear Ololon's "name" in this way is to register the possibility of a "place" or a mode of utterance outside of or not yet inscribed in the patriarchal Symbolic Order. The nature of that "place" is what is at issue in *MIL/TON*, and the problem is how to find it and multiply it. The "place" will be metaphorically gender-specific for cultural and historical reasons, but if it is too specific it will not be a point *inside* the

Symbolic Order that can function, like the "void," as a point *outside* that order; it will be the already all too familiar concept or signified of the feminine, "stampt" like Oothoon in *Visions of the Daughters of Albion* with Bromion's signet. It will be the female desire that answers Freud's famous question (what does woman want?) by *reflecting* the object-specific limited forms of phallogocentric desire.[3] Ololon can be interpreted as an attempt to represent the Other as a genuine libidinal and linguistic *materia prima*, before it takes on a codified proscriptive form within the patriarchal Symbolic Order. "Can it be?" Blake asks at the beginning of *Jerusalem*, chapter 2, and that question governs the interpreter's problem in engaging the text of *MIL/TON*. If it *can* be, how to find it, and how to articulate it?

II

Most attempts to comment on Ololon's "name" reflect how *not* to comment on it. In a recent article Donald Reiman and Christina Krauss have criticized the proposal of Frye and Bloom that the name should be heard as a cry of lamentation, arguing instead that "Ololon" must be heard as "a cry of joy or a cry to the gods," and that the name has "traditional historical or linguistic bases." Their emphasis on alternative ways of hearing the "name" is useful, but their desire to inscribe it as a name reduced to a specific mode of lexical meaning and to a specific lexical meaning within that mode misses the point. It is not surprising, then, that in their view *MIL/TON* becomes yet another version of the culturally preinscribed Family Romance, "the story of a journey from a pre-sexual state through childhood/motherhood to the full awareness of adult sexual maturity" (84). Thus Ololon's "descent," marked by a cry of joy, is mistakenly inscribed by them within the limits of what Nietzsche calls "Greek cheerfulness," or the "hunger for insatiable and optimistic knowledge" governed by "paternal descent from Apollo, the god of individuation and just boundaries." Her "name" should instead be heard neither as one of

---

3. Lacan has given graphic emphasis to a point made long before him by many others: "~~The~~ woman does not exist" (*Feminine Sexuality* 48). The context of this observation is the argument that "the woman" supports a male phantasy of oneness, that "she" exists *only* as excluded by the nature of things, i.e., the nature of words, or language. See *Feminine Sexuality* 137–61 passim.

"lamentation" nor of "joy" but as a polyvalent evocation of what Nietzsche describes as "the curious blending and duality in the emotions of the Dionysian revelers," reminding us "of the phenomenon that pain begets joy, that ecstasy may wring sounds of agony from us. At the very climax of joy there sounds a cry of horror or a yearning lamentation for an irretrievable loss" (98, 72, 40).[4] Her "name" should challenge our mode of hearing, rather than conform to some predisposition or expectation that we bring with us.

> *Is that trembling cry a song?*
> *Can it be a song of joy?*
>   ("HOLY THURSDAY," *SE*)

MIL/TON includes a vivid representation of the negative predisposition of the ear, locating its source in the hermeneutic semiosis of the "Shadowy Female," who strives to articulate the poem as a lamentation, a deadly bodily "articulation" that cannot perceive human form as Living Form:

> *And thus the Shadowy Female howls in articulate howlings*
>
> *I will lament over Milton in the lamentations of the afflicted*
> *My Garments shall be woven of sighs & heart broken lamentations*
> *The misery of unhappy Families shall be drawn out into its border*
> *Wrought with the needle with dire sufferings poverty pain & woe*
> *Along the rocky Island & thence throughout the whole Earth*
> *There shall be the sick Father & his starving Family! there*
> *The Prisoner in the stone Dungeon & the Slave at the Mill*

---

4. This is not an unusual reaction to the sounds made by women in the Mediterranean mode of mourning. In his recent novel, Gabriel García Márquez describes women "wailing with such high-pitched shrieks that they seemed to be shouts of joy" (186). The "ologroaning" of the Irish Catholic pilgrims to Station Island on Lough Derg provides an instance closer to home. For Lacan, "mourning" is a form of work that takes place in a breach, "performed to satisfy the disorder that is produced by the inadequacy of signifying elements to cope with the hole that has been created in existence, for it is the system of signifiers in their totality which is impeached by the last instance of mourning" ("Desire" 38). But the very utterance which asks to be heard as rupturing the structured system of signifiers, with a polyvalence that can only exist "outside," can also be explained as a cultural linguistic inscription. Louis Gernet's study traces the incidence of shrill ritual cries in the ancient and modern Mediterranean area, relating the Greek *ololuge* to the Berber *iou-iou*, and rejecting the possibility that the collectiveness of the phenomenon can be adequately explained as a "spontaneous" emotional response: "Nous avons affaire . . . à un usage social du cri: celui-ci fait partie de l'expression obligatoire des sentiments; il est d'ordre institutionel" (259).

I will have Writings written all over it in Human Words
That every Infant that is born upon the Earth shall read
And get by rote as a hard task of a life of sixty years

(18.4–14)

These howlings threaten to drown out and cover all alternatives with a semiosis of woe, a woe-ven verbal garment, a "needle-work / of emblematic texture" that seems to be ascribed to a "feminine" source.

It cannot be overemphasized in response to lines like these that what we are encountering here is not an hypostasized/allegorized feminine principle, an *élan négatif* as a personified "Nature," but a system of meaning posited as primal, preinscribed, proscriptive, and definitive. The system goes back to the particular mode of the triumph of the figural over the literal that Augustine learned from Ambrose:

> I was pleased to hear that in his sermons to the people Ambrose often repeated the text: *The written law inflicts death, whereas the spiritual law brings life*, as though this were a rule upon which he wished to insist most carefully. And when he lifted the veil of mystery and disclosed the spiritual meaning of texts which, taken literally, appeared to contain the most unlikely doctrines, I was not aggrieved by what he said.
>
> (115–16)

Augustine's "conversion" to Christianity was prompted by his learning a powerful interpretive system that includes "both a stipulation of what meaning there is and a set of directions for finding it, which is of course a set of directions—of interpretive strategies—for making it, that is, for the endless reproduction of the same text" (Fish 170).

Behind the conversion of Augustine is the author of the words ("The written law inflicts death") that were the leitmotif of Ambrose's sermons, the Saul/Paul whose "conversion" figures so insistently in the background of Blake's *MIL/TON* as a warning that conversion and change of name do not necessarily generate the desired transformation. Especially important in this context is the fusion in Paul's thought of his negative attitude toward the physical world and his mode of interpretation. In his famous allegorical interpretation of Abraham's two wives, Hagar and Sarah, Paul wrote:

> Tell me, ye that desire to be under the law, do ye not hear the law? For it is written, that Abraham had two sons, the one by a bondmaid, the other by a freewoman. But he who was of the bondwoman was born

after the flesh; but he of the freewoman was by promise. Which things are an allegory; for these are the two covenants; the one from the Mount Sinai, which gendereth to bondage, which is Hagar. For this Hagar is Mount Sinai in Arabia, and answereth to Jerusalem which now is, and is in bondage with her children. But Jerusalem which is above is free, which is the mother of us all. . . . What saith the Scripture? "Cast out the bondwoman and her son: for the son of the bondwoman shall not be heir with the son of the freewoman." So then, brethren, we are not children of the bondwoman, but of the free.

(Gal. 4)

Paul's allegorical "freedom" under the law is to be accomplished not by freeing the mother from the bondage of allegorical interpretation but through the "adoption of sons" into the Symbolic Order, which will be accomplished at "the time appointed of the father" when the son will become "a heir of God through Christ." It is the Name-of-the-Father, or the son acting in the Name-of-the-Father, who will assure legitimation under the rule of law; the bondwoman and her son will not be redeemed but will be cast out of the allegorical abode.[5] Paul's persistent denigration of the physical in favor of the spiritual, of the literal in favor of the allegorical, is for Blake not only the result of a system of misogynist morality (in which "Sinai . . . gendereth to bondage") but is also constitutive of an epistemic system of meaning and interpretation that like Urizen is "self balanc'd stretch'd o'er the void" of "Natures wide womb," a semiosis constantly confirming the system that gave it rise.

In the poem, simultaneous with the entry of the falling star into Blake's left foot ("falling on the tarsus enterd there") is the emergence of a black semiotic cloud: "But from my left foot a black cloud redounding spread over Europe."[6] The "False Tongue" that plays so prominent a part in this poem speaks of the "fibrous left foot black"

5. Paul's drastic solution to the problem of interpreting on the literal level is always simply to "cast out" the "literal" signifier. In Galatians 5, wrestling with the problem of the possible "meaning" of the practice of circumcision, he says: "For in Jesus Christ neither circumcision availeth anything, nor uncircumcision. . . . I would they were even cut off which trouble you."

6. *Tarsus* is both the name of an articulation of the foot between the leg and the metatarsus and the name of the birthplace of Paul. Among the other significant aspects of the star in this context is the etymological one; *desire* comes from *desiderare*, "to long for," by analogy with *considerare*, "augury that consults the stars" (*sidus, sideris*, n., "star, planet").

rather than the alternative vision in which "all this Vegetable World appear on my left Foot, / As a bright sandal formd immortal of precious stones & gold" (21.12–13). For Blake this misperception is a *méconnaissance* (or false augury, mis-consideration) comparable to Paul's misperception of the meaning of the incarnation and the consequent "black cloud" of his doctrine. Misreading of the Biblical scripture is compounded with misreading of the book of nature, where interpretation of the natural as black is the "reading" of an imposed cultural meaning, of "Writings written all over it in Human Words." The ensuing system of morality and aesthetics is coded in the form of puritan dress, a *human* sartorial semiotics that is then aped by nature and history:

> *The Famine shall clasp it together with buckles & Clasps*
> *And the Pestilence shall be its fringe & the War its girdle*
> *To divide into Rahab & Tirzah that Milton may come to our tents*
> *For I will put on the Human Form & take the Image of God*
> *Even Pity & Humanity but my Clothing shall be Cruelty*
> (18.16–20)

The aesthetics of the "black cloud" is also the Miltonic poetics of "all our woe," which called for a theodicy to illuminate "what in me is dark" by retelling the myth that mankind was lost because of the first mother and can only be saved by the appropriation of the mother's body as the vehicle for "spiritual" redemption. It is the poetics of Miltonic melancholy (literally, "black bile") that dominated eighteenth-century poetry in the form of the "False Tongue" for which "most musical" and "most melancholy" were indeed synonymous. How to hear—or *not* to hear—this synaesthetic black cloud spread over Europe is one crux of the problem of Blake's poem, which must avoid participating in it and reinscribing it in yet another form of the "Idol Virtues of the Natural Heart" (38.46).

III

Paul's function for Blake's *MIL/TON* is comparable to that of those authors Michel Foucault calls "founders of discursivity," because they produce in addition to their own works "the possibilities and the rules for the formation of other texts" ("Author" 154). Others, such as

Luther, Calvin, and Milton, have taken their places as revisionary interpreters and codifiers within the same rule of interpretive law, which holds out as one of its chief enticements an illusory model of "conversion" that functions as a veil for the continuation of the same system:

> *Satan! My Spectre! I know my power thee to annihilate*
> *And be a greater in thy place, & be thy Tabernacle*
> *A covering for thee to do thy will, till one greater comes*
> *And smites me as I smote thee & becomes my covering.*
> (38.29–32)

For Milton's "unexampled deed" to be a true conversion rather than a repetition within the system, he must redeem his Emanation from the bondage of an allegorical system in which the feminine exists only as an object for an interpretive practice that continually writes the same text. He must "rename" her by "un-naming her," reclaim her by hearing her "name," her call, as it is implied in the anagrammatic force of *Emana*tion as an inversion of *name*.

> *And then & then alone begins the happy Female joy*
> *As it is done in Beulah, & thou O Virgin Babylon Mother of Whoredoms*
> *Shalt bring Jerusalem in thine arms in the night watches; and*
> *No longer turning her a wandering Harlot in the streets*
> (33.19–22)

In one sense we can see a form of agreement between Blake and Paul, in that freedom from bondage is to be imaged by a relationship to a "Mother" who is not in bondage but is free. But for Paul that freedom is "above" in an allegorical Symbolic Order legitimated by paternity; for Blake the freedom is "below," requiring "descent" on Milton's part—and Ololon's—in order to free her from the bondage of an allegorical system. If we are to follow in Milton's track, we must follow the double hearing of his unexampled deed, first of the Bard's prophetic song and then—accompanied by the Lark and Wild Thyme, the two "witnesses" of the new revelation—the voice of Ololon: "Mild was the voice, but more distinct than any earthly / That Miltons Shadow heard" (37.6–7). What he hears in the Bard's song is his own poetic legacy, the "high" song of the intertextual strife of the patriarchal discourse, resounding with successive names and striving for the certainty of a univocal judgment. The exhibit presents itself as a par-

ody of his own style, his own ambitions, his own contamination by
the Greek and Roman models he presumed to have gone beyond, and
as an example of the presumptuous "Bardity" that infected his eighteenth-century heirs. What Milton "hears" in the song includes the
gaps and omissions that lead Los to declare that "this mournful day /
Must be a blank in Nature" (8.20–21). To hear the voice of Ololon, as
"Emanation," is to hear a contrary voice:

> are we Contraries O Milton, Thou & I
> O Immortal! how were we led to War the Wars of Death
> Is this the Void Outside of Existence, which if enterd into
> Becomes a Womb?
>
> (41.35–42.1)

The sense of Ololon and Milton as contraries here is comparable to
Nietzsche's "tremendous opposition" between the Apollonian art of
sculpture and the Dionysian art of music, "two different tendencies"
that "run parallel to each other, for the most part openly at variance;
and they continually incite each other to new and more powerful
births . . ." (33). The encounter between the two physiological forces
is imaged by Nietzsche as a "rupture of the Dionysian reality" (59).
Milton's unexampled deed is to open and enter that same void in himself that is both a place and an emanative modality.

> Here in these Chaoses the Sons of Ololon took their abode
> In Chasms of the Mundane Shell which open on all sides round
> Southward & by the East within the Breach of Miltons descent
>
> (34.40–42)

A discursive sense of what it means for Milton to open this
"Breach" and to find his Emanation there must include the full force
of both meanings of *breach*. The "Chasms" as gaps or breaches in
structure (the "cracks, clefts, fissures, voids, blanks" of the *OED* definition) can be imaged as the "track of Miltons course" or "Miltons
Track"—both consequence and evidence of his "Breach" as an active
assault, which the *OED* characterizes as an irruption into, an infringe-
ment upon, a breaking of relations or continuity, or the active viola-
tion of a communal rule or code. But a *breach* can also be the physically broken or ruptured condition of something, or the disrupted
place, gap, or fissure caused by the act of separation. Blake's image of

the "Breach of Miltons descent" includes both meanings, since it is both act and rupture, causing and constituting the gap in the Symbolic Order that is the "Moment in each Day that Satan cannot find" (35.42). Plate 16 (fig. 18) shows Milton's foot "breaching" the word "Selfhood," echoing and reinforcing the breach of the stone tablets in the center of the plate.[7]

What Milton finds in his "descent" (a word Blake uses only four times, all in *MIL/TON*) is the suppressed gap in his own discourse and creativity that constitutes the space ("if space it may be calld") that is an internal void that must be entered if he is to recover his Emanation.[8] "Emanation" is one of a cluster of words that stems originally from *ma* as an imitative root derived from the child's first utterance, interpreted as a cry for the breast (*mama*, "the thing cried for").[9] *Manare*, the intermediate root for *emanation*, means "to trickle or

7. A comparably powerful and ambiguous sense of the word may be found in Melville's description of the "breaching" of Moby Dick on the third day of the chase, the fulfillment of the "enormous act" that is Ishmael's prefigurative interpretation of the allegorical painting he encounters in the Spouter Inn at the beginning of the novel. Alan Bass chooses "breaching" as his translation of Freud's *Bahnung* ("pathbreaking," from *Bahn*, "road") for a similar emphasis, because "it is crucial to maintain the sense of the *force* that breaks open a pathway, and the *space* opened by the force" (Derrida, *Writing* 329). Although considerably less poetic, Ehrenzweig's discussion of "inarticulate form experiences" that "appear to be altogether empty, like 'gaps' or interruptions in the stream of consciousness" is pertinent here, especially his discussion in chapter 6 where he explains how those gaps in our surface perception of articulate speech are revealed and "filled" by listening to human speech played backward on recordings. It is an interesting coincidence that *London* is the word he chooses to illustrate his points (3, 96–115).

8. The phrase "if space it may be calld" is from *MHH* 19, and it shows Blake's sensitivity to gaps in discourse. In 1745 Swedenborg had traveled through the whole solar system, recording his findings in the *Treatise on the Earths in the Universe*. The Universe at that time included only the six visible planets; in 1781 *Georgium Sidus* (now called Uranus) had been found in "the void, between Saturn and the fixed stars" (*MHH* 19; see Howard 47–48). The notion of the Emanation located in a special space is emphasized in Revelation 6 ("And the woman fled into the wilderness, where she hath a place prepared of God") and 14 ("And to the woman were given two wings of a great eagle, that she might fly into the wilderness, into her place, where she is nourished for a time, and times, and half a time, from the face of the serpent"). The woman in Revelation is identified by Swedenborg as "the New Jerusalem," which will "emerge" from its space in the wilderness (*Apocalypse* 583).

9. It is perhaps also related to the root *ma* meaning "good," in the sense of occurring at a good moment, timely or early (*mane*, "in the morning; mature"). Roman Jakobson has observed that in almost all languages some variation of *mama* is the familiar term for "mother" (538–45). Coleridge anticipated Jakobson in a 1794 Notebook entry: "Smile from subrisus. B and M both labials/ hence Infants first utter a Ba, pa, a, milk—. In Greek the W (V) rendered by Ου & by β, not by Φ. So Ουργιλιος., Βιργλιος.. As B for W so M for W. Mit = with" (4 1.5).

18. *MIL/TON*, pl. 15

flow." *Matter* and *material* and *matrix* stem from *mater* (mother), which comes from the baby-talk *ma* with the added kinship-term suffix *-ter*. It is as if beneath these significant words is a prelinguistic primal scene in which crucial oppositions are collapsed: fixity and flowing, word and thing—an unformed, moist (*madere*, "to be wet") region suffused by an undifferentiated, qualitative state of being, a breaking of the experientially syntagmatic structure of the signifying chain of language, a "zero degree" like that of animal language in which there is a one-to-one relationship between signal and place, between signifier and signified, and in which the enunciation has no other content than the act by which it is uttered. To attempt to imagine such a place is to attempt to imagine a place marked by the absence of figuration or representation, a physical and linguistic Beulah in which one might actually hear the sounds of Bowlahoola as the unmediated physiological music of one's own bodily processes. In Revelation 10 the angel bringing the little book places "his right foot upon the sea, and his left foot on the earth," a stand suggestive for the emphasis I am trying to bring to Blake's poem. The location of one foot on the sea suggests the fluidity of the contrary state of the Emanation, not as an "object" of desire but as a contrary mode of being. "There is in Eden a sweet River, of mild & liquid pearl, / Namd Ololon" (21.15–16) and "to redeem the Contraries" Milton must "come in Self-annihilation" in order "to bathe in the Waters of Life" (40.33, 41.2, 1).

As redeemed Emanation, Ololon is not an "object" of desire, defined in a structured Symbolic Order of object-choice, but a modality of the libidinal economy that is prior and contrary to the modality of external object-choice, ego-differentiation and linguistic suppression.[10] Her/its/their "place" is at that internal source "where Thames currents spring / From the rivers of Beulah; pleasant river! soft, mild,

---

10. Freud's basic notion of what guides object-finding in sexual desire is the attempt to resurrect a lost pleasure and revive past satisfaction. Our earliest erotic satisfaction is presumed to be at the mother's breast, in the anaclitic state of completely eroticized existence. In his *Three Essays on the Theory of Sexuality*, Freud claims that suckling at the breast is the "prototype of every relation of love" and that "the finding of an object is the refinding of it" (22). It is important for Blake's sense of the Emanation to emphasize that what is at stake is not the recovery of an "object" but of a state before or contrary to object-ification—a state like the form of art that Kant describes as an imitation of the "productivity" of Nature rather than the object-mimesis of the "products" of Nature.

parent stream" (*J* 53.2–3), and her mode is the Emanating mode of Mary on recovering "Infant Love" in *Jerusalem*:

> *Then Mary burst forth into a Song! she flowed like a River of*
> *Many Streams in the arms of Joseph & gave forth her tears of joy*
> *Like many waters, and Emanating into gardens & palaces upon*
> *Euphrates & to forests & floods & animals wild & tame from*
> *Gihon to Hiddekel, & to corn fields & villages & inhabitants*
> *Upon Pison & Arnon & Jordan. And I heard the voice among*
> *The Reapers Saying, Am I Jerusalem the lost Adulteress? or am I*
> *Babylon come up to Jerusalem?*
>
> (*J* 61.28–35)

The contrasting mode is one in which "piteous Female forms" are "compelld / To weave the Woof of Death!" (*M* 35.7–8) in

> *the External Spheres of Visionary Life*
> *Here renderd Deadly within the Life & Interior Vision*
> *How are the Beasts & Birds & Fishes, & Plants & Minerals*
> *Here fixd into a frozen bulk subject to decay & death[?]*
> *Those Visions of Human Life & Shadows of Wisdom & Knowledge*
> *Are here frozen to unexpansive deadly destroying terrors[.]*
> *And War & Hunting: the Two Fountains of the River of Life*
> *Are become Fountains of bitter Death & of corroding Hell*
>
> (*M* 34.51–35.3)

This textural and textual rigidification may be read as a form of what Luce Irigaray calls the "hegemony of the solid" in masculinist discourse; an earlier vision of its origin had been written by Blake in the form of Urizen's quest for "a joy without pain, / For a solid without fluctuation" because he preferred the "petrific abominable chaos" of "A wide world of solid obstruction" to the libidinal economy of "unquenchable burnings" (*BU* 4.10–11, 3.26, 4.23). But there is no anticipation in *Urizen* of the problem of the Emanation and of the revision of the imagined fall necessary before change can be imagined at the juncture of language and libido:

> *In the Wars of Babel & Shinar, all their Emanations were*
> *Condensd. . . .*
> *All the infant Loves & Graces were lost, for the mighty Hand*
> *Condens'd his Emanations into hard opake substances;*
> *And his infant thoughts & desires, into cold, dark, cliffs of death.*
> . . . .
> *Every Emanative joy forbidden as a Crime*
>
> (*J* 8.42–9.2; 9.14)

When Blake wrote *Urizen* neither the word "Emanation" nor its structural dynamics had entered his poetic vocabulary. In fact, the word "Emanation" does not appear in Blake's work before *The Four Zoas*, and in that poem it appears only in places that can clearly be regarded as late additions.[11] The word "Beulah," which is featured so prominently in *MIL/TON*, would seem at first to have a more secure venue in *The Four Zoas*, since it appears there a total of fifty-three times. Of these, however, at least thirty-seven clearly can be shown to be additions.[12] Thus it would seem that around the time of the Felpham stay, beginning with revisionary work on *The Four Zoas* and continuing with the writing of *MIL/TON*, Blake radically revised or reconceived the nature of his project.

There is even more evidence to support this conjecture if we follow the fortunes of Orc—both as name and persona—during this period.

---

11. "Emanation" appears five times in Night 1, on MS pages 19, 20 (twice), 21, and 22. G. E. Bentley, Jr., has argued convincingly that MS pages 19–22 are "clearly from all considerations a late addition" (*Vala* 195). The only other appearance of "Emanation" is on MS page 56, where it is in lines written over an erased passage. "Emanations" appears six times in Night 1. Four of these are on MS page 4, where two instances are written over erased passages; one is sideways in the left margin, and the other sideways in the right margin. It appears twice on MS page 7, in lines written over an erased pencil passage that had been written over erased copperplate hand. It appears once on MS page 10, in a line inserted between two regularly spaced lines. Its only appearance after Night 1 is on MS page 85, where it is written sideways in the right margin. Since these revisionary additions of "Emanation/s" are almost all in Night 1, and probably date from the 1802–3 Felpham period of "My Spectre around me night & day" (in which "Emanation" also appears), it might be conjectured that after discovering the importance of the Emanation Blake began recasting the whole poem to take into account his new discovery. Bentley's attempt to argue for Blake's revision of the poem in terms of late "Christian" additions shows the danger and complexity of such a compositional fiction, but it does seem possible—from the evidence I have cited—that Blake may have conceived and written almost the whole poem without recourse to the notion of the Emanation.

12. Twenty-six are textual emendations or additions; eleven more are in Night 8 (one of these a marginal addition), which probably took its present form later than the other Nights. In the remaining fifteen instances there is relatively little resemblance to the Beulah of *MIL/TON*. See, for example, the four instances on MS page 83, where Urizen grew up on the "plains" of Beulah, which later "fell." I find Bentley's argument that the present form of Night 8 took shape after 1804 convincing, based on its use of lines found also in *MIL/TON* and other evidence (*Vala* 164–65). His discussion of "Beulah," however, is mystifying. He says that "if the lines over the erasure on page 4 are ignored the name *Beulah* first occurs on page 50, Night IV, and does not occur in Nights I, II, III, V, and VI" (171), and that "this name appears on only two pages before Night VIIb" (172). There are, however, twenty-one instances of "Beulah" before Night 4, twenty of them in Night 1, including the one on MS page 4 that Bentley proposes to ignore, and one in Night 2 added in a stanza break on MS page 25.

At a crucial point in *MIL/TON* Los recollects "an old Prophecy in Eden recorded . . .

> *That Milton of the Land of Albion should up ascend*
> *Forwards from the Ulro from the Vale of Felpham; and set free*
> *Orc from his Chain of Jealousy*
>
> (20.57, 59–61)

On plate 22 Rintrah and Palamabron echo this verbal interpretation of Milton's descent ("knowest thou not that he / Will unchain Orc?"), and on plate 23 they warn, "Lo Orc arises on the Atlantic. Lo his blood and fire / Glow on Americas shore," and they argue at length for permission to "descend & bring him chained / To Bowlahoola." Rintrah and Palamabron are correct in their formulation here, but completely wrong in their interpretation of the consequences, as if they were basing their interpretation on Blake's earlier work without understanding what is going on in *MIL/TON*. What it means to "unchain" Orc has changed—is changing in the poem—from what it meant earlier in Blake's oeuvre: the beginning of yet another "Orc cycle" in the violent eruption of repressed desire. The change in libidinal economy effected by the recovery of the Emanation is totally different from Blake's previous anticipations and attempts, and an understanding of *MIL/TON* must find a way to deal with that difference.[13]

Blake's ability to revise and work through the "Orc problem" in *MIL/TON* is another dimension of what it means to redeem the Emanation, and a confirmation of the prefigurative lines in *The Four Zoas*:

> *And now fierce Orc had quite consumd himself in Mental flames*
> *Expending all his energy against the fuel of fire*
>
> (126.1–2)

Thus previous instances of Orc's "revolt" may be seen as a breaking of "chains" on one level—the unleashing of repressed libidinal energy—

---

13. There are sixty-three instances of the name "Orc" in *The Four Zoas*, and only *one* rather insignificant one in *Jerusalem*: "He views the Cherub at the Tree of Life, also the Serpent, / Orc the first born coild in the south" (14.2–3). This marks a rather spectacular change in Blake's "system," and I suggest that *MIL/TON* is in large part the working ground of that change. The name "Orc" appears seventeen times in the poem, all but two minor instances coming in book 1, and of those remaining fifteen appearances almost all are in the context of a misunderstanding of the action of the poem comparable to that of Rintrah and Palamabron already mentioned. On plate 18, for example, where the name occurs five times, the context is that of the regressive Shadowy Female's attempt to rewrite the poem in earlier terms.

but as securely "chained" on the level of discourse, where the revolt was preinscribed within the dynamics and structure of the Oedipal triangle and a sexual rivalry with the father that defined the woman/ mother as the object of desire and possession. As a preinscribed revolt, or Oedipal manifestation, it reflects the desire to change places or relations within a structure so that the channeling of the libidinal impulses or desire sustains rather than transforms the inherited structure of the Oedipal script. The Lacanian notions of the Symbolic Order and the Name(*nom/non*)-of-the-Father provide a mediating scheme that makes it possible to speak of both libidinal analysis and linguistic categories in a single conceptual framework, transliterating the Oedipus complex into a linguistic phenomenon, where the discovery by the subject of the Name-of-the-Father is a transformation of the physical parent into the abstraction of the paternal role, as the possessor of the woman/mother and the place of the Law as a *non*.

The naming function is associated with the acquisition of an alienating identity whose rigid structure (the Selfhood under the Law of the Name) limits the subject's entire mental and emotional development. The Law governs a Symbolic Order of abstraction that separates the paternal function from the biological father and holds out the promise ("I know my power thee to annihilate / And be a greater in thy place . . . till one greater comes / And smites me as I smote thee" [*M* 38.29–32]) for the child to take the father's place in his turn, reinscribing the circuit described in Blake's "Mental Traveller." In this circuit the breaking of the "chains" of Orc is governed at a higher level by the structuring power of a "signifying chain" (Blake calls it the "Chain of Jealousy") that prevents any "change" except the taking of a different position within the limiting triangular scheme. "So the signifying chain becomes a vicious circle, and the story of the norm itself, of the Symbolic Order, is not that of a 'happy end,' but rather of a perpetual alienation" (Jameson, "Imaginary" 374).

To break this circle Blake must simultaneously "breach" his own discourse and find the "breach" or gap in his prior cyclical "system." His previous attempts had been symptomatic of the system rather than therapeutic or transformative, and he, like Milton before him, had been turning the wheels of the system, repeating it even while thinking he was working for change. To trace the function and appearance of words like "Emanation" and "Beulah" and "Orc" as I have done is another form of following Milton's "track" as he finds the "space" in *MIL/TON* where he can redeem his Emanation and engage it as contrary, opening the discourse to the active presence of a contrary modality in order to begin the "marriage" anticipated in *The Marriage of Heaven and Hell* and curiously aborted in *Visions of the Daughters of Albion.*[14] It is important to see the process of reclaiming the Emanation as a double journey or marriage of contraries. The "Mental Fight" in Book I is still for the most part waged within the Symbolic Order, and it is both necessary and appropriate that this is so. But the struggle with the "Sons" who want another father figure in the patriarchal discourse, or with the "souls" in the Vintage who want definitive closure ("O God deliver us to the Heavens or to the Earths" [25.13]) needs the aid of a dimension that can only be provided by the "marriage" with Ololon, a marriage of contraries made possible by a recovery of what she represents.

IV

What *does* she "represent"? Here the temptation to "name" Ololon is difficult to resist, but it is crucial that we do so. To give her a name, especially one based on a univocal hearing of "Ololon" (*either* as "lamentation" *or* as "joy") is both to limit by naming (to define) and to privilege the *énoncé* over the heterogeneously polysemous state of the subject of the enunciation—to "hear" her, in Humboldt's distinction, as ἔργον (*ergon*, or produced object) rather than as ἐνέργεια (*energeia*, or the force of linguistic production itself). If we succumb to the temptation to name her as the Feminine, the Spontaneous, the Body, the Mother, the Natural, and so on, we should do so only in the most self-conscious and erasive manner possible, recognizing the nature of the Symbolic Order as it is manifested in its onomastic power, and remembering Derrida's warning that "the very form of your proposi-

---

14. In that poem there is no transformation because Oothoon's speech takes precisely the form that Theotormon is most defended against—the seduction of the sirens, Circe, Eve, Dante's Beatrice, and a host of other nonsubversive voices (Marcuse? Reich? N. O. Brown?) that can be allowed to speak at length because they reinforce the status quo rather than threaten or transform it. See Foucault's discussion of "The Repressive Hypothesis" in *The History of Sexuality*, vol. I, for an interesting discussion of this process of confrontation and mutual reinforcement in their tracings of *"perpetual spirals of power and pleasure"* (45).

tion, the 'is' ['est'] affiliated with *trying-to-say*, essentializes the text, substantializes it, immobilizes it" (*Dissemination* 350).

One must write, in this context, on a razor's edge between, on the one hand, a nostalgic and simplistic *Lacanisme* that would appropriate and valorize a reductive notion of the Imginary as the completely adequate answer to the ills of the Symbolic and, on the other hand, its counterpart in producing yet another disguised manifestation of the signifying chain of the Symbolic Order in which the woman *as* blank (to be ploughed and planted, written on, named) is always already *represented*, serving discourse as a commodity of exchange rather than participating as a source.[15]

> To redeem John Milton's dualism, Blake, therefore, structured *Milton* in two books, with Book I being the male journey and Book II, the female journey. Since the feminine virtues . . . are "the weak," Book II is shorter, "weaker" than Book I, and Ololon's journey depends on Milton's journey.
>
> (Easson and Easson, *Milton* 161)

Dualism is not "redeemed" by the strategy of excluding the Other on the level of representation in order to reappropriate it into the discourse to fulfill its function in the place prepared for it. An excluded representation, like Milton's Satan, is not only not excluded (*not a* "void") but is an integral part of the structure, accommodated to and by the system as that which allows it to accede to the "Truth" of a limited and symmetrical binary oppositional system in which each "part" is defined in terms of the other. *MIL/TON* is profoundly engaged in the problematic of a system in which "man calls himself man only by drawing limits, excluding his other—the purity of nature, animality, primitives, childhood" (Derrida, *Grammatology* 244). Beulah is a place in which this pervasive binary logic can be suspended, not a "place" but a different set of relationships where differences are joined in "marriage." As such it is not the final goal of a struggle in which "the Negation must be destroyed to redeem the Contraries" (40.33) so much as a mediating stage of that struggle. The feminiza-

---

15. See Gayatri Spivak's discussion of the "symbolic clitoridectomy" and the "effacement of the clitoris," which she argues are necessary to mark the woman or the category of the feminine as "blank" and ready for inscription or commodity exchange in patriarchal culture and masculinist interpretation (181).

tion of Ololon and the use of the marriage metaphor are not absolutes but rather indices of the inevitable historical determination to which structures dealing with "otherness" are subject. The struggle with a system that generates endless hierarchical structures in order to subordinate all forms of difference to the interests of the dominant group runs the risk of being subsumed by the very structures it fights. The endless turns of Blake's "Orc cycle" seem to have been examples of this phenomenon, and *MIL/TON* is in part the result of Blake's recognition of this fact.

Within those historical determinants of the forms of binary opposition, none is perhaps more important than the concept of gender, as it reflects the domination of culture over biology and determines the shape of our metaphysics as well as our sexual politics. There is always a dangerous possibility, in speaking of gaps and voids, and of entering them, that one is (whether Blake or his interpreter) only repeating a fantasy of penetration/being penetrated as the only form of gratifying desire, playing both roles in a narcissistic economy of self-penetration in which the feminine is still only a category constructed around the phallic term or concept as transcendental signified, reproducing "Ainsoph, this upright one, with that noughty besighed him zeroine" (Joyce 261).[16] The fantasy dualism is repeated in the role of the "female" Other in this scenario, since it must fulfill the role of object to be possessed and void to be penetrated. Is there a different way to imagine and enter the void, another (not an Other) object of desire that is not an "object," a desire that is not satisfied by objects or representations of objects? Milton was "unhappy tho in heav'n." What desire or hunger *moved* him from his place at the "eternal tables"? To imagine this as a scenario of desire, we must imagine Milton to have an *excess* of desire that is not satisfied by the available "objects," which are defined as available to a definite mode of identity, a conceptual and libidinal Selfhood. This excessively available desire is not being fulfilled for Milton, even though we must imagine him as having entered his own situation of imagined fulfillment, of total adequation

16. For Freud the fantasy of female desire is that she must "want" what she lacks, the instrument of penetration. The girl enters the Oedipal triangle (i.e., takes her place in the Symbolic Order of structured desire) by her desire for the father's penis; she can only solve the problem by "having" it in a different sense, in the reproductive intercourse that produces her baby/substitute.

between desire and object. Blake imagines Milton experiencing the consequences of the closure of a discourse (moral and polemical) that has achieved as much systematic and conceptual coherence as is possible. His "system" and its assumptions are therefore open to the deconstructionist maneuvers that can invoke *différance* in order to uncover the usual contradictions inherent in any totalizing metaphysical project. Blake's tactic, however, as Steven Shaviro has argued, is not simply to rest with a negative and critical unmasking of *différance*, "as that which compromises the totalizing project from within," but to move also to affirm the potency of "that which, after the totalization has in fact been accomplished, still remains irreducibly exterior and prior to it" (236), making a "positivity of this perpetual lack of closure which Blake privileges as Creation or as Imagination . . ." (235). Thus both his personality (the Selfhood of his imaginatively limited sexual identity) and his systematizing phallogocentric discourse are seen to have reached the same crisis of successful closure, the only situation in which (de)creative rupture can occur.

Milton imagined the creation of woman to be for the function of "Race" ("Male he created thee, but thy consort / Female for Race"), which means for sexual reproduction, which means her appropriate function and pleasure will be that of the consummated act of reproduction, in which she exists as a blank on which future generations are inscribed by the male. This function is the same, whether the inscriber be an actual male person or the divine Logos written on the virgin womb in the incarnation. Milton's concept of "Race" condenses into one word Freud's view that "women represent the interests of the family and of sexual life" (*Civilization* 50). The question of "female" pleasure is at least as old as the fate of Tiresias, but in this respect Milton would seem to agree with Freud that the reproductive pleasure of "vaginal" orgasm is the only appropriate one within a goal-oriented regulation of the libidinal economy. There is a "gap" in this view, which is both anatomical and libidinal.

> Male and female sexuality are asymmetrical. Male orgasmic pleasure "normally" entails the male reproductive act—semination. Female orgasmic pleasure (it is not, of course, the "same" pleasure only called by the same name) does not entail any one component of the heterogeneous female reproductive scenario. . . . The clitoris escapes reproductive framing. In legally defining woman as object of exchange, passage,

or possession in terms of reproduction, it is not only the womb that is literally "appropriated"; it is the clitoris as the signifier of the sexed subject that is effaced. All historical and theoretical investigations into the definition of woman as legal *object*—in or out of marriage; or as politico-economic passageway for property and legitimacy—would fall within the investigation of the varieties of the effacement of the clitoris.

(Spivak, "French Feminism" 180–81)

Spivak is here emphasizing the strategies that produce the woman as "legal *object*," but the same strategies—at least in a metaphoric or symbolic sense—can be seen to govern woman as an object of representation in patriarchal discourse. At the most fundamental level, the problems of sexual identity and the problems of literary representation as a fulfillment of desire cannot be separated, so that from the viewpoint of the male author the fact that "das Ewig-Weibliche zieht uns hinan" will always be reflected in both personal identity and artistic practice.

It would be possible to assemble here a collection of "great passages" from literature and philosophy to show how, unobtrusively but crucially, a certain metaphor of woman has produced (rather than merely illustrated) a discourse that we are obliged "historically" to call the discourse of man. . . . The discourse of man is in the metaphor of woman.

(Spivak, "Displacement" 169)

It is clear that a change in the mode of representing the woman will reflect changes on the most fundamental level, will indeed be a change in the Selfhood. What is not so clear, as we shall see, is the answer to Spivak's question in this context: "Is it possible to undo this phallocentric scenario by staging the efforts of a critic who seeks to discover the name of the *mother*?" (176).

The "gap" in Milton's Selfhood and in his discourse is not the fully represented gap of woman as void, for that "place" was already filled by the hermaphroditic Shadowy Female. The gap is something missing in Milton himself, a lack that has governed his self-representation and his attempts to represent "the" woman. What symbolic "object" can represent that missing part, which is not literally an anatomical part but is a quality of surplus desire unfulfilled by the libidinal economy of his artistic practice? To pronounce the name "Ololon" is to *create* an oral void, an "O" (like an echo of Milton's "All our wo-o-o-o-e") and to fill that void with one's tongue.[17] In doing so one feels the presence of the tongue in a way different from that in any other phonetic articulation, and especially different from the articulation of the "False Tongue" with its endless lamentations, or the "gross tongue that cleaveth to the dust" (20.15).[18] The emphasis on voice and sound associated with Ololon reflects a change in the symbolic topography of the feminine for Blake; no longer a mute body or object, or the spectral howling of the male hidden in the female, but itself a source or the vocal trace of a source comparable to but different from (as its contrary) the Bard's claim of inspiration: "Every Natural Effect has a Spiritual Cause" (26.44). The identification of the tongue as a non-phallogocentric source of pleasure, or of expression that transcends the categories of pleasure and pain, locates a functional part of the body that is nongenital, that escapes "reproductive framing" in Spivak's phrase, in the double sense that it is free from a biological compulsion for reproduction and free from the discursive imperative for the production of univocal meaning.

V

Here the argument might well stop, content with having assembled a few more hints leading toward a gratulant reading of Blake's poem.

17. Saussure argued that "phonation, i.e. the execution of sound-images, in no way affects the [language] system itself" (*Course* 18). This view assumes that a particular phonation is merely the performance of an ideal phonation already included in the system; it may be an instance of the "False Tongue" that is part of the matter of *MIL/TON*. Culler claims that "the poet makes himself a poetic presence through an image of voice and nothing figures voice better than the pure O of undifferentiated voicing: 'the spontaneous impulse of a powerfully moved soul'" (142). If there is any possibility of creating "presence" through "an image of voice" it may be in the voice-void of Saussure's formulation, the "Void Outside of Existence, which if enterd into / Becomes a Womb" (42.37, 43.1).

18. The *l* figures prominently in many words of echoic origin. The effect can be that of howling or lamentation, as in the Latin *ululāre*, French *ululer*, Gaelic *aililiú*, English *ululate*, *ululation* ("Los howld . . . bellowd his Dolor . . . in ululation waild his woes upon the wind"; *FZ* 49.7–10), but it can also have the opposite effect, of soothing, as in the Latin *lallāre* (to sing to sleep, as in *lull* and *lullaby*). In *MIL/TON* the "softly lilling flutes . . . make sweet melody," and "the hard dentant Hammers are lulld by the flutes lula lula" (24.56–57, 64). Certain qualities of Bowlahoola and Beulah seem to be evoked by their names; the Lark "leads the Choir of Day" with its "trill, trill, trill, trill" (31.31), and the name "Milton" breaks after the *l*. The effect of Poe's Lorelei, and even more his Eulalie ("My soul was a stagnant tide / Till the fair and gentle Eulalie became my blushing bride—/ Till the yellow-haired young Eulalie became my smiling bride") deserve comparison here, along with Stevens' Eulalia.

But the nature of commentary such as this tends to restore the text to a propositional discourse and in doing so to recreate the void in the discourse that the poem was trying to overcome or enter. Assuming the "real" subjective position that corresponds to the poetic discourse is quite another matter, both for the reader and for the reader-as-commentator. To ignore the difficulties of Blake's attempt is to ignore one of the most important aspects of the poem, crucial to its "meaning" as a representation of experience. *MIL/TON* does not conclude with the end of time, but with the hoped-for beginning of a moment that can be multiplied. One does not so easily escape the historical and linguistic determination of the Name-of-the-Father or annihilate the Selfhood in a reorganization of one's libidinal economy and artistic practice. Blake was well aware of the psychological dangers and fears that beset such a quest, and of how artistic representation can be a way of mediating or keeping at a distance the subjective position that is desired.

> *O how can I with my gross tongue that cleaveth to the dust,*
> *Tell of the Four-fold Man, in starry numbers fitly orderd*
> (20.15–16)

> *for man cannot know*
> *What passes in his members till periods of Space & Time*
> *Reveal the secrets of Eternity: for more extensive*
> *Than any other earthly things, are Mans earthly lineaments.*
> (21.8–11)

The problem of *representing* the experience, of naming it, and of *achieving* it inevitably fuse and become one in this context, where the floating of desire free from objects is a menace to coherent self-definition, and the inevitable strategy for defense—the Urizenic impulse—is to plot the immobilization of desire, to change the clay to marble or to keep the "furrows" in the marble from being filled with living clay. Those who enter Beulah and go to sleep there can be lured "down / The River Storge (which is Arnon) into the Dead Sea" (34.29–30).[19]

But the dangers associated with entering an undifferentiated and object-free psychic state may only exist in fantasy, in the face of the

---

19. Critics who remember Freud's speculations on the Medusa will no doubt recognize castration anxiety in the Urizenic "Rocky Form," and in the multiplication of substitute images for the thing whose loss is feared (Polypus as "many feet"). The Angel of Revelation is careful to put only one foot on the water.

manifest impossibility of "returning" to an archaic, preverbal stage of development. Freud argued that no matter how far back we go in our imagined history of the psyche, we cannot conceive of a source (as instinct or drive, *Triebe*) as existing in a pure state without some form of ideational representative (*Vorstellungsrepräsentanz*) that constitutes the fantasies or objects to which they are bound. Freud is emphatic in his insistence that the instinct will always be represented by an idea or group of ideas in this sense, and the analogy that he uses to clarify his meaning is the instinct's relationship to its "representative" and the inscription of a sign. This inscription for Freud involves a "primal repression" (*Urverdrängung*) that results in establishing a *fixation* so that the representative in question persists unaltered from then onward and the instinct remains attached to it. Although he is insistent on the permanence of the primal repression at the origin of the first unconscious formations, he is less clear about the nature of the mechanism of "anticathexis" (*Gegenbesetzung*) that effects it, conjecturing that it must be due to "an excessive degree of excitation and *the breaking through of the protective shield against stimuli*" (*Inhibitions* 20.94; emphasis added).[20] Thus for Freud, although there must once have been an excess of stimulation—an instinct, drive, or desire not bound to an ideational representation and which therefore "breached" the representational defense—a recurrence of such a breach after the metaphoric inscription that constitutes the "primal repression" is impossible. It is "representation" itself, understood as a psychic process, that will protect—or prevent—us from reenacting or reexperiencing the breaching. The congruence of Freud's neurological fable with Blake's fable in *MIL/TON* is a striking one, with Freud's amounting to a denial of the thrust of Blake's.[21]

Or can we read Freud's fable as a self-confirming defense against

20. Under the appropriate entries in *The Language of Psychoanalysis*, Laplanche and Pontalis provide useful discussions of these terms and a guide to other contexts in Freud where they appear. Derrida discusses these areas of Freud's "problematic of breaching" as a "neurological fable" about a "writing machine" (*Writing* 200).

21. A similar attitude in Freud can be found in his various discussions of the relationship between "thing-presentations" (*Sachvorstellungen* or *Dingvorstellungen*) and "word-presentations" (*Wortvorstellungen*). A "presentation" revives and recathects a memory trace, but verbalization is essential for the bringing of anything to consciousness. It is only by becoming associated with a verbal image that the memory-image can be registered in consciousness. "The conscious presentation comprises the presentation of the thing plus the presentation of the word belonging to it, while the unconscious presentation is the presentation of the thing alone" ("The Unconscious" 300). See also *The Ego and the Id*, chapter 2.

precisely the point of Blake's poem that is the crucial one—that there still is or can be an excess of desire not bound by our most ambitious attempts at representation? The question here is whether or not the structure of the subject (of Selfhood) can be breached or put into motion by the movement of a desire experienced as an excess beyond representation, imaged as a *parole* or act of enunciation that both breaches and constitutes the gap in the structure of language. If Ololon, accompanied by the Lark and the Wild Thyme (as the two messengers of Revelation), can be seen as a "new" signifier (not merely another instance of the "female" as blank) then she/they/it could be taken as the *revelatory sign* of a new "system," a linguistic *materia prima* as *energeia* that invokes and cries out her/its/their semiotic nature as a mode of primal truth or authenticity, a linguistic *acte gratuit* that is its own source and not a repetition or translation of the already written. At issue here is the question of whether language is an autonomous master structure, a psychological and cultural anticathexis, that always precedes the human subject and preinscribes its *parole*, or whether there "really" is a void or gap in language that makes possible a "Divine Revelation in the Litteral Expression." And *if so*, can it be "represented" in a literary text that does not in the very process of literary mediation reveal its absence? Can we name an unnamed subjective state without engaging in that process whereby the state in receiving a name is transformed into nothing more than a representation of itself?

C. S. Peirce argued that a third element or "interpretant" will necessarily be involved in the relationship between a sign and its object, so that

> the meaning of a representation can be nothing but a representation. In fact, it is nothing but the representation itself conceived as stripped of irrelevant clothing. But this clothing never can be completely stripped off; it is only changed for something more diaphanous. So there is an infinite regression here. Finally, the interpretant is nothing but another representation to which the torch of truth is handed along; and as representation, it has its interpretant again. Lo, another infinite series.[22]

$$(1.171)$$

---

22. Derrida discusses Peirce's formulation in terms of the deconstruction of the transcendental signified. "There is thus no phenomenality reducing the sign or the representer so that the thing signified may be allowed to glow finally in the luminosity of its presence. The so-called 'thing itself' is always already a *representamen* shielded from the simplicity of intuitive evidence. . . . The *represented* is always already a *representamen*" (*Grammatology* 49–50).

Does Peirce's pronouncement mean that Milton's desire "to take off his [Albion's] filthy garments, & clothe him with Imagination" (41.6) is only to change to "something more diaphanous" in the form of the "Clouds of Ololon folded as a Garment dipped in blood" (42.12)? Must Nanzia Nunzio's claim ("I am the woman stripped more nakedly / Than nakedness, standing before an inflexible / Order, saying I am the contemplated spouse") always be met by Ozymandias' answer: "The spouse, the bride / Is never naked. A fictive covering / Weaves always glistening from the heart and mind" (Stevens, "Notes Toward a Supreme Fiction")?

The issue may by its very nature forever remain a matter for conjecture and assertion, and nowhere is that more the case than in a critical commentary that, by *its* very nature, assumes the function of Peirce's "interpretant" to become a "representation" of the poem in the form of a discursive doubling. The reader or interpreter can adopt the celebratory posture of a Mircea Eliade, and assert that the "symbol" is an autonomous mode of cognition that provides the viewer/reader/celebrant/worshiper with an unmediated *experience* of eternal truth, making him "contemporary with the mythical moment of the beginning of the world" and satisfying "the need of returning to that moment as often as possible in order to regenerate himself" (*Cosmos* 76–77). For Eliade, "One thing alone is important: That *every new valorization has always been conditioned by the actual structure of the Image*, so much so that we can say of an Image that it is *awaiting* the fulfillment of its meaning" (*Images* 159–60). But this formulation merely returns us to the problem: that the potential for experience is already structured by the image, and that the celebrant in the ritual or myth is transformed by the image into a mere representation of the subject.

In his "Finale" to *L'Homme nu*, Lévi-Strauss argues that the attempts of "ritual" to achieve an undifferentiated immediacy are always bound to fail because the "undifferentiated" will itself always be a construct made from objects already differentiated by language and artificially pieced together. Myth, on the other hand, can in his view embody a principle of differentiation that is genuine because it is identical with human thought and language. René Girard concurs with this view of ritual, but he argues that there is a "standard profile" that governs both ritual and myth:

> In order to achieve this undifferentiation, myths, as well as rituals, resort to make-believe. They, too, piece back together entities that, "in

reality," are already distinguished by language. . . . Is it reasonable to describe the incentive for plunging a postulant into the undifferentiating waters of baptism as a "nostalgia for the immediate"? The postulant will not stay in there forever; he will drown only symbolically in order to reach the shore of a new differentiation.

(156–57)

VI

Part of the issue, as I see it, is whether or not in the writing of the poem Blake entered or experienced the regressive state of "Beulah." But that part may be bracketed—perhaps indefinitely—while we consider whether or not the reader can follow Milton's track into the breach and "hear" the music of Bowlahoola in its full somatic implications.[23] Milton's track is the track of phonetic and morphemic concretization and fluidity, down South "Molton" Street into the "molton" ore of Los's ladles, avoiding the "melting cadences that lure" (34.29) in order to enter the "rough basement" of English where "Los built the stubborn structure of the Language, acting against / Albion's melancholy, who must else have been a Dumb despair" (*J* 36.58–60).

Beulah is a place or state where the rest and play that is part of Blake's project can occur as a "Rest before Labour" (*FZ* 2) and where one can perceive the concrete possibility of rearranging the substance of "Babylon" into the living form of "Albion," both as a playful possibility and as the vehicular dimension of the transformation of consciousness that it may signal as yet to come. As such, it will inevitably be frowned upon by "serious" adults and by literary critics who have purely "spiritual" notions of the sublimated mode of existence of the literary text. Freud emphasized how language in dreams becomes

---

23. In a future article I shall argue that the importance of Bowlahoola (as the noise/music made by the body) demands much more attention than the occasional embarrassed comment it has received so far. In the meantime, I quote Michel Serres' useful emphasis on

> the direct pathetic tie we maintain constantly with our own body [which] must always function as languages. On the one hand, at the cellular or molecular level, a proto-language (stereospecific information and thermal noise) is already functioning; on the other hand, at the most highly integrated level, a language is still functioning, but now as individuated signals equipped with something like meaning: calls for desired objects or warnings against dangerous ones. And again, because chiasms and ambiguity complicate matters, we can find a refusal of desire and a call for suffering.

(78–79)

concrete, and this is a dimension of the textual Beulah as an intermediate state of wish-fulfillment, as the articulation of a *Wunsch* for de- and re-articulation. But for Freud, and even more emphatically for Lacan after him, the dream is not pure, does not escape the structured operations of those processes of desire and of the mechanisms that inform the structure of subjectivity. Blake's Beulah can be imagined as a textual experience, as the place of the wish before it is structured in the economy of a language, or a place where its unstructuring, its *morcellement* can occur. To enter Beulah in our reading is to risk the censure of theorists like Wellek and Warren, who would urge a different phenomenology of reading:

> Actually, all experience shows that . . . we grasp printed words as wholes without breaking them up into sequences of phonemes and thus do not pronounce them even silently. In reading quickly we have no time even to articulate the sounds with our vocal cords. To assume besides that a poem exists in the reading aloud leads to the absurd consequence that a poem is non-existent when it is not sounded and that it is recreated afresh by every reading.
>
> (132)

This phenomenology of reading is compatible with the linguistic "science" of Saussure, in which language is a form rather than a substance, and where there is an unbreakable link between signified and signifier in the "unity" of the sign: "It is impossible for sound alone, a material element, to belong to language. It is only a secondary thing, substance to be put to use" (120). But if the imagined constituent element of language is the phoneme before difference, or sound before thought, with the signified being only the effect of the combination and interaction of signifiers, then the "rough basement" of the language may be an imagined "place" that exists *before* the collection of signifiers is constituted by the structure of language. Such a place would be before the subject of desire is determined by the discourse of the Other, before the structure that is assumed by Lacan to be prior to the subject's entry into the speech act determines the possible modes of all subjectivity. If the "rough basement" is also a scene of writing, it will include graphic elements addressed to the eye that do not need to be transposed into the phonetic substance of air in order to be grasped or perceived—the "molton ore" of the Or-*Ul*ro that can move toward Be*Ul*lah or toward "*sorrow*," in the creative Archetexture of the "rough basement," an Archetexture that can "su*rro*und the Passions with p*ORC*hes of iron & silver / Creating f*orm* and beauty ar*ound* the dark regions of s*orrow*" (28.1–2, emphasis added). When Michael comes to Adam and Eve in book 11 of *Paradise Lost* he comes "to send them forth, though sorrowing, yet in peace," and to teach them how to "see the Morn" of their new world of woe by reading the "mute signs in Nature." In the Bard's song, after Satan has taken over the "Harrow of the Almighty" artist (7.10), "Michael sat down in the furrow weary dissolv'd in tears" (8.37). It is the "furrows" of that track of writing that Blake is trying to rewrite, letter by letter, joining the "Harrow" of the artist's graver to his "Arrows of desire" to write "morning" instead of "mourning," to make audible those "mute signs."

Wallace Stevens' mariners arrive in "the land of the lemon trees" and declare that they are "back once more in the land of the elm trees, / But folded over, turned round" ("An Ordinary Evening in New Haven," section 29). They have experienced "an alteration / Of words that was a change of nature."

> The countrymen were changed and each constant thing.
> Their dark-colored words had redescribed the citrons.
>
> (487)

Words formed of letters may be, in one respect, only representations of the acoustic signifiers that constitute language. But once they are written down they take on a separate power of their own, becoming sources of sounds we make with our mouths or in our heads. Stevens explores this interchange in his poem "Certain Phenomena of Sound."

> Eulalia, I lounged on the hospital porch,
> On the east, sister and nun, and opened wide
> A parasol, which I had found, against
> The sun. The interior of a parasol,
> It is a kind of blank in which one sees.
> So seeing, I beheld you walking, white,
> Gold-shined by sun, perceiving as I saw
> That of that light Eulalia was the name.
> Then I, Semiramide, dark-syllabled,
> Contrasting our two names, considered speech.
> You were created of your name, the word

Is that of which you were the personage.
There is no life except in the word of it.
I write Semiramide *and in the script*
I am and have a being and play a part.
You are that white Eulalia of the name.
(*Collected Poems*, 286–87)

Eulalia, like Ololon, is the phenomenon of "a sound producing the things that are spoken." Hence she is created "of" her name, a word "of which" she is the personage. Semiramide is *in* a name too, "in the script" of the written name/word. "I" and "am" "play a part" in the play of the written letters of the name. One version of the play might be "See me I am," or even "See me, I am, I die" as the letters get "folded over, turned round," in a writing that may produce the letter that kills if it lacks a divine revelation in the "litteral" expression.

The realm of the absence of the signified, as the realm of *play*, is the realm both of labor and of rest, the contraries that need each other for the full engagement in Mental Fight. As such the realm is a mediating space, like that of Barthes' pleasure of the text. If it is to be found and entered, and the Emanation reclaimed, it must be on the level of experience rather than of abstract thought, a textural as well as a textual Beulah. What this means is that if Blake "found" it, it would be in the *writing* of his text, as a writing not yet inscribed in the book "of" Urizen, not as the spectral representation of something always already absent, but as a "sourcing" component of his writing, the rest before labor and the rest during labor. The reader cannot "know" this unless s/he too can *experience* Beulah in a participatory or writerly reading, not as "images drawn from experience" (41.24) but in that mode preferred by Blake:

> If the Spectator could Enter into these Images in his Imagination approaching them on the Fiery Chariot of his Contemplative Thought if he could Enter into Noahs Rainbow or into his bosom or could make a Friend & Companion of one of these Images of wonder which always intreats him to leave mortal things as he must know then would he arise from his Grave then would he meet the Lord in the Air & then he would be happy. General knowledge is Remote Knowledge it is in Particulars that Wisdom consists & Happiness too.
>
> (*VLJ*, E560)

I am convinced that the main tendencies brought to the reading of Blake are among those tendencies in literature—and in his own artis-

tic efforts—that he was struggling to overcome in the only way he
could imagine overcoming them; not through a writing as allegoresis,
a writing that pointed away from itself toward "an allegorical abode
where existence hath never come" (*Eur* 6.7) but a writing as mode of
praxis, the writing of a full word rather than a univocal word. The
goal is not to escape "Albions land: / Which is this earth of vegetation
on which now I write" (*M* 14.40–41) but to experience it as a home, to
be at home in it, to be human in it—which means to be creative, to be
an artist, to labor in a material medium:

> *as the Plowman or Artificer or Shepherd*
> *While in the labours of his Calling sends his Thought abroad*
> *To labour in the ocean or in the starry heaven. So Milton*
> *Labourd in Chasms of the Mundane Shell, tho here before*
> *My Cottage midst the Starry Seven, where the Virgin Ololon*
> *Stood trembling in the Porch:*
>
> (39.54–59)

Their feet are on the ground. Their hands are in the clay. Their labor
is a constant test of the possibility that "every Natural Effect has a
Spiritual Cause, and Not / A Natural" (26.44–45). "Golgonooza is
namd Art & Manufacture by mortal men" (24.50), and one is "in" Golgonooza when one is engaged in the Blakean *praxis* of art, whether
producing it or productively reading it: "Guide thou my hand which
trembles exceedingly upon the rock of ages / While I write of the
building of Golgonooza" (*J* 5.23–24). "And they builded Golgonooza:
terrible eternal labour!" (*J* 12.24). The Golgonooza he/they/we build is
"continually building & continually decaying desolate! / In eternal la-
bours:" (*J* 53.19).

Blake's workshop is "in" English, the rough basement, which is
both "litteral" and revelatory. In it he works with letters and sounds,
and the eternal tension between the Symbolic Order of language and
the sourcing of the Imaginary, where the results of the labor may be
spectral if the practice is not emanative. It is a constant struggle of
"terrible eternal labour!" to reclaim the Emanation so that the "hollow
reed" can write words that are full, words that "Every child may joy
to hear" even to the point of weeping while "their sweet round
mouths sing Ha, Ha, He" ("Laughing Song," *SE*). To experience his
work can be both labor and the experience of delight that so pleased
Blake in the "Children who have taken a greater delight in contem-

plating my Pictures than I even hoped" (E703). It may be part of Blake's vision of that becoming like little children that is essential to entering the Kingdom of Heaven.

> concrete art aims to transform the world. it aims to make existence more bearable. it aims to save man from the most dangerous folly: vanity. it aims to simplify man's life. it aims to identify him with nature. reason uproots man and causes him to lead a tragic existence. concrete art is an elemental, natural, healthy art, which causes the stars of peace, love and poetry to grow in the head and the heart. where concrete art enters, melancholy departs, dragging with it its gray suitcases full of black sighs.
>
> (Arp 53)

I do not think that for Blake the experience of Beulah alone constituted the Golden Age or the Kingdom of Heaven; his notion was more problematic, and more dangerous.[24] But like Dante's terrestrial paradise, and like Bunyan's Beulah, it is both a goal of the terrestrial journey and a gate for the spiritual one. The "track" toward that goal is a difficult one, punctuated by its own self-conscious criticisms and those we must bring to it in our efforts to understand, judge, and follow. But as a goal, it may remain intact even if we find its particular articulation unsatisfactory or ineffective.

24. The "melting cadences" of Beulah can "lure the Sleepers of Beulah down / The River Storge (which is Arnon) into the Dead Sea" (34.29–30). What is "beneath" Beulah would more than provide matter for another essay. The River Storge is the vision of a desire that, in locating its existence and origin solely in sexual reproduction, becomes only mortal, bound to the biological conditions of human life and to the "Sexual Machine" (J 39.25). We can imagine it as a mode or realm "beyond the pleasure principle," in which sexual reproduction is a detour to the eternal death that inhabits vegetative life and where the body, and sexual reproduction, are no longer a "vehicle" for the meaning or promise but the limiting determinants of subjectivity.

7

Illuminated Printing: Toward a Logic of Difference

STEPHEN LEO CARR

In the last complete version of *Jerusalem* (copy F), Blake carefully revised the left margin of plate 36 [40], transforming it into a clearly delineated tree by wiping the plate's border almost clean of ink, outlining the print's margin to construct a trunk, and altering and adding to the lines at the top to define further branches (fig. 19). This monochrome plate offers a more definite representation of a tree than does the sole illuminated version (E). Yet both late revisions establish a similar thematic contrast with the scene in the right margin: its exuberant human activity and ripe grapes are now counterbalanced by a stark, almost leafless (lifeless?) tree. The newly formed tree also plays off numerous other marginal designs, especially in *Jerusalem* 34 [38], whose chainlike vegetation is echoed at the top of plate 36, and in *Jerusalem* 49, which depicts a similar desolate tree. Blake's revisions thus have iconographic implications, or at the very least they stimulate hermeneutic activity, for they produce significant new visual relationships that require interpretation. Yet if this revised marginal detail can substantively alter some aspects of *Jerusalem*, how should we understand earlier versions of the poem that lack a fully naturalistic representation of a tree in this margin? We could, perhaps, try to avoid this problem by deciding retroactively to "see" some sort of tree in earlier versions, for example in the border of copy D, which was reworked slightly in a way that may suggest intertwining vines or branches. But in copies C and especially in A, the left border can be naturalized as a "tree" only through a very prejudiced retrospection that reads backward from a determinate to an ambiguous or even

Los shudderd at beholding Albion, for his disease.
Arose upon him pale and ghastly: and he called around
The Friends of Albion: trembling at the sight of Eternal Death
The four appeard with their Emanations in fiery
Chariots: black their fires roll beholding Albions House of Eternity
Damp couch the flames beneath and silent, sick, stand shuddering
Before the Porch of sixteen pillars: weeping every one
Descended and fell down upon their knees round Albions knees
Swearing the Oath of God! with awful voice of thunders round
Upon the hills & valleys, and the cloudy Oath rolld far and wide

Albion is sick! said every Valley, every mournful Hill
And every River: our brother Albion is sick to death.
He hath leagued himself with robbers: he hath studied the arts
Of unbelief! Envy hovers over him! his Friends are his abhorrence!
Those who give their lives for him are despised!
Those who devour his soul, are taken into his bosom!
To destroy his Emanation is their intention:
Arise! awake O Friends of the Giant Albion
They have perswaded him of horrible falshoods!
They have sown errors over all his fruitful fields!

The Twenty-four heard! they came trembling on watry chariots.
Borne by the Living Creatures of the third procession
Of Human Majesty, the Living Creatures wept aloud as they
Went along Albions roads, till they arriv'd at Albions House

O! how the torments of Eternal Death, waited on Man
And the loud-rending bars of the Creation ready to burst:
That the wide world might fly from its hinges, & the immortal mansion
Of Man, for ever be possessed by monsters of the deeps:
And Man himself become a Fiend, wrap'd in an endless curse,
Consuming and consumd for-ever in flames of Moral Justice.

For had the Body of Albion falln down, and from its dreadful ruins
Let loose the enormous Spectre on the darkness of the deep,
At enmity with the Merciful & filld with devouring fire.
A nether-world must have reciev'd the foul enormous spirit
Under pretence of Moral Virtue, filld with Revenge and Law.
There to eternity chaind down, and issuing in red flames
And curses, with his mighty arms brandishd against the heavens
Breathing cruelty blood & vengeance, gnashing his teeth with pain
Torn, with black storms, & ceaseless torrents of his own consuming fire:
Within his breast his mighty Sons chaind down & filld with cursings:
And his dark Eon, that once fair crystal form divinely clear:
Within his ribs producing serpents whose souls are flames of fire.
But, glory to the Merciful-One, for he is of tender mercies!
And the Divine Family wept over him as One Man.

And these the Twenty-four in whom the Divine Family
Appeard; and they were One in Him. A Human Vision!
Human Divine, Jesus the Saviour, blessed for ever and ever.

Selsey, true friend! who afterwards submitted to be devourd
By the waves of Despair, whose Emanation rose above
The flood, and was nam'd Chichester, lovely mild & gentle! Lo!
Her lambs bleat to the sea-fowls cry, lamenting still for Albion

Submitting to be call'd, the son of Los the terrible vision:
Winchester stood devoting himself for Albion: his tents
Outspread with abundant riches, and his Emanations
Submitting to be call'd Enitharmons daughters, and be born
In vegetable mould: created by the Hammer and Loom
In Bowlahoola & Allamanda where the Dead wail night & day.

(I call them by their English names: English, the rough basement.
Los built the stubborn structure of the Language, acting against
Albions melancholy, who must else have been a Dumb despair.)

Gloucester and Exeter and Salisbury and Bristol: and benevolent
Bath

19. *Jerusalem* (copy F), pl. 36 [40]

amorphous feature.[1] The left margin needs some special articulation in order to be recognized as a significant shape, as is evident from the simply printed posthumous copies of *Jerusalem*, which do not suggest any determinate form. The network of visual allusions set into play by this marginal revision in the last versions of this poem is thus unavailable in the earliest versions. And if there are alternative structures or patterns of meaning woven throughout different versions, then what authorizes or legitimates an interpretation of *Jerusalem* based only on one of several possible realizations or performances of the work? The play of different treatments would seem to undermine the authority accorded any single version as a privileged standard for determining the poem's meaning or aesthetic value.

From a certain magisterial perspective, variations in minute detail pose no unresolvable problems: they may be deemed ultimately insignificant changes of emphasis, too slight or subtle to affect the fundamental structures or meanings of *Jerusalem*. After all, the representation of a tree in the margin of some versions of one page may not obviously affect our understanding of the large and complex constructions of this ambitious text. Yet any such studied indifference even to small changes ignores the deliberate labor that produced all variations, and determines in advance that some central core of meaning or form remains untouched by "minor" or "marginal" revisions. Indeed, it seems generally accepted that unless a variant surpasses some tacitly understood threshold of iconic value, it can have no significance; it makes no difference. Even the best bibliographic surveys of different treatments effectively obscure the aesthetic or hermeneutic implications of variation through their lists of, say, the way clothes are colored, through simple enumerations that elide questions of how variants interrelate, of how they participate in larger verbal-visual interactions.[2] The dismissal or reduction of difference gains implicit

1. The fullest discussion of this design is in Erdman, *Illuminated* 315. For full bibliographic information on the various copies here designated by their *Census* letters, see Bentley, *Books* 224–65.

2. Erdman (*Illuminated*) and Bentley (*Books*) rely heavily on simple lists, which is partly, of course, dictated by space constraints. For the simultaneous acknowledgment and dismissal of differences, see Erdman's comment: "Monotony Blake loathed, and when we consider how much variety he introduced into the printing and painting of his works, how distinctive each copy is in coloring and in the finishing of details, it is surprising how few truly variant details are to be found" (15).

support from the still common assumption that an essentially homogeneous (noncontradictory) "system" or "myth" underlies Blake's art, guaranteeing that each illuminated book is finally a performance of the same, a marginal deviation or derivation from some *ur*-text or "vision."[3] This stabilizing originary structure is to be recuperated by reading each Blakean text in the context of all others, a practice that tends always to direct attention to large, underlying structures of meaning and to minute details only in relation to such structures.

Beyond interpretive decisions peculiar to the study of Blake, the literary institutions of our culture offer several bibliographic and critical methods for adjudicating the competing interpretive claims raised by variable treatments of detail. Thus, if we adopt a standard editorial practice and arrange versions of the left margin of *Jerusalem* 36 in their probable order of composition, it is possible to trace a steady progression from a rather lumpy margin sprouting an incongruous tendril or chain in A (fig. 20), through increasingly "treelike" representations in C and D, to a more naturalistic tree in E and F. This neatly linear series might well seem to suggest a gradual unfolding of the design's "intrinsic" potential or even Blake's slow self-realization of his "original intention," and either understanding would sanction interpreting earlier versions as latent or unconsciously proleptic manifestations of the page's primary structure or full meaning. Of course, most variations in detail across versions of a page do not follow such a reasonable logic: what rule governs the coloring of clothes in successive copies of the *Songs*? What law generates the continual fluctuation of detail in *Urizen*? But in most cases, some "logic" of bibliographic or critical decision can be elaborated in order to organize variants into subordinate relationships to a privileged treatment of a page, whether it be the first, last, most highly wrought, or most representative version. Such editorial judgments, though rarely explicitly defended, have long influenced discussion of Blake's verbal-visual art, generally lead-

---

3. Basing interpretation on a knowledge of some Blakean "system" is undoubtedly the dominant feature of twentieth-century criticism of his art. Since the publication of *Blake's Sublime Allegory* (1973), there has been an increasing awareness of the dangers of systematization, and several critics (e.g., W. J. T. Mitchell, *Composite*, and Christine Gallant) have argued that Blake had an ambivalent attitude to the systems he invented. Yet the habit of defining a detail through comparison with a wide range of similar details still remains a procedure that effectively privileges recurrent features over what seems eccentric, obscure, or inexplicable. The most recent argument for the priority of some extratextual basis in the production and interpretation of Blake's art is Leopold Damrosch, Jr., *Symbol and Truth in Blake's Myth*.

Los shudderd at beholding Albion, for his disease
Arose upon him pale and ghastly: and he calld around
The Friends of Albion; trembling at the sight of Eternal Death
The four appeard with their Emanations in fiery
Chariots: black their fires roll beholding Albions House of Eternity
Damp couch the flames beneath and silent, sick, stand shuddering
Before the Porch of sixteen pillars: weeping every one
Descended and fell down upon their knees round Albions knees,
Swearing the Oath of God! with awful voice of thunders round
Upon the hills & valleys, and the cloudy Oath rolld far and wide

Albion is sick! said every Valley, every mournful Hill
And every River: our brother Albion is sick to death
He hath leagued himself with robbers! he hath studied the arts
Of unbelief! Envy hovers over him! his Friends are his abhorrence!
Those who give their lives for him are despised!
Those who devour his soul, are taken into his bosom:
To destroy his Emanation is their intention:
Arise! awake O Friends of the Giant Albion
They have perswaded him of horrible falshoods!
They have sown errors over all his fruitful fields!

The Twenty-four heard! they came trembling on watry chariots.
Borne by the Living Creatures of the third procession
Of Human Majesty. the Living Creatures wept aloud as they
Went along Albions roads, till they arrivd at Albions House.

O! how the torments of Eternal Death, waited on Man:
And the loud-rending bars of the Creation ready to burst:
That the wide world might fly from its hinges, & the immortal mansion
Of Man, for ever be possessd by monsters of the deeps:
And Man himself become a Fiend, wrapd in an endless curse.
Consuming and consumd for-ever in flames of Moral Justice.

For had the Body of Albion falln down, and from its dreadful ruins
Let loose the enormous Spectre on the darkness of the deep,
At enmity with the Merciful & filld with devouring fire.
A nether-world must have recievd the foul enormous spirit
Under pretence of Moral Virtue, filld with Revenge and Law.
There to eternity chaind down, and issuing in red flames
And curses, with his mighty arms brandishd against the heavens
Breathing cruelty blood & vengeance, gnashing his teeth with pain
Torn with black storms, & ceaseless torrents of his own consuming fire:
Within his breast his mighty Sons chaind down & filld with cursings:
And his dark Eon, that once fair crystal form divinely clear:
Within his ribs producing serpents whose souls are flames of fire.
But, glory to the Merciful-One, for he is of tender mercies!
And the Divine Family wept over him as One Man

And these the Twenty-four in whom the Divine Family
Appeard; and they were One in Him. A Human Vision!
Human Divine, Jesus the Saviour, blessed for ever and ever.

Selsey, true friend! who afterwards submitted to be devourd
By the waves of Despair, whose Emanation rose above
The flood, and was namd Chichester, lovely mild & gentle! Lo!
Her lambs bleat to the sea-fowls cry, lamenting still for Albion.

Submitting to be calld the son of Los the terrible vision:
Winchester stood devoting himself for Albion: his tents
Outspread with abundant riches, and his Emanations
Submitting to be calld Enitharmons daughters, and be born
In vegetable mould; created by the Hammer and Loom
In Bowlahoola & Allamanda where the Dead wail night & day.

I call them by their English names; English, the rough basement.
Los built the stubborn structure of the Language, acting against
Albions melancholy, who must else have been a Dumb despair.)

Gloucester and Exeter and Salisbury and Bristol: and benevolent
Bath

20.   *Jerusalem* (copy A), pl. 36 [40]

ing, for example, to preferences for illuminated over monochrome versions (as is the case with *Jerusalem*) or for sharply delineated over more indeterminate treatments (especially with ambiguous or ill-formed designs like the "Tree of Jesse" compartments in the "Introduction" to *Innocence*).

Methods for containing variation within a hierarchy of meaning or value may seem entirely reasonable within the general institutional and ideological constraints of "practical criticism" or in terms of the more peculiarly Blakean concerns of defending a writer regularly charged with being obscure, inchoate, or mad. But such conventional procedures accommodate the differentiation of visual detail in Blake's art to categories and methodologies developed for the study of more standardized forms of artistic production. And this inhibits sustained inquiry into one of the most remarkable qualities of Blake's works of illuminated printing—that each "copy" of a work differs from all others. This radical variability is embedded in the material processes of producing illuminated prints, and thus always enters into the verbal-visual exchanges generated within each page. The characteristic variation of detail in Blake's art challenges aesthetic beliefs deeply associated with conventional modes of producing books and prints. And beyond this, it points to Blake's innovative production (or reproduction) of artistic qualities, which needs to be more fully elaborated if the distinctive features of his art are to be appreciated.

For most works, both graphic and verbal, designed for mechanical reproduction, variation from the primary text or master copy occurs as an undesirable intervention in the normal productive process, as an accidental departure from the original or an extra-ordinary revision by author or editor of the initial invention. The logic of mechanical reproduction is one of identity: it leads to a multiplication of the same, to a mass publication of what are taken to be identical copies. For a variety of technical and commercial reasons (in terms, for example, of manufacturing time and cost per unit), it is always easier to base this production on an economy of simple repetition extended as far as mechanically possible. And this standardization tends to replicate itself on higher levels, as uniform artistic styles and highly conventionalized choices of subjects, for similar technical and commercial reasons related to the ease of producing, marketing, and consuming—or interpreting—recognizable, more or less "identical" objects.

Blake, of course, was well aware of the artistic consequences of the logic of identity as manifested through technological and economic imperatives.[4] In his polemical notes on art, he anatomizes the relationship of economics, the standardized techniques of reproductive engraving, and aesthetic beliefs, elaborating the crucial insight that "Commerce Cannot endure Individual Merit its insatiable Maw must be fed by What all can do Equally well" (E573). Evidently, variation in detail helps to define an artistic practice significantly in opposition to historically dominant modes of artistic production. But to articulate this significance and its implications for our understanding of Blake's art, it is not enough simply to note the fact of variation, for differences or "errors" inevitably infect the mass dissemination of any text or image, even those mechanically reproduced under the aegis of a logic of identity. Variation must be understood in terms of its significance within a specific system of production and reception, in terms of the logic of signification peculiar to that system.[5] Thus, within most forms of mechanical reproduction, and most especially within conventional book publication or eighteenth-century reproductive engraving, vari-

---

4. The most detailed and far-reaching discussion of Blake's aesthetic in terms of its relationship to technology and commerce is Morris Eaves, "Blake and the Artistic Machine: An Essay in Decorum and Technology."

5. Robert N. Essick, in his excellent response, elaboration, and (at times) challenge to this essay, argues that variation occurs in conventional prints and that connoisseurs and collectors have always appreciated such material differences among prints. He believes, therefore, that Blake's ever-varying graphic productions differ from traditional prints only "in emphasis and detail, not in the nature of the phenomena." Essick suggests an innovative materialist understanding of connoisseurship, and usefully reminds us that variation in Blake's art has analogies with traditional forms of artistic production. Yet I still contend that variation in Blake's printmaking process sets into play its own characteristic logic of signification; its importance—both historical and theoretical—cannot be understood as merely a change "in emphasis and detail" from that found in other systems of production. Most variations in conventional print and book publication achieve their significance only in and through an economy of scarcity. Within this market economy, variations among different versions are used to articulate a range of values that directly correspond to a version's availability. Though sometimes versions may differ in ways that are of aesthetic or interpretive interest (e.g., the difference between a published proof and the completed version of a print), all that is strictly necessary to attract a connoisseur's attention is any mark, *however insignificant*, by which versions can be distinguished (e.g., the change in an engraved date, or moving from open to closed letters in the inscription). Variations in Blake's art, however, immediately and significantly alter the design: material differences introduced in reproduction themselves produce alternative construals or performances of a page. Their value or interest is always "semiotic" and never simply "economic." Though variation inevitably occurs in any system of production, its function in Blake's printmaking process differs in kind and not in degree or "emphasis" from that in other modes of artistic production.

ation is effectively controlled and marginalized. Artistic labor is divided into a series of discrete operations, each with a precisely defined task and a determinate relationship to the original invention. Those factors characteristically introduced at each successive stage (e.g., size of page or type; method of reproductive engraving) are judged to be insignificant variations precisely because they can almost always be separated from direct authorial involvement. Moreover, the division of labor usually makes it possible to locate the exact stage where an original changes more substantively (e.g., alteration of a word or pictorial detail), to determine the degree of authorial involvement in that stage, and then to judge the relative authority of all newly introduced variants.[6] Traditional forms of mechanical reproduction thus operate under a governing opposition between an authoritative original and its ghostly and imperfect reflections. Within the terms established by this system, variation always seems a derivative and insubstantial phenomenon.

Variation in Blake's art must be understood in radically different terms, indeed in terms of a radical difference, for his mode of production disrupts the very possibility of simply repeating some authoritative version of a design over and over again. The multiplication of differences is a distinctive feature of every stage of Blake's printmaking process, and is fundamentally integrated into his characteristic manner of developing and completing a work of illuminated printing.[7] Even the mundane task of printing a design using the technique of re-

6. My account, of course, oversimplifies the often irreducible complexities besetting textual editing, but I now wish only to indicate the general attitude toward artistic variability that both emerges from and supports mechanical reproduction.

7. Essick challenges this claim, noting that "Blake's major graphic innovation, the relief-etched copperplate, is a more stable matrix, more resistant to purposeful or accidental change, than conventional copperplate engravings." But this observation in no way affects my larger argument. Though as a physical artifact a relief-etched plate is indeed "more resistant" to change, as an element in Blake's printmaking process such plates always engender variation. Technically, since ink on relief-etched plates is not "packed" into distinct channels incised into the plate, the medium enforces minute changes in every print pulled from such plates. Moreover, in terms of what the medium is capable of representing, relief-etched plates cannot achieve the fine delineations and linear discriminations possible in intaglio engraving since thin relief areas are liable to break down under printing pressures because of "foul biting" from acid that literally undermines thin relief plateaus. Relief-etched plates thus can never convey as much visual information as intaglio, and it is this relative paucity of visual information that facilitates or even makes possible significant alterations in later stages of the printmaking process.

lief etching that Blake invented significantly alters the image it produces. Relief printing is far more prone than work in intaglio to slight
uncertainties in the marriage of paper and ink, to foul printing, blur-
ring, and uneven or imperfect inking. This delicate alteration to
printed detail is raised several powers in Blake's experiments with
color printing, which may entirely obscure and/or substantively revise large etched details (as in several versions of *Urizen* 24 and 25),[8]
and which always change in a somewhat aleatory fashion the visual
qualities of every minute particular on a page. Blake's habitual
"touching up" of prints with ink or scratchwork and, most especially,
his ever-changing manner of illuminating a page further differentiate
every version of a design, producing not only large-scale iconographic variants but also a subtler alterity in background details, figures' lineaments and expressions, and the visual relationships linking
together pictorial elements.[9]

Blake's publication process itself, then, extends and accentuates
the play of differences. Variation is the necessary condition of the production of a work of illuminated printing. It supplements the network
of signification in each individual "copy," re-marking each mark, not
simply in an accidental, ad hoc manner that can be cleanly isolated
from the initial inscription but through the requisite global re-vision
or re-making set into play by each act of making. The stereotyped
"original" on the etched plate exists only as an idealized abstraction.
A plate design may establish certain technical and artistic limits (of
"Opakeness" and "Contraction") on the material processes of differentiation, but it does not constitute a privileged, canonical version.
Indeed, it is sometimes nearly impossible to reconstruct the "plate
state" of a design, especially, for example, with the heavily color-
printed pages of *Urizen*.[10] The significance of radical variability does

---

8. On both pages, the appearances and even the number of figures change considerably across versions. See Erdman, *Illuminated* 206–7.

9. For a discussion of the methods and effects of variation in uncolored versions,
see my "William Blake's Print-Making Process in *Jerusalem*." The best reading of the
subtle changes in illumination from version to version is Myra Glazer-Schotz and
Gerda Norvig, "Blake's Book of Changes: On Viewing Three Copies of the *Songs of Innocence and of Experience*."

10. For work on the "plate states" of *The Book of Urizen*, see John W. Wright, *William
Blake's Urizen Plate Designs*. Some of Blake's prints have very little or no etched foundation, and thus cannot be said to have a "plate state": the best discussion of the graphic
techniques this involved is Essick, *Printmaker* 128–35.

not depend, however, on the practical difficulty of recuperating an "original," nor even on the number, extent, or value of individual variants with some formal or iconographic burden. These issues may show how variable Blake's pages are, and suggest how infinitely laborious the task would be of discovering some stable form beneath their constantly fluctuating surface. But the continual differentiation of detail gains its specific importance because it reveals the ultimate impossibility of determining some underlying authoritative structure that stabilizes the field of verbal-visual exchanges. This is not solely an empirical difficulty, a problem of organizing a large number of variants in some hierarchical order of significance; it is a basic condition of the production of verbal-visual interactions within Blake's system of production. Variation is a result of the constitutive doubleness of each signifier on an illuminated page, of the double "origin" of each sign both in time (at the etching of the plate and at the production of a page) and in its material inscription (as a printed character that is subsequently altered by illumination). This double determination generates a logic of difference informing the production of Blake's pages: each stage of the printmaking process is displaced by the articulations of other stages. The final product is the result of different artistic imperatives, each of which is never fully able to realize itself because it must always interact with other construals of the design. Variation is the material mark or trace of this conflict within the system of production.

Precisely because each signifier on an illuminated page is doubly inscribed, it always emerges as the product or remainder of a double intention. Its precise signification seems to emanate from somewhere "between" each specific construction of its features. But this, of course, is only a "virtual" point of origin, an imaginary effect of the structural relationship of two intentional acts of meaning, a relationship that generates an irreducible complexity or conflict in the production of meaning in Blake's works of illuminated printing. There is no simple determination of the meaning or aesthetic value of an illuminated page, no single authoritative point of reference, whether it be defined as some extratextual, analytically reconstructed "system" or "myth" or some idealized authorial "vision" or intention. The unauthorized (or multiply authored) operations of a logic of difference, especially as set into play by technical processes of inking, printing, and coloring whose effects are never perfectly predetermined, continually open new possibilities of meaning that are articulated as individual variants. Every illuminated page is thus overdetermined by processes that bifurcate, revise, and complicate its originary or initial configurations.

My formulation of this "logic of difference" and its implications bears certain obvious resemblances to the idioms and insights associated with deconstruction, most especially to what Derrida labels *différance* in order to designate

> the movement of play that "produces" (and not by something that is simply an activity) these differences, these effects of difference. . . . Différance is the nonfull, nonsimple "origin"; it is the structured and differing origin of differences.
>
> ("Différance" 141)

The virtual or imaginary origin of meaning constituted by the double inscription of an illuminated page exemplifies the "nonfull, nonsimple 'origin'" of *différance*. Of course, Derrida's formulation leads us to explore the ways each of these double inscriptions also differs inevitably from itself, from what we may imagine to be Blake's intention at each stage of his printmaking process. But rather than directly following this line of thought, I prefer to focus on the way *différance* is related to the contradictory impulses of reproduction, to the repetition necessary for representation, in ways that further clarify the import of the logic of difference embedded in Blake's process of reproduction.

The movement of *différance* is inextricably bound up with the necessary iterability of any sign, with its capacity to remain significant when repeated in other contexts than the situation in which it was initially employed.[11] The ability of a sign to function in the absence of its author, to effect new meanings when reproduced in different contexts, always distances a signifier from its origins: it reveals the systematic working of some irreducible quality that is not solely determined by the initial inscription and that prevents, therefore, the sign from simply manifesting a single intention. As Derrida and others have argued, the power of signs to differ from themselves when they are repeated is characteristically suppressed by a variety of ideologies

11. Derrida marks the relationship between *différance* and repetition most clearly and extensively in his essay, "Limited Inc abc. . . ."

and rhetorical and interpretive strategies. What distinguishes the logic of difference from the general operations of *différance* is that Blake's mode of production recapitulates materially an abstract condition of language that is usually manifest only in the dislocations and absences *différance* produces. The play of differences enters into Blake's printmaking process in relatively accessible ways, leaving traces that do not so much simply subvert attempts at closure as make moments of structural indeterminacy available for artistic revision.

This underlying logic of difference engenders a radical change in the aesthetic status and function of illuminated pages, which may best be explored by again contrasting them with mechanically reproduced art. As Walter Benjamin has argued, mechanical reproduction leads to the destruction of art's "aura," its authoritative presence that he defines as "the unique phenomenon of a distance." Mass production overthrows this authority by making a work generally accessible, and this "reactivates the object reproduced," renewing its connections to social needs and desires (221–22). In a certain sense, the destruction of "aura" by mechanical reproduction is understandable in Derridean terms as the effect of *différance* as set into play by repetition: the sign's continued power to signify when reproduced in radically new and unforeseen contexts reflects the lack of total determination by its origin. Mechanical reproduction, however, manifests the operations of *différance* despite itself, as a disruption of its logic of identity. Its goal of mass producing exact copies epitomizes in material ways the effacement of differences, and thereby perpetuates the illusion that a text or image is ever originally and adequately present. Moreover, in ways that Benjamin essentially ignores, mechanical reproduction helps to constitute the very "aura" that it undermines. In obvious ways, reproductions always refer to something outside of themselves, and thus locate their value or meaning at a distance; indeed, they mark off the idealized distance defining an original's "aura," their own imperfect existence signaling the endless difficulty of reaching or realizing art from the past. In some sense, only after an original has been reproduced, only after it has revealed its power to be disseminated indefinitely, does its historical authority become operative or even visible. Mechanical reproduction, therefore, does not simply demystify the status of an original: a necessary countermovement preserves the privilege accorded the initial invention, making it seem even more remote and ideal.

The displacement of aesthetic value from a reproduction to its distant original often manifests itself in a peculiar self-effacement of the reproduction's modes of signifying. Consider, for example, eighteenth-century reproductive engravings. Each print marks its distance and its derivation from what it reproduces, and not only through its homage to the superior original in its title nor by its double signatures that distinguish inventor from executioner. Eighteenth-century attempts to capture the nuances of the different painterly media by graphic means (the invention of mezzotint, stipple, and aquatint, the refinement of linear systems of reproduction, and so on) implicitly locate the criteria of aesthetic value and correctness outside the graphic medium. Appreciating a print's virtuosity requires, in effect, a comparison with the image and medium it recollects. And since even the most successful and ingenious graphic techniques produce manifestly imperfect copies, the discrepancy between how a print is designed to appear and how it does appear always marks off the distance between a copy and its original. To a modern eye, these reproductive prints may appear so unlike the image they repeat that it is nearly unthinkable that they could be seen as accurate reproductions. Of course, there are good historical and technological reasons why they were accepted as such, but these reasons do not obviate the effect on ways of looking at images entailed by treating imperfect copies as truthful reproductions. Within the terms of a logic of identity, looking *at* a reproduction really means seeing *through* the copy to a distant, invisible original, an imaginary process that is far less plausible, far less based in phenomenological experience than Blake's "seeing thro'" the eye to identify the sun as a host of heavenly angels. The reproductive process that makes the original accessible thus also idealizes it, produces its "aura," abstracts art away from its material execution. And just as a technical standardization facilitated a conventional uniformity in the arts, so too does the abstract idealization embedded in the system of reproduction tend to repeat itself on higher levels, as, for example, Platonic doctrines that locate the value of all art in some extrasensory, ideal realm.

The play of differences in Blake's pages inhibits this abstract idealization, for it highlights the materiality of each mark on an illuminated page. In general terms, the novelty of Blake's works, their radical difference in appearance from other artistic productions, focuses attention on the physical characteristics of their minute particulars, and invites the eye to linger on their execution. Such close attention must quickly move beyond the appreciation of mere connoisseurship. Instead of the fine delineations and "Clean Strokes" of conventional prints, Blake's pages offer not only the "crude" or "simple" outline drawings characteristic of his relief prints but also an equally "primitive" manner of reworking and illuminating printed details that does not hide their revisionary transformation under a smooth overall neatness of "high finish." We cannot easily see "through" these marks to some ideal invention. Insofar as the structure of a double inscription is made apparent (through, for example, outlines or illuminations that alter the underlying print without entirely obscuring it, or through details that clearly have no etched foundation), Blake's pages insistently signal that they are not transparent mediums for some canonical "vision." In addition to their individual formal or iconic contributions, variations also help to define the conditions of representation within illuminated printing. They point to an ongoing, open-ended production of meanings rather than a re-presentation of an original meaning.

Insofar as variability itself has been recognized as a significant aspect of Blake's art, it has been primarily in social-economic contexts, in terms that contrast Blake's methods to the monotonous uniformity of commercial reproductive engraving. But the significance of radical variation in this context can be too easily subsumed in a general ethos of "imaginative freedom," which evokes post-Romantic notions of the alienated artist who strives to "express" freely an individual consciousness. The play of differences certainly offers occasions for the exercise of imagination, but this activity is always embedded in a system of production, within the structure of double inscription that deflects and complicates its expressive value. The logic of difference shows how Blake inhabits a system of production that mediates and structures his art while still criticizing the entrapment such systems enforce: like Los, Blake is "Striving with Systems to deliver Individuals from those Systems" (*J* 11.5). The variation engendered by Blake's productive processes is thus a symptomatic mark of a necessary mediation that permeates every aspect of his art. Its implicit social critique leads to an innovative discursive and artistic practice.

Because the play of differences marks a new discursive practice, it challenges the way we understand the bibliographic—or chalcographic—"fact" of variation.[12] Blake's methods of production undermine those institutional practices and beliefs that generate the fundamental distinctions of bibliographic study. "Substantive" and "accidental" variants, for example, can only be systematically distinguished because of the division of labor between author and printer (or designer and engraver). Similarly, the possibility of rejecting some variants as lacking authority derives from the isolation of the author from the productive process, from his lack of intimate involvement with the material execution of an invention. Any direct application of these categories, or even an implicit acceptance of the general model in which an artist intrudes only occasionally to make a substantive revision, inevitably distorts Blake's art because it requires in advance that the vast majority of variations be understood as insignificant, as simply "accidental." An approach responsive to how the logic of difference effects signification in Blake's art must reconceive traditional editorial categories and methods. It should foster a skeptical wariness toward even the most seemingly neutral descriptive terms; how can we talk of "copies" of Blake's works of illuminated printing when no two are identical? Why should we identify Blake's art as "illuminated

12. In his extensive review of *Blake Books*, Robert N. Essick has also argued that traditional bibliographic methods cannot handle the variation occurring throughout Blake's art. But he then proposes a hierarchical typology of variation in terms of "chalcographic significance" (180), which is, I believe, a reification of traditional printmaking methods into universal categories.

Essick defends this earlier position when he suggests in "How Blake's Body Means" that "we should not take alarm if the distinguishing of variants sometimes replicates traditional bibliographic or chalcographic procedures." If he means only that all "archeological reconstructions" (a wonderfully apt metaphor) of graphic production are alike in their attempt to locate variants at the stage in production in which they originated, then we very much agree. What I object to in his earlier review essay is his effort to establish a *hierarchy* of significant variants to determine a priori that, say, an addition to the printed design would always be more important than an emphatic underscoring within it. To decide this in advance is to approach Blake's art with a critical/scholarly apparatus abstracted from a different system of producing prints. And this risks simply falling into a habitual way of appropriating prints that remains blind to variants deemed relatively "marginal" or "insignificant." I take it that a primary concern of both our essays is to direct attention to graphic qualities of illuminated pages too often ignored or dismissed: to do this, I believe it necessary to rethink and redefine our critical and editorial procedures.

21. "The Little Boy found" (*Songs of Innocence*, copy P)

22. "The Little Boy found" (*Songs of Innocence and of Experience*, copy F)

books" if his practices ultimately challenge the hegemony of the "book" as a social and artistic institution? And beyond such self-critical scrutiny, this approach must attend to the unique productions of meaning entailed by Blake's idiosyncratic system of production, to the constitutive differentiation and re-doubling of an invention always generated by its execution.

I will end this discussion of the logic of difference by considering an already much discussed work, "The Little Boy found" in *Songs of Innocence*, in order to distinguish the ways variation supplements the fundamental structures of an illuminated page. The design at the top of the page shows two figures, an adult and a child, walking through a dark forest (fig. 21). The traditional interpretation treats the larger figure as male and identifies him as Christ. In one version (*SI* P), Blake added to printed detail so as to represent Christ very definitively or unambiguously: a somewhat scraggly beard is inked in, and an unusually full halo is further emphasized by numerous inked rays of light emanating from it. But even when the figure is not marked so strongly as a saintly male, it still sufficiently resembles other Blakean depictions of Jesus that its identification as Christ can seem plausible. Moreover, if we see the design as illustrating the poem, that is, if we assume that text and design are representations of the same, then we may imagine that we are seeing "God ever nigh" leading the little lost boy "by the hand." And this leads to a comforting reading of the illuminated print as an expression of the benevolent divine guardianship of Innocence.[13]

Yet in several versions (for example, *SI* B, C; *SIE* A, I, T, Z, AA), the larger figure is distinctively feminine (fig. 22). Its facial lineaments have been softened, the waviness and/or length of its hair emphasized, and the curves of a full bosom suggested by subtle alterations in shading and illumination. Thus, for example, in one copy (*SIE* F) flesh tones soften the printed detail of the face, shading above the waist suggests a girlish bosom, and the figure is given long, flowing blond hair. Such variants suggest an alternative identification of the figure as the boy's mother. Though this interpretation opens several

---

13. The main terms of this interpretation have been laid down by Gleckner, *Piper* 98–102, and Hirsch, *Innocence* 186–88. Hirsch offers one of the first identifications of the large figure in the design as Christ.

interesting perspectives on the page, it seems to have been totally rejected, and its reading of the figure as the boy's mother, or even as a
female, dismissed.[14] A compromise position—treating the figure as
androgynous—turns out to be no compromise at all, for this apparent
complication can be readily resolved by slightly expanding the
boundaries of Christ's sexuality, thereby permitting the traditional
interpretation to remain essentially unchanged.[15]

Throughout the critical debate about this page, substantive differences in Blake's treatment of the print have been effectively ignored,
or else seen as problems to be explained away. The fact that plausible
alternative interpretations could arise has never seriously been taken
to be meaningful in itself: ambiguous details are understood as purely
local problems within a stable field of meaning, and not as marks defining the ways meaning becomes generated throughout the field.
Some primary structure, determined in this case by textual allusions
that seem to authorize seeing the design as an illustration and by
"standard treatments" of various details and themes, predetermines
critical understanding so much that it becomes difficult even to see
the sex of the large figure as significantly problematic.[16]

This dismissal of differences goes beyond the issue of whether one
sees the adult as male or female. Other potentially significant variants
that do not directly bear on the question of the figure's sexual identity
are simply ignored, even though they can alter our sense of the transaction being represented. In copy B of *Innocence*, for example, the tree
trunk at the right has been broadened so that the child's outstretched
hand seems to rest on or behind it, as though he were using the tree

14. Thomas E. Connolly and George R. Levine first identified the figure as the boy's
mother in "Pictorial and Poetic Design in Two *Songs of Innocence*." John Grant's heated
critique of this article and defense of the Christ identification elaborates the arguments
and methodological decisions for the traditional interpretation. Erdman treats the figure as Christ without mentioning its occasional feminine appearance (*Illuminated* 55).

15. In the reproduction of the *Songs of Innocence and of Experience* he edited, Sir Geoffrey Keynes notes that the figure probably is "one of Blake's not infrequent androgynous figures" (plate 14). Yet this acknowledgment does not affect his immediately
previous identification of the figure as "a person in the image of God." Grant veers
toward accepting androgyny, but again this does not change the essentials of his
interpretation.

16. See, for example, David Bindman's dismissal of the entire issue in a footnote: "It
is inconceivable to me that the figure leading the boy could be anyone but Christ" (*Blake*
235). See also Zachary Leader's brief discussion of this controversy, which concludes
that this page "is another of Blake's attempts to do too much" (49–50).

for leverage in order to resist being led in the direction the adult is moving. This possibility is always latently available in the design because the child stands with his leading right leg crossed over in front of his left leg. His peculiarly convoluted posture conveys the kinesthetic impression of a turning away, which is reinforced by the symmetrical opposition of the stance of the adult, whose leading left leg is crossed over in front of the back right leg. The resulting subliminal sense of opposing movements is often counterbalanced by making the background trees form a containing oval frame for the two figures (see *SIE*, copies B, T). But even when this particular visual tension is resolved or downplayed, the larger issue of how the two figures interact is continually reopened for interpretation by other variables, by the presence of haloes over one or both figures, or by facial expressions connoting either an unsympathetic or a friendly exchange. Such differences in detail challenge the self-evidence of the traditional interpretation: they establish a range of treatments of visual detail, all of which cannot equally well be contained within a single interpretation. Variation thus invites alternative and even antithetical readings that might, for example, stress the dangers of being led by either a "wand'ring light" or a seemingly benevolent hand, or that could use the anomalous haloes to read the page in terms of the typology of Christ's separation from his parents.

I do not wish to elaborate any of these interpretations now. Merely outlining some possible lines of development will suggest, I hope, the hermeneutic richness produced by variation. Moreover, though more developed readings might better elucidate the particular verbal-visual exchanges in this poem, in some sense attempts to achieve a more comprehensive interpretation, to interrelate as many variable treatments as possible within some encompassing framework, may obscure the radical quality of the play of differences across Blake's pages. Variation does not simply produce a range of emphases within a single unified network of signification: attention to diverse treatments shows that incompatible interpretations will often be generated, as in the case of "The Little Boy found." But the alternative interpretations made available by surveying different versions do not exhaust the field of possible verbal-visual interactions. The double inscription of each signifier necessarily reconstitutes significant relationships within a work of illuminated printing, and this revisionary transformation always has the potential to introduce entirely new aesthetic qualities. The development of "The Little Boy Found" in copy E of *Innocence*, for example, exceeds the thematics associated with the adult's sexual identity or with the quality of the transaction between the two figures. In this version, both figures are uncolored, their lineaments faintly marked by light orange-brown printing ink, while the surrounding area is entirely colored in a dark and mysterious copper. The remarkable effect is to make the ghostly figures seem to have emerged directly from a copperplate, a self-reflexive comment on the medium of illuminated printing and the effects of representation it engenders that invites a reading of the poem as an allegory of artistic production and reception, of a work's entrance into the world and the responses it provokes and requires.[17]

Again, I am not so much interested in advancing a particular new interpretation as in exploring the general conditions of encountering works of illuminated printing.[18] Blake's printmaking process necessarily involves re-vision, and is therefore a form of reproduction that breaks free from simple repetition. The initial invention is always open to an execution that can substantively alter its configurations, to a new articulation that may depart in unpredictable ways from other versions. The material characteristics of Blake's art require an interpretive willingness to enter into the play of differences, to see the double inscription of illuminated printing as generating an openended proliferation of verbal-visual exchanges, and to join in the strenuous imaginative activity of producing and reproducing each page.

17. Though he makes no reference to this version, David Simpson notes that the child is "being led out of the plate," moving "towards us, in what almost seems to be a frontal confrontation with the reader and his world" (*Irony* 49).

18. Though I repeatedly try to avoid simply using variants as a basis for new readings, Essick correctly complains that this essay focuses on "those variants that seem to alter representation, and thus may have the most iconographic potential." In my treatment of both "The Little Boy found" and the marginal "tree" in *Jerusalem* 36, I am seeking to direct attention to variants that now fall below what I earlier called "some tacitly understood threshold of iconic value" but that are still close enough to this "threshold" to require explanation. Variation must first be made visible as a significant aspect of Blake's art before its full implications can be appreciated. For a brief discussion of "meaningless" variants and what they suggest about Blake's artistic practice, see Carr (536–37).

8

How Blake's Body Means

ROBERT N. ESSICK

The recent intensive study of Blake's graphic techniques has pro-
ceeded along two tracks. Some scholars, employing traditional historical research methods coupled with studio experiments, have endea-
vored to recover the specific materials and procedures Blake used to
produce his relief and white-line etchings and his color prints, both
relief and planographic.[1] Others in this new field have sought out the
ontological and epistemological consequences of Blake's habit of creating his words and images in and through these unusual, even
unique, media. The illuminated books in particular have been viewed
as medium-reflexive, their means of production as a constitutive part
of their meaning, and their departures from conventional publications as a critique of those conventions. Stephen Leo Carr's essay in
the present collection is the most recent, and in many ways the most
intellectually challenging, representative of this interpretive perspective.[2] Using his work as a central statement, I intend to make explicit
some of Carr's most fruitful implications, developing from these a
more historically oriented view of graphic production (both intaglio
and relief) and thereby laying a few spur lines between the main
tracks of research and commentary. Finally, I will suggest some ways
a consciousness of graphic forms and processes might evolve into a
hermeneutics based on medium-specific definitions of "sign," "meaning," and "intention."

Much of Carr's argument depends upon a binary opposition be-

---

1. Representative texts are Essick, *Printmaker* 85–164, and Viscomi.
2. The editors kindly supplied me with texts of all essays in this volume before I
wrote my contribution. Predecessors of Carr's work include Eaves, "Machine," and
Sherry.

tween identity and difference, the first the province of reproductive graphics, the second a hallmark of Blake's relief etchings. Carr judiciously avoids claiming that impressions from intaglio copy plates really are identical, but he takes that as the goal of a reproductive medium forever seeking to be unmediated, which is thus its representative characteristic within the logic of his commentary. Yet this doomed attempt at double identity, both among impressions and between any one impression and the object (painting, drawing, and so on) it pictures, signals for Carr the very opposite—the difference between original and reproduction, and between ideal identity and real difference, both as fact and as implicit aesthetic judgment. The analysis is structurally similar to Derrida's deconstruction of the Saussurean sign, in which the "/" of the signifier/signified relationship is granted ascendancy over the sacrificial intentionality of the signifier, and to Paul de Man's deconstruction of the romantic symbol (like copy engraving, another late eighteenth-century failure at unmediated reproduction).[3] Since conventional graphics generate both the concept of identity and the perception of difference, Blake's ever-various prints must be seen not as the absolute opposite of copy engravings but in terms of a shift in emphasis. What is repressed in one erupts so insistently above the threshold of perception in the other that it cannot be denied. Conversely, Blake's graphics must embody a residual desire for identity for the perception of difference to avoid chaos. This is only to say that two impressions of plate X of an illuminated book have more in common than any impression of plate X and any impression of plate Y. Further, all of Blake's prints show representational images, even if only letters, and thus they gesture toward forms existing outside of and prior to the work itself through some sort of functional or formal similitude, however meager. We may be right in perceiving relief etchings as less heterotelic than Woollett's or Schiavonetti's high-finish intaglio prints, but this does not make Blake's work absolutely autotelic. Both types of prints, when viewed as manufactured objects rather than as the vehicles of reified abso-

3. See Derrida, *Speech* 129–60, and de Man, *Blindness* 187–228. The latter's thesis is further developed in Hamlin, "Temporality." One could also point to the self-heroes of Shelley and Byron as other romantic "types" (in both senses) whose will to identity through union with the forever-other never bridges the irony of difference.

lutes, reside in a vast middle ground, the habitation of "similarity" and "variation," terms that each contain the other as they glance, Janus-like, toward both identity and difference.

Carr's logic of difference (which necessarily assumes a logic of identity) has an implied plot, a history of opposition, as well as a structure. Parts of this drama may have been performed in the late eighteenth century, when differences between Blake's books and conventional publications were probably apparent to anyone who cared to make a comparison, but the final acts must await the present, a time when copies of Blake's illuminated books have been gathered into accessible institutions and widely reproduced so that differences among impressions can be perceived, minutely described, and ruminated upon in the shadow of Derrida. I have proposed a slightly different paradigm of similitude and variation. It remains to be seen if the plot implied by this formulation can be acted out in an eighteenth-century context. In particular, was variation purposefully introduced into conventional graphics and valued as such by the consumer? And is there a structure of similitude within Blake's prints essential to the play of differences Carr explores so incisively?

As a conventional copy engraver labors over an intaglio plate, he alters its appearance with each stroke or dot, however minute. To see how his work is progressing, the printmaker generally finds it useful to pull impressions several times during the plate's development. These "proofs" are thus selected, discrete points, or "states," in what is almost a continuous process. They are important to the printmaker as records of work done *between* proofs, and thus have something of the process- or medium-reflexivity attributed to Blake's unique graphics.

Blake's engraving of William Hogarth's *Beggar's Opera, Act III* is a typical reproductive print. Its five known states record the following intermediate activities:

1. Etched image, incomplete but with signatures and imprint ("Publishd October 29: 1788: by Ald^m Boydel & C° Cheapside").

2. Image completed with the addition of a great many engraved lines. Blake's signature changed from "Etch'd by Willm Blake 1788" to "Engrav'd by Willm Blake 1788."

3. Title inscription and two further lines of text added below image. Dates removed from signatures and changed to "July 1.st 1790" in imprint.

4. Open letters of title filled in with horizontal lines; "Size of the picture 24$_{\shortmid}$ by 30$_{\shortmid}$ long" added. All letters strengthened with the graver.

5. Much worn image recut with a few new lines, apparently in an attempt to restore the plate to its earlier appearance.

The second through the fourth states come closer than the first (unfinished) and the fifth (decayed) to the impossible goal of identity with the original painting. If the contemporary customers for the *Beggar's Opera* (and similar copy prints) were interested only in its reproductive capabilities, the first state would be of no value. The differences in lettering would be of no consequence, except that the fourth state might be preferred because it gives the most verbal information about the painting. Yet these very inscriptions show that the exact opposite pertained in the contemporary marketplace. The presence of an imprint or publication line on the first state indicates that it is a "published" proof, printed in multiple copies (at least seven still extant) and sold to the public.[4] More specifically, they were sold to collectors who desired unfinished states and were willing to pay more for them than for later, completed impressions. Similarly, the distinction between open-letter and closed-letter states indicates that the former was pulled prior to the latter and thus was more valuable—not because it was a better reproduction, but because it had qualities *as a print* (tone, sharpness of line, and so on) that degenerate with every printing from the copper.[5] The purposeful production of variation be-

---

4. The Engravers' Copyright Act of 1735 required imprints only on impressions intended for public sale, not on working proofs pulled for the printmaker's own uses or on plates intended for private distribution.

5. As is typical of the genre, many of Blake's own separate reproductive plates exist in open-letter and closed-letter states; see Essick, *Plates* 125–26, 130, 139, 142, 158, 165–66. The 1829 sale of impressions of Blake's engraving of John Opie's "Romeo and Juliet, Act IV, Scene V," originally published by John and Josiah Boydell, indicates how differences in state were translated into currency. The London firm of Moon, Boys, & Graves offered "Prints" for 4s., but "Proofs" cost 7s.6d. (1829 catalogue 65). The difference between plain and color-printed or hand-colored impressions was always given financial acknowledgment; see, for example, the prices of prints, including three by Blake, in [Macklin], *Prints*.

tween states extended to press runs of the same state, distinguished by differences in paper, inking, and color. Finally, individual impressions were (and still are) evaluated by the print connoisseur on the basis of unavoidable characteristics that accrue over time: presence of foxing or tears, verso blemishes, appearance of a watermark, collectors' stamps indicating a distinguished provenance, and so on. These features rarely affect the reproductive function of the image but rather indicate its process of production or subsequent history. The copy engraving, like fine-art photographs in our day, thereby takes on the "aura"[6] of an original, a self-reflexive production rather than a reproduction, through a sequence of variations introduced both purposefully and accidentally throughout the life of a print. This history of a reproductive engraving reveals the same differential pattern as the multilayered production of variation in Blake's unconventional etchings. The differences are in emphasis and detail, not in the nature of the phenomenon, and in our tendency to consider its presence in copy engraving as a matter of "mere connoisseurship" (to use Carr's phrase) while granting great consequence to the same processes in Blake's work. We need not accept the connoisseur's hierarchy of values to acknowledge a logic, an aesthetic, and an economy of variation operative in the production, inscribed in the material body, and acted out in the marketing of conventional graphics.

The history of book production and distribution reveals a similar presence of variation underlying a system of values. Individual copies are distinguished by different bindings, by wear and damage, by inscriptions, bookplates, and by a long list of other "points," including histories of ownership. Very few of these points disturb a book's representational capabilities—that is, its readability. These features of a book are of course of little interest to literary critics and are left to the materialistic attentions of booksellers, collectors, and children. Accidents are dismissed in the pursuit of essence—the "text" as a transcendental category never to be confused with its necessarily but inconsequentially physical representatives or merely decorative packaging. Such distinctions, operating under the aegis of sound Platonic and Lockean principles, are imbedded in our institutions of "higher" (the word takes on special significance in this context) learning and

---

6. Like Carr, I take this term from Benjamin (217–51).

modes of publication.[7] This same idealizing spirit is at work when we neglect variations in Blake's illuminated books or decide that some are "meaningful"—more on that issue later—and others are not.[8] On this point, I trust I am in complete accord with Carr, and at least companionable with Derrida's critique of the transcendental signified, although I have come at the matter from a rather different direction.[9] My addition to Carr is simply that differences in the illuminated books may indeed distinguish them from conventional publications, both engraved and typographic, in degree of variation, but Blake's books should also remind us of the often suppressed and generally neglected presence of that same phenomenon in conventional prints and books.

The very feature of Blake's illuminated books to which Carr so rightly draws our philosophical attention is the point at which they swerve beyond the range of most modern literary scholars and make contact with the collector and bibliophile who, with nearly philatelic passion, are always seeking for the one and only "best" copy, for the unique impression, and for other printed objects inscribed with difference. There may be resistance to the notion that Blake's inventions speak in any fashion to "the Cunning sures & the Aim at yours" (*Notebook* 40, E510) of his day or ours, but it must be remembered that

7. Compare, for example, the implicit concept of "text" in *PMLA* with what a book is for the contributors to *The Book Collector*. It is not advisable to try building a successful career as an English professor in America by writing essays, however definitive, on bindings and bookplates for the latter journal. The institutional distinctions are frequently given semantic justification by distinguishing between "book" and "literature." Similar oppositions are legion, including craft and art, material and meaning, body and soul, conception and execution, and other divisions Blake attacked.

8. Erdman's comment, quoted by Carr in his second footnote, exemplifies the latter tactic. The passage continues in a similar vein: "The variants that do exist are often extremely interesting, but it is important, if sometimes very difficult, to distinguish true [i.e., significant] from more or less accidental [i.e., insignificant] ones" (Erdman, *Illuminated* 15).

9. Derrida's discussion of the residual transcendentalism of Husserl's phenomenology, his demystification of the equation of iteration with transcendence (e.g., *Speech* 52), and his occasional recognition of the materiality of signification (e.g., *Speech* 38) offer the closest contacts with my discussion—and, I believe, with Carr's. I feel less comfortable with Carr's identification of differences among signs, or between one appearance of the "same" sign and another, as representative of *différance*, which I understand to be a function of the signifier/signified relationship intrinsic to the sign. In particular, the sense of deferral, an important component of *différance*, does not seem relevant to the differences between any two impressions pulled from one of Blake's relief plates, since neither is the signifier of the other.

what few contemporary purchasers Blake had (as distinct from the fictive audiences he addresses in his writings) came by and large from that class, not from the masses or the literary intelligentsia.[10] I am led by my attempt to supplement Carr to the even odder observation that deconstruction and *histoire du livre*, Derrida and the collector, share a small patch of common ground even if they rarely speak each other's language.

The economy of variation in conventional graphics leads one to consider the presence of its mirror image: an economy of similitude in Blake's graphics. A relief-etched copperplate may be "an idealized abstraction" (Carr's phrase) for those who attempt to reconstruct its minute reticulations on the basis of impressions from it, but we can recover the general properties of what was for its maker an irreducibly material object. At the end of *The Ghost of Abel*, Blake refers to his first relief etching as a "Stereotype" (E272). He thereby associates his invention with plates mold-made from standing type that look somewhat like relief-etched copperplates. More significant is the implication of a functional similarity. Stereotypes were invented to permit reprinting even after the initial setting of type had been distributed. They had the additional advantage of permanence and more resistance to accidental alteration than movable type, but they could not accommodate purposeful revision other than deletion.[11] Blake's own "types," as he calls them in *Jerusalem* 3.9, share these characteristics.[12]

Even though relief etching permits the elimination of relief plateaus with a few strokes of a sharp tool, it is very difficult to add new printing surfaces on the plate.[13] Conventional etched or engraved plates are much more flexible in this regard, for lines defining an in-

10. Although a member of the liberal Joseph Johnson circle in the late 1780s and early 1790s, Blake did not find his customers there. *The French Revolution*, Johnson's only known attempt to publish Blake through regular channels, seems not to have progressed beyond page proofs. William Hayley is not known to have purchased any illuminated books; indeed, he tried to turn Blake's hand to more conventional projects. Robert Hunt's withering review of Blake's 1809 exhibition of paintings offers a final example of liberal literary opinion in Blake's day (*The Examiner* [17 September 1809]; see Bentley, *Records* 215–18).

11. Although its early history is uncertain, stereotyping was developed specifically because of these properties. See Kubler, *Stereotyping* 14–15.

12. "Type" in the inscriptions on "The Chaining of Orc," a relief-etched separate plate of 1812 or 1813, would also seem to be a reference to Blake's medium linking it with stereotyping.

13. For a brief discussion of technical problems, see Essick, *Printmaker* 109–11.

taglio image can be very easily added. Removing lines with scraper and burnisher takes more time but is only slightly more difficult. Given these technical parameters, it should not be surprising to find that Blake altered his relief plates less frequently and less extensively than he changed his original intaglio plates, many of which he thoroughly revised years after their original execution.[14] The slightest scratch on an intaglio plate will register in an impression from it, whereas small scratches or pitting on a relief plate rarely show in impressions. If accidental marks are in uninked etched areas, they will not print at all. If they are on relief surfaces, small indentations will be filled with ink forced into them by the dabber and become indistinguishable from their printed surroundings in impressions. Blake exploited this characteristic of his medium to disguise the presence of platemakers' marks on many of his plates.[15] In these ways, Blake's major graphic innovation, the relief-etched copperplate, is a more stable matrix, more resistant to purposeful or accidental change, than conventional copperplate engravings. Variation is a function of the later stages of production, which, with the exception of Blake's method of color printing, are standard procedures.[16] For these reasons, I must question Carr's claim that "multiplication of differences is a distinctive feature of *every* [emphasis mine] stage of Blake's printmaking process." There is, after all, some basis in those material processes for Blake's idealization of them:

> Reengravd Time after Time
> Ever in their Youthful prime
> My Designs unchangd remain
> Time may rage but rage in vain
> For above Times troubled Fountains
> On the Great Atlantic Mountains
> In my Golden House on high
> There they Shine Eternally
> (Notebook 87, E480–81)

14. See the record of second and third states in Essick, *Plates* 3–97. The intaglio plates of *The Gates of Paradise* were reworked at least once, and probably twice.

15. These marks are identifiable as such only in posthumous pulls, not in those printed by Blake. His monochrome impressions indicate that the masking of the marks occurred at the inking and printing stages of production.

16. Inking with a dabber, relief printing, and hand drawing and coloring on impressions began in the very early history of woodcut and metal-plate printing.

The recognition of an interplay of similitude and variation as a phenomenon intrinsic to Blake's graphic processes leads to a dialectical perspective on his productions. Our attention should focus on neither identity nor difference alone, nor on them as absolute opposites, but on their unfolding relationship in the production and perception of images. The application of ink to the plate, and the imposition of paper over the plate beneath the rollers of the press, outline the general character of the graphic dialectic. The relatively stable and continuous identity of the copperplate is supplemented in its inking and printing by activities of enormous variability and absolute discontinuity. Carr claims that these "different artistic imperatives" never fully "realize" themselves because they "always interact with other construals of the design." I find the realization of the imperatives of the medium precisely through that interaction. We can locate thereby a continuity between the dialectics of Blake's texts and the medium through which he delivers many of them to us.[17]

When comparing two impressions from one of Blake's relief plates, we should complement the perception of differences with an attempt to understand as precisely as possible what happened between those two fixed and discrete points to generate the variations. This is not to transcendentalize the printed objects or cast them into a hypostatized notion of the printmaker's mind, but rather to situate them in their phenomenal origins and subsequent history. We can then make further discriminations between different types of variations depending on their source within the production process and how they came into being. It is possible, with a degree of probability equal to that of most archaeological reconstructions, to tell if a particular variant is the result of purposeful changes made on the plate, of wiping ink from a relief plateau or its deposition in an etched valley, or of handwork on the impression itself. The media-reflexivity of a variant detail refers us to the specific procedure that generated it, but to the entire production process only through synecdoche. Variants themselves can be stable and repeatable or radically nonrepeatable. The signifi-

17. The fullest study of contrariety and dialectic in Blake's poetry is Punter, *Blake, Hegel and Dialectic*. Thorslev's strictures in his "Dialectic" are similar to my objections to a simple binary opposition between identity and difference noted earlier. Thorslev's arguments do not seem relevant to Punter's discussion of either Blake or Hegel—nor, I trust, to my concept of dialectic in graphic processes.

cance of a variant within any interpretive undertaking should be determined by these phenomenal distinctions.

We should not take alarm if the distinguishing of variants sometimes replicates traditional bibliographic or chalcographic procedures. Such parallels are not necessarily "a reification of traditional
printmaking methods into universal categories" (Carr's note 12), but
they may be the result of actual similarities between Blake's processes
and their sources in traditional techniques.[18] But as Carr implies, mis-
conceptions arise if we do not attend to the media-specificity of terms
such as "variant," "accident," and "intention." The fact that Blake
managed all stages of production does not mean that his control over
his productions was absolute. Each medium has physical properties
that influence the nature of the signs that can come into being within
it. Graphic media have, as it were, an intentionality or *telos* of their
own that establishes a dialectic between the artist's will and the materials and procedures he uses (and that use him). Anyone who has
ever printed an etched plate knows how the process itself takes
charge at the crucial moment of actual printing when metal, ink, and
paper establish their transactions within the press, quite beyond the
reach or even observation of the artist. The "deliberate labor that produced all variations" (Carr's phrase) is frequently the deliberation of
the medium and not of the artist as a presence separable from the processes he initiates, oversees, but does not totally control.[19]

Blake's management of both relief and intaglio processes is remarkable for the freedom he gave to the media to express themselves, allowing even those flaws and accidents suppressed by more conventional practitioners to become part of his images. In some cases, such

18. In the eighth note to his essay in this volume, Paul Mann makes a similar point:
"Much has been made of the differences between Blake's books and industrially produced books, but often at the expense of noting essential similarities."

19. Cassirer, *Language* 59–60, describes the way this independence of media from
their creator gives rise to a myth of transcendent origins: "It may be observed that as
soon as man employs a tool, he views it not as a mere artifact of which he is the recognized maker, but as a Being in its own right, endowed with powers of its own. Instead
of being governed by his will, it becomes a god or daemon on whose will he depends.
... An implement, then, is never regarded as something simply manufactured, something thought of and produced, but as a 'gift from above'." This sort of logic—which,
pace Cassirer, does have a factual basis in the phenomena of mediation—may have motivated Blake's "myth" that relief etching was revealed to him by his dead brother in a
"visionary" experience (Smith, *Nollekens* 2:461; Bentley, *Records* 460).

as the tree in *Jerusalem* discussed by Carr at the beginning of his essay, we can trace interrelated variants through a sequence of impressions. When a series of variants can be identified as the result of Blake's purposeful activities, such as the three-step addition of white lines in plate 4 of *Europe*, we can observe the evolution of an image. Such patterns reveal an intention extrinsic to the process, in the sense that the artist must will his hand to act, but neither that action nor the image exists outside of or prior to the medium.

The vast majority of variants observable in Blake's relief etchings do not fall into purposive sequences; they are "accidents" in the sense that they arise freely within the process whether the artist desires them or not. The printmaker's control is limited to the establishment of procedures that aid or hinder the generation of variants, and he can accept or reject them *post facto*.[20] Blake's small press runs and printing on a per-book rather than per-plate basis further militated against uniformity. Color printing injected another element of sheer randomness into the production of illuminated books and separate plates. The repeatable matrix of the copperplate was largely effaced when Blake printed colors from both relief and etched surfaces. In the planographic color printing he developed in the mid-1790s, the stable etched image disappeared completely as book and print production evolved into Blake's painting techniques of the late 1790s.[21] Hand drawing and coloring restore direct authorial control over the image and permit some degree of repeatability, as in the traditional hand coloring of intaglio prints developed into an assembly-line industry by Rudolph Ackermann in the early nineteenth century. Yet Blake's habit of coloring each illuminated book as a separate unit gave rise to an enormous number of variants among copies. Blake's hand and eye (or his wife's) directed each stroke of pen or brush, but individual differences between one copy and another, colored and sold years be-

20. It would be interesting to peer into Blake's waste basket and see which sorts of color printing variants he rejected. He seems to have been more receptive to the propagation of variations than any printmaker before Gauguin, although Blake's planographic color-printing processes bear some interesting similarities to Alexander Cozens' method of blotted landscapes in which accident plays a central role. Cozens described and illustrated his technique in *A New Method of Assisting the Invention in Drawing Original Compositions of Landscape* (1785).

21. Several important discoveries have been made since my description of the evolution of Blake's color-printing techniques (Essick, *Printmaker* 121–35, 147–51), but the general outline remains essentially the same.

fore, cannot be attributed to the artist's intentions unless we invent a "Blake" whose art is based on memory. All we can say is that Blake selected a mode of production and handled it in a way that allowed differences among finished impressions to be invented, executed, and proliferated by the medium itself. Under these conditions, the divisions between invention and execution, artist and artifact, subject and object essential to a traditional model of intentionality begin to collapse in on themselves—as Blake insisted they must in any artistic activity.[22] Carr's phrase, "an invention always generated by its execution," nicely characterizes part of the graphic dialectic by reversing the conventional order of cause and effect.

The dispersal of intentionality throughout the system of production disrupts the a posteriori presence of a self as the center and continuous origin of production. It becomes increasingly difficult to treat every feature of the products as a reference to "ideas" in the mind of the artist, or to justify our inability to do so by opening a gap between conception and execution. "Blake" is only one component for whom "Opposition" with the materials and processes of the medium is the "true Friendship" necessary for "progression"—to adopt the language of *The Marriage of Heaven and Hell* (E34, 42). Any attempt to separate Blake the artist from that process is to give Blake the man a mode of being he did not have independent of his media. Such reifications create a "false Body" (M 40.35) and an "Abstract objecting power" (J 10.14) that, like the Spectres of *Milton* and *Jerusalem*, prevent the labors of the artist and obfuscate our perception of his emanations.[23]

The problematics of intentionality, intrinsic to all media but so fully dramatized and explored in Blake's graphics, lead to the problematics of signification. Carr points out how many variants are filtered from our interpretive activities if they do not surpass "some tacitly understood threshold of iconic value." This strategy presupposes that the interest in any part of a design, variant or not, depends upon its level

22. See the discussions of the unity of conception and execution, lying at the heart of Blake's aesthetic, in Eaves, *Theory* 79–91. Eaves also explores the integration of artist and artifact, or as he calls it, "artists expressing themselves as works of art" (45).

23. The Spectre's blockage of dialectic is indicated in the passage from *Milton*: "The Negation must be destroyd to redeem the Contraries / The Negation is the Spectre; the Reasoning Power in Man" (40.33–34).

of iconicity—that is, the extent to which the image can be treated as though it were a verbal sign or could be translated into one. Most people who write on Blake are English teachers, and thus it is not surprising that they extend their logocentrism (or grammocentrism?) to the study of pictures and pay little more attention to letter shapes, paper, and ink color in Blake's books than in their study of conventional ones. The problem, however, goes deeper than professional inclinations.

The general thrust of Carr's consideration of the significance of variation in the illuminated books applies to all types of differences. But the examples of variant details he chooses hint at a narrower focus within the theoretical inclusiveness. Both the tree in *Jerusalem* and the different appearances of the figures in "The Little Boy found" relate directly to representational variants. These are introduced because of their potential "iconographic implications" within "the verbal-visual exchanges generated within each page." The privileging of those variants that seem to alter representation, and thus may have the most iconographic potential, is inconsistent with Carr's astute questioning of other language-centered systems for selecting only a limited range of differences. There would appear to be some tacitly understood threshold of representation that must be surpassed for any feature of an illuminated book to enter the arena of interpretation, even for Carr. The "verbal-visual exchanges" always seem to become one-way streets: the conversion of all that is visual or tactile into the verbal. The inconvertible are left out of the system of exchange.

To look at the matter from a purely quantitative perspective, in order to avoid predetermined qualitative judgments, it is safe to say that most of the differences among Blake's relief prints are not representational in the sense that they picture nothing in the world other than themselves. Such variations are not simply neutral (and therefore inconsequential) presences in a design's iconography or a text's meaning. They actively thwart iconicity by disrupting the stability and repeatability basic to the way verbal signs and their visual representatives (letters or iconic images) ideally function. The countless and ever-varying droplets of ink, printed from both relief and white-line surfaces, offer an obvious example, but even many changes made by the printmaker's arm and graver affect *how* something is represented and not *what* is represented. The addition, for example, of white-line hatchings to the man's stomach in the second and third states of *Europe* plate 4 does not make it any more or less a "man's stomach" in the conversion of image into linguistic sign. Unlike the absence or presence of a tree, or the conversion of a hat into a halo, such changes have a low iconic yield and thus rarely find their way into interpretive discourse. Perhaps the most difficult feature in the illuminated books is color, even if we ignore its enormous variability. Blake's colors are generally representational, in the simple sense that leaves are green, skies are blue, flesh is flesh, and so on, but they do not have much iconic potential. In the linguistic exchange, color becomes a name in description but is forced only with great difficulty into an interpretive structure.[24] Indeed, it is precisely because Blake's colors are representational, and in that sense motivated by the world, that they seem not to constitute a symbolism motivated by his ideas.

The availability of Blake's colors, ink droplets, and textures to the senses, and their resistance to conceptualization, may indicate one of their functions in the illuminated books. In his 1793 prospectus "To the Public," Blake says nothing about the iconography of his productions or the meaning of their texts. He does, however, claim that his books are more "ornamental" than any before published—a term that, in the mouth of a critic, would be taken as a trivialization of Blake's art. Ornamentation in a book is irrelevant to verbal meaning. By so emphatically including a great deal of ornament in his books, Blake directs his reader to experiences offered by his productions other than iconographic and verbal meanings. It is almost impossible to overcome the pejorative connotations of "ornament," but surely Blake intended something positive in his advertisement. A famous passage in *The Marriage of Heaven and Hell* suggests why. The opening of man's perceptions to the "infinite . . . will come to pass by an improvement of sensual enjoyment." Illuminated printing—"printing in the infernal method"—will assist in this process by expunging "the notion that man has a body distinct from his soul" (*MHH* 14). By making books with a physical presence, a body, that we cannot ignore, Blake tries to prevent his readers from separating out a "soul" of verbal meaning and leaving the body behind. To make such a separation

24. The boldest, most procrustean effort is still "The Symbolism of Colour" in Ellis and Yeats (1.309–14).

is both cause and consequence of man's narrowing of his senses "till he sees all things thro' narrow chinks of his cavern" (*MHH* 14). This narrowing results in the definition of "book" as nothing more than "text" by discarding as a mere husk, an unavoidable but inconsequential physicality, all that is not a visual/verbal text.[25] The illuminated book can open those chinks through its sensual, physical, and ornamental qualities precisely because they so stubbornly resist conversion into a text. Once again, it is the child or uneducated collector, illiterate in the language of Blakean interpretation, who is most receptive to these extra-textual experiences.[26] They have known all along that Blake's books are unreadable. But while this audience revels in textures and colors for their own sake, those who seek to write about such things are working against their intrinsic significance. The result is commentary that frequently slips into belletristic mumblings about intensity, richness, or, worst of all, beauty.

In the face of such hazards, one can all too easily conclude that Blake's colors, textures, white-line hatchings, and most of all ink droplets are not signs and thus do not "mean" anything. The hegemony of verbal signification must be reduced if many features of Blake's graphic works, including most of the differences among impressions, are to become part of their meaning. If such things as ink drops and brush strokes are signs, they signify only their material selves and their coming into being. This hypothetical sign offers some intriguing characteristics. It constitutes a semiotic phenomenon, but not a symbolic system.[27] It resists translation from one medium to another—or, to put it another way, it is the nontranslatable part of any sign. It refuses identical iteration, for it exists only as a spatial/temporal performance. Its relationship to the linguistic sign is subversive

25. "Text" here includes the iconic signification of representational images, for to interpret (or "read") their meaning is to convert the image into a verbal text.
26. In his letter to Dr. Trusler of 23 August 1799, Blake defends his artistic practices. "I am happy," he writes, "to find a Great Majority of Fellow Mortals who can Elucidate My Visions & Particularly they have been Elucidated by Children who have taken a greater delight in contemplating my Pictures than I even hoped" (E703). Surely such elucidating (*elucidare*, "to make light or clear") is a kind of sensual "delight" or enlightening, not the verbal interpretation of iconography.
27. I borrow the distinction between "semiotic" and "symbolic" from Kristeva, *Desire* 134, 136. Kristeva associates the semiotic with the body, the sensual, in a way similar to my location of the extralinguistic function of the "ornamental" within the book/body expansions of *MHH* 14.

and dialectical, much as the instability of Blake's printing procedures both subvert and complement the repeatability of his copperplates. This sign does not escape *différance*, but it is a *différance* constituted only by the difference between the sign's being in space and its becoming in time.[28] To analyze the physical properties of this sign and trace its history is to interpret it, for these constitute what it signifies. Like Blake's sense of the immanence of spirit within the body, for which Christ is the paradigmatic type, such a sign contains the signified within the material presence and history of the signifier. It is incarnational, not transcendental.

The evolution of a Blake-induced media consciousness into an alternative semiotics offers the possibility of studying other media from this perspective. The greatest challenge is that other medium with which Blake wrestled—language. The task is complicated by the unavoidable presence of language, as a meta-medium, in perception, and the impossibility of studying it in terms other than those language itself determines. I am proposing not that we bang our heads against those walls but only that we make a few extrapolations from the strategies used here, and, I believe, in Carr's essay, for the investigation of the intrinsic properties of graphic media and Blake's exploitation of them. A first step, like the distinction between "book" and "text" implicit in the illuminated books, might be to distinguish between "word" and "sign" as a structure of referential (signifier/signified) meaning. The focus would then fall on those properties of a word, and on the processes of language as a whole, that stand outside of its significative component. This distinction bears some obvious similarities to Saussure's division between *langue* and *parole*, but with

28. From a certain magisterial perspective, one might argue that this hypothetical sign would avoid *différance* through the identity of being and becoming, or the collapse of one into the other, along a space-time continuum. Yet I think this strategy would convert the sign into a pure signified, or pure being rather than "being for," and thus subject the theory to the same objections Derrida levels against Husserl's use of the distinction between *Sinn* and *Bedeutung* to construct "a layer of prelinguistic or presemiotic (preexpressive, Husserl calls it) meaning whose presence would be conceivable outside and before the work of *différance*, outside and before the process or system of signification" (Derrida, *Positions* 31). In a similarly idealizing vein, one might conclude that my hypothetical sign is motivated because it signifies its own material presence, which is physically inscribed with its history of production. However, I wish to retain within the signified those elements of the sign's production and subsequent history, including its reception (sales price, ownership records, and so on), which are arbitrary in the sense that they are not present in the sign's materiality.

an emphasis on the latter as the more encompassing term rather than as an "accessory and more or less accidental" performance of the former.[29] This shift means that we concentrate on the accidents (as distinct from the supposed essence) of language, its surfaces and material presences as aural or visual images, and the ways Blake may or may not have exploited that materiality to generate meanings within an alternative semiotics of the type I have outlined here for his graphic media—meanings that are phenomenological and incarnational rather than structural and transcendental.

Treating language as a medium (but not as a medium "of" something else) runs counter to the psychologizing mainstream of linguistic philosophy, in particular the various theories that identify language with mind, consciousness, the unconscious, or other transcendental signifieds.[30] A brief passage from Saussure will exemplify this contrariety:

> Consider, for example, the production of sounds necessary for speaking. The vocal organs are as external to language as are the electrical devices used in transmitting Morse code to the code itself; and phonation, i.e., the execution of sound-images, in no way affects the system itself. Language is comparable to a symphony in that what the symphony actually is stands completely apart from how it is performed; the mistakes that musicians make in playing the symphony do not compromise this fact.
>
> (18)

From the perspective I am suggesting, Saussure's metaphors make nonsense of his argument. The "electrical devices" establish the nature of the code (i.e., dots and dashes) that comes into being only within those devices. I'm not sure what a symphony "is" for Saussure

---

29. Saussure, *Course* 14. Saussure's language (or at least his translator's) in this passage is reminiscent of the tactics used to dismiss from the meaning of Blake's images the accidents caused by inking and printing.

30. Saussure's objections to defining language as a medium all apply to the "medium of . . ." model, much as I have argued against the idea that Blake used relief etching as a way of reproducing images first produced in some other medium (or in no medium at all). In the later sections of his *Course*, Saussure similarly suggests that certain significative features of language do not transcend its physical presence. For example, he writes that "to think that there is an incorporeal syntax outside material units distributed in space would be a mistake" (139).

(probably something that "does not exist in the world"),[31] but for a media-oriented semiotics it is audible sounds arranged in a certain sequence. What it is includes the "mistakes" of each performance that make the symphony different each time it comes into being.[32] The physical properties of the medium (i.e., sound) and the method of production (violins, hands, lungs, flutes, and so on) determine in large measure what a symphony *is* and hence what it "means" to the audience. The same may be said of language *qua* medium, including its establishment of the parameters of meaning and, like Blake's graphic methods, its ability to produce effects (often labeled "mistakes" or "accidents") whether the user of the language wills them or not. To what extent does Blake's use of language exploit such effects, and do they in any sense contribute to meaning by subverting and supplementing the referential significations of his writings?

Some answers to these and related questions are offered by several essays in this volume. Thomas Vogler considers "writing as a mode of praxis" and asks us to consider the "rough basement" of the signifier in its visual as well as acoustical extensions. His psycho-sexual perspective on "the recovery of the Emanation" leads him to a concern with the role of the body in the construction of dialectical and incarnational forms of signification. David Simpson appeals to "a wider range of discursive options" than is "containable" within such "traditional yardsticks" as "meaning demonstrably produced out of conscious free will." Paul Mann, in response to "Blake's intense awareness of the materiality of his productions," finds that "in Blake's text in general, most attempts at transcendental [but not incarnational?] projects are doomed to failure." Even Donald Ault, a reader with a strong commitment to deep structures, notes that "the surface narrative is primary" and that the way the *Four Zoas* manuscript reveals the compositional processes that created it constitutes part of its mean-

---

31. As Derrida writes of an "identity, which is but another name for the permanence of the same and the possibility of its repetition" (*Speech* 52). Saussure's implicit concepts of the Morse code, a symphony, and language would seem to be this sort of ideality transcending any single embodiment of it. Saussure's neoplatonism could not be clearer.

32. Long before Saussure, Wilhelm von Humboldt argued for the importance of a somewhat different, but related, form of performative variation: "No one when he uses a word has in mind exactly the same thing that another has, and the difference, however tiny, sends its tremors throughout language" (*Grundzüge des allgemeinen Sprachtypus* [1824–26] in Humboldt, *Anthology* 235).

ing. The main focus of these essays is on Blake's language, yet they exhibit the questioning of conventional notions of intentionality and self-presence, the antitranscendental tendencies, the emphasis on the signifier rather than the signified, and the concern with process more than with stable structure characterizing the media-consciousness raised by Blake's graphics.

The division of "me-/-tals" between two lines on plate 4 of *The Book of Urizen* offers a particularly intriguing example of how meanings arise at the intersection between Blake's graphic and linguistic media.[33] Once Blake had determined the width of the right-hand column of his plate (left-hand in an impression), his line length was determined before he began to write the penultimate line in reverse. When he met the left margin and had not completed a word ("metals") already begun, hyphenation was the only recourse short of dramatically reducing the size of his letters in the middle of a word or removing the entire line of letters already written in acid-resist. The physical differences between etched script and movable type (which allows for justification without resetting an entire line) create a situation in which hyphenation is more likely to occur than in conventional book production—unless the printmaker takes special steps to avoid it. There is no evidence that Blake prepared mock-ups of his plates in which such matters as exact letter size and spacing could be determined before writing on the copper. Indeed, that type of preparatory operation would introduce the very sort of standardization that his printed but ever-various calligraphy consistently subverts. All he required for his autographic medium was a completed text on paper, such as those we find in his *Notebook*. Thus the fact that plate 4 contains lines of approximately the same length but with more (necessarily smaller) letters than line 24 (ending in "me-") does not indicate an unmediated intention to hyphenate "metals" free from physical constraints. Blake could only make a rough guess as to how small he should draw his letters to fit them all into one line. When he guessed wrong, the medium dictated hyphenation as the easiest solution. Blake's books are not just "formd of me-/-tals" (*BU* 4.24); they are formed *by* the very nature of those metals and the material processes

33. The verbal significance of this division is discussed in Hilton, *Imagination* 250–51, and noted by the editors in their introduction to this volume.

he employed. As is typical of Blake's approach to all his innovative graphics, he allowed the medium to express its own tendencies. In the case of "me-/-tals," the graphic inclination generates textual meanings because of an unavoidable feature of language: words are composed of a sequence of phonemes or graphemes, any part of which may also be a word.

An "accident" resulting from an essential feature of Blake's method of publication has produced a word ("me") with its own associations and contributions to the *Book of Urizen*. Blake did not have to hear voices to have some of his poetry dictated to him.[34] He needed only to receive the messages of his medium. We usually think of activities whereby verbal meanings come into being as a function of the compositional process as a poet works over his lines in early drafts, discovering and creating significant coincidences of sound and sense. Blake's remarkable graphic medium allowed this evolution of verbal meaning to continue right through the publication process. It should be no surprise that no typographic edition of *The Book of Urizen* repeats the meaningful division of "me-/-tals." In such texts, one medium (relief etching) has been translated into another (movable type). The conventions of the latter overrule the nature of the former, changing "me-/-tals" to "metals," and thereby altering the matrix of meaning.

I have concentrated on this one incident because it serves both as a transition from graphic to linguistic concerns and as an example of the practical application of a media-oriented hermeneutics. But we do not require promptings from printmaking to know that words have sounds and shapes independent of (because arbitrarily related to) their referential function as signs. Words also have an etymology— that is, the history of their production—inscribed within their aural/ visual presence.[35] These features of words as material objects associ-

---

34. In a letter to Thomas Butts of 25 April 1803, Blake notes that he had written a poem "from immediate Dictation twelve or sometimes twenty or thirty lines at a time without Premeditation & even against my Will" (E729). See also my note 19 on the transcendentalizing of physical processes.

35. Most studies of the etymologies of Blake's words focus on his manufactured (as distinct from inherited) proper nouns. The usual strategy is to find meaning in these names by associating their sounds with "real" words out of which they were supposedly constructed. A media-oriented hermeneutics might treat Blake's made-up words as records of how words come into being, through various transformations of sounds

ate them with words with similar sounds, visual forms, or histories whether the poet consciously wills such associations or not. The importance of these subtle and shifting patterns in Blake's texts and their contributions to meaning have been demonstrated by Nelson Hilton's recent book, *Literal Imagination: Blake's Vision of Words*. Like the ever-various inking and coloring of Blake's relief prints, these linguistic effects play over the surfaces of Blake's poetry and establish a dialectical relationship with the more structured and conventional referentiality of his words. *Horse*, for example, is the signifier of the same signified idea of a thing wherever it appears in or out of one of Blake's texts, but as a sound or linear form in that syntagmatic context it establishes associations with other words, such as *hoarse*, different from—and thereby extending—the paradigmatic referentiality of *horse*.[36] To dismiss such patterns from the interpretation of Blake's texts on the basis of a model of authorial intention, based in turn on distinctions between accidents and essences proposed by rationalist philosophers Blake explicitly rejects, falls into the same problems of transcendentalism (or, to use a more Blakean word, "abstraction") that burden those who would ignore ink droplets and brush strokes in the perception and interpretation of Blake's graphics. Our definition of "Blake" should be wider, not through some further reification of what "he" really "meant," but through a productive recognition that the only "Blake" actually existing in this world now is the various, recalcitrant, and material body of the manufactured objects he had a role in producing.

---

or shapes and their sequences, and how these transformations may or may not take on meanings in the context of their use. Blake had to create words within the phonemic and graphemic circumference of language (remember, only twenty-six letters), and in that way they can indicate the nature of that circumference. Something of this approach finds application in De Luca, "Names," and Fogel.

36. On "Horse/hoarse," see Hilton, *Imagination* 248–49. Any single example of such punning is vulnerable to the skeptic, but Hilton's accumulation of many such patterns and their extensions of meaning is difficult to dismiss.

9

A Wall of Words:
The Sublime as Text

V. A. DE LUCA

I give you the end of a golden string,
Only wind it into a ball:
It will lead you in at Heavens gate,
Built in Jerusalems wall.

(J 77)

Blake is still conspicuously difficult to read, even in a critical climate in which all readings are said to be problematic. This difficulty is my theme. I want to concentrate on those elements of Blake's texts that tend to withdraw from referential function altogether. Where these elements operate, the text becomes iconic, a physical *Ding an sich*, not a transparent medium through which meaning is easily disseminated. In *Jerusalem*, particularly, the thread of thematic continuity is subject to snagging on these verbal outcroppings, and there are indeed passages in the poem where such outcroppings mass themselves into a solid wall of words. Most readers of Blake have spent a lot of time pacing before these ramparts, the golden string slack in their hands.

I want to pursue this notion of a Blakean "wall of words" in the context of the Romantic sublime, in which natural walls, steep and lofty cliffs, have a preeminent place. For the Romantics, these towering forms interpose a barrier to the continuities of travel, substituting elevation for the planned destination. In the theory of the period the sublime experience is typically presented as a three-fold moment: an encounter with the stimulating object, an episode of discontinuity (usually described as vertigo or blockage or bafflement), and a sudden and ecstatic exaltation. In all sophisticated theories of the sublime, this outer confrontation betokens an inner drama; the sublime experience is said to sift the mind, dividing it into two unequally privileged faculties, one consigned to pain and deprivation, the other admitted to an exalted sphere of delight. The terms for these faculties vary from writer to writer—for Wordsworth "the light of sense" goes out as "Imagination, dread power" rises up; for Kant the Imagination is itself the faculty of deprivation, and Reason the faculty of plenitude—but their relative functions remain the same. Although he is not often included among the theorists of the sublime, Blake also gives us a psychology of the sublime as constituted from a similar division of faculties. Speaking of his own work as a "Sublime Allegory," Blake goes on to amplify his terms: "Allegory addressed to the Intellectual powers while it is altogether hidden from the Corporeal Understanding is My Definition of the Most Sublime Poetry" (E730). The barrier to the faculty allied with sense is an avenue to its more privileged counterpart. Conceived dynamically, the sublime stimulus operates as a kind of psychic traffic light that directs energy denied to the Corporeal Understanding into the released Intellectual Powers. Such a barrier is needed to channel and concentrate energy, and this economy explains why Blake deems a privilege afforded to one of two faculties as more sublime than privileges afforded to both.

At the barrier is a point of indeterminacy, a moment between stop and go, a state of incomplete disengagement between the Corporeal Understanding and the Intellectual Powers. The barrier seems to flicker before the eyes, now opaque, now translucent, at once forbidding and yielding. The sublime object presents a towering face and yet offers a conspicuous invitation to ascent, or it holds back and teases with the promise of penetration, or it hints at ineffable possibilities of Presence and then defers them. It is not surprising therefore that recent critics, increasingly sensitive to the perplexed role of language as both a conductor of meaning and an agency of blockage, have, like Blake, described the sublime experience as if it were an encounter with a difficult text.[1] For even the material world affords ob-

---

1. See, e.g., Hartman, *Fate* 120: "The structure of the act of reading . . . is the structure of the sublime experience in a finer mode"; Hertz (68–70); and, most elaborately, Weiskel (26–31 and passim).

jects that function as signs or the settings for them. The walls and their aggrandized equivalents so prominent in the literature of the sublime—lofty cliffs, great architectural piles, monumental slabs, standing stones, ruins, and the like—seem to beg to be read, blank as they are. For this reason, many artists working in the tradition of the sublime betray a fascination with inscription, as if responding to a call latent in their grand but mute material. The point where writing begins to appear on the wall is the point of indeterminacy, the point where the flicker of opacity and translucence starts, of presentation and deferral. Before the *mise en abyme* of recent deconstructionist talk became a scene of reading and writing, it was literally a scene of the eighteenth-century and Romantic material sublime with its steep drops and dizzying heights. Blake's own textual sublime, to be fully understood, should also be located within the larger tradition of walls and inscriptions that prevailed in his age.

II

Let us begin with an actual *mise en abyme*, a toehold on the steep side of the abyss. It is a famous drop, already a set piece of sublime descriptive poetry by the time of the Augustans. I refer to Edgar's imaginary recreation of Dover cliff in *King Lear*:

> Come on, Sir, here's the place: stand still; how fearful
> And dizzy 'tis to cast one's eye so low!
> The crows and choughs that wing the midway air
> Show scarce so gross as beetles. Half way down
> Hangs one that gathers samphire—dreadful trade!
>
> (4.4.11–15)

Commenting on this passage, Dr. Johnson found himself dissatisfied. He denied its sublime effect because the described drop, he felt, is not dizzying enough:

> He that looks from a precipice finds himself assailed by one great and dreadful image of irresistible destruction. But this overwhelming idea is dissipated and enfeebled from the instant that the mind can restore itself to the observation of particulars, and diffuse its attention to distinct objects. The enumeration of the choughs and crows, the samphire-man and the fishers, counteracts the great effect of the prospect, as it peo-

ples the desert of intermediate vacuity, and stops the mind in the rapidity of its descent through emptiness and horrour.

(Shakespeare 695)

Later, on the same subject, Johnson was to growl to Garrick, "It should be all precipice—all vacuum. The crows impede your fall" (Boswell 1.365). "All precipice—all vacuum"—a neat oxymoron: wall or nothing, or rather wall *as* nothing, a blank face, a vertical causeway to oblivion.

Johnson's distaste for the busy detail of the Shakespearean scene, his preference for an unbroken height or sheer drop, conforms to a neoclassical aesthetic that associates the sublime with a massive and uniform simplicity. The same preference leads his friend Reynolds in the first of his *Discourses* to divorce "minute accidental discriminations of particular and individual objects" from the "grand style," which, he says, "improves partial representation by the general and invariable ideas of nature." "Minute Discrimination is Not Accidental," Blake retorted in the margin; "All Sublimity is founded on Minute Discrimination" (E643). One imagines that Blake would be receptive to the crows and other "distinct objects" of the Dover cliff passage as contributing to its sublimity. Indeed, there is a curiously similar passage, perhaps rebuking Johnson, in Blake's own work:

> When I came home; on the abyss of the five senses, where a flat sided steep frowns over the present world. I saw a mighty Devil folded in black clouds, hovering on the sides of the rock, with corroding fires he wrote the following sentence now perceived by the minds of men, & read by them on earth.
>
> > *How do you know but ev'ry Bird that cuts the airy way,*
> > *Is an immense world of delight, clos'd by your senses five?*
>
> (MHH 6–7)

The Devil's rhetorical question turns Johnson's complaint inside out. It is not that the little birds of the midway air interrupt our sense of immensity but rather that a taste for vacuity automatically closes the mind to perception of the immensity inherent in every particular, diminishing such particulars to irrelevant empirical clutter.

Whether or not one hears a Shakespearean echo in the passage from the *Marriage*, the ingredients of Blake's scene match, with certain visionary aggrandizements, those of Dover cliff. The precipice in each instance is not the unbroken descent that Johnson would have liked but a place where suspension is possible midway, a "hanging" (Shakespeare) or "hovering" (Blake) that corresponds to the indeterminacy of the middle phase of the sublime moment. The samphire-man inscribes the cliff at Dover as surely as Blake's Devil inscribes his flat-sided steep. The "dreadful trade" of gathering a living from the cliff face is oxymoronic; the purposiveness of "trade" is poised against the disablement of "dread" so that as a minutely discriminated detail in the awesome scene the samphire gatherer becomes a miniature emblem of the contraries of the sublime experience. Like the crows and choughs about his head, his midway presence articulates the cliff face's own sublimity. Blake's mighty Devil, hovering in his black clouds, seems to amalgamate the black crows and the samphire-man of Shakespeare, while the Shakespearean birds reappear in Blake's scene as a kind of suspended message. The mighty Devil—as well as the man of "dread" trade at his printshop in Lambeth who stands behind him—turns this message against the blank face of nature on which it is inscribed. A text is substituted for the birds of the midway air, and the birds themselves enact the ecstatic liberating phase of the sublime as their *mid*-way becomes an "airy" way. The Shakespearean and the Blakean sublime inhere in the minutely discriminated figures on the face of natural grandeur, in the writing on the wall, not in the height of the wall itself or in the "vacuum" it measures—which is, after all, not really a vacuum but a cavern closed by the "senses five" of neoclassical expectation.

With the waning of a neoclassical taste for "general and invariable" masses or spaces as settings for the sublime, inscribed or figured walls and steeps frequently appear to take their place. A number of salient examples, both literal and metaphoric, occur in Wordsworth: monumental letters carved upon the turf, cliffs that *impress* thoughts on the rest of the scene, rocks that speak as if a voice were in them, and everywhere a fascination with inscriptions and epitaphs.[2] These encounters are linked easily to the sublime experience in ways familiar to Romantic critics: the inscribed surface halts the wayfarer, disrupts his sense of continuity, throws him into an abyss of self-consciousness, but finally elevates him to sublimities of the spirit. Part of

2. See *The Prelude* (1850) 6.631, 12.241–45; "Tintern Abbey," lines 5–6.

the power of the verbal inscription comes from its ability to rivet the eye, as do the crows and choughs of Dover cliff, and to offer a point of translucence amid the opaque expanse of wall, steep, or slab. But this effect is possible only if the verbal element calls attention to the surface on which it is inscribed. As Geoffrey Hartman has said in his seminal essay on Romantic inscription, inevitably it comes to seem "conscious of the place on which it [is] written" and turns into "iconic verse" (*Formalism* 207, 212). Words take on the look of stone and place as they speak of stone and place, or, conversely, stone and place speak to the inner ear stony words.

Blake has little to do with this kind of sublime discourse. His Devil inscribes on the side of the rock a message intended not to commend the rock but to obliterate its dominion, for the message promotes the immense inward delights of the particular against the pretensions of the abyss of the five senses to represent the sublime. The inscription thus is similar to that prototype of all sublime wall writing, the divine characters on the wall of Belshazzar's palace, which announce the imminent destruction of the empire—a destruction of the palace wall itself. It is one thing for Romantic poets and artists to interest themselves in speaking walls, quite another for them to admire the material surface for assimilating the living word to its own substance. Such admiration evidently underlies the prominence of inscription in much Romantic nature poetry; according to Hartman, "the setting is understood to contain the writer in the act of writing: the poet in the grip of what he feels and sees, primitively inspired to carve it in the living rock" (*Formalism* 222). This formulation would horrify Blake: the poet in the grip of what he sees would be a description of Urizen petrifying—he becomes what he beholds. What he beholds is the Body of Death, and in this sense the tradition of inscription always betrays traces of its original kinship with the epitaph, which, in the words of one recent critic, is "the gravesite of the sublime" (Fry 433).[3]

For a sense of Blake's position on the sublime trope of the mural inscription, we may turn to some Romantic visual representations. If

---

3. The whole of this passage deserves quotation: "[The epitaph] is at the furthest extreme in manner and purpose from the vocality of the sublime; it is not the pursuit of voice but the burial of voice, a concession to the tomblike bar between signifier and signified that leaves only the bar itself as theme and place of presentation. The epitaph is the gravesite of the sublime."

The morning comes, the night decays, the watchmen leave
    their stations;
The grave is burst, the spices shed, the linen wrapped up;
The bones of death, the cov'ring clay, the sinews shrunk & dry'd.
Reviving shake, inspiring move, breathing! awakening!
Spring like redeemed captives when their bonds & bars are burst.
Let the slave grinding at the mill, run out into the field:
Let him look up into the heavens & laugh in the bright air;
Let the inchained soul shut up in darkness and in sighing,
Whose face has never seen a smile in thirty weary years;
Rise and look out, his chains are loose, his dungeon doors are open
And let his wife and children return from the opressors scourge;
They look behind at every step & believe it is a dream.
Singing. The Sun has left his blackness, & has found a fresher morning
And the fair Moon rejoices in the clear & cloudless night;
For Empire is no more, and now the Lion & Wolf shall cease.

23.   *America*, pl. 6

24. Piranesi, *Carceri*, title page (second state)

plate 6 of Blake's *America* (fig. 23) is compared with the second-state title plate of Piranesi's *Carceri d'invenzione* (1760), general similarities are apparent. Both works are indebted to that common convention of tombstone carving in which a human figure is elevated to the head of a slab or plaque covered with text; there is even a superficial resemblance in the posture and orientation of the figures in the two plates. At first glance Blake's design seems more blandly conventional, an eighteenth-century headstone with decorous italic script supporting a common resurrection motif, a naked youth rising from the grave; all that is lacking is the usual hovering angel blowing the last trump. Although the figure of the soul's triumph over the grave is related to, and perhaps the origin of, the sublime trope of blockage and elevation, the plate does not present itself as visually sublime. By contrast, the Piranesi title page (fig. 24) is all Romantic sublimity, busy with minute discriminations, fully in revolt against a taste for undifferentiated heights and drops. Its monumentality appears figured not only with inscribed letters but with even more drastic versions of those mid-air suspensions that Shakespeare used to dramatize the height of Dover cliff. Yet a Blakean reading of the plate would find in it only a sinister parody of the sublime. Piranesi's prisoner, chained to the top of the inscribed slab, is held not only by the chains but also by the impassability of the drop and so is imprisoned literally in "height," *hypsous*, the sublime of the *mise en abyme*.[4] And what of the inscription? Since, in our Blakean reading, the victim is imprisoned in delusion, the abyss of the five senses, the inscription appropriately designates its own ground as a prison for the imagination and becomes self-referential; the words *carceri d'invenzione* are themselves imprisoned in the stony grip of what they signify. Signifier collapses into signified and is emptied, for from the Blakean standpoint, the signified is "all vacuum."

The task of a sublime artist and poet such as Blake is to liberate the signifier from the signified, word from surface—and the Intellectual Powers, reflected in words, from the grip of death toward which the Corporeal Understanding tends. Conceptually more sophisticated

---

4. On the sublimity of Piranesi's *Carceri* see Eitner (19–26). These prisons represent an antihuman sublime: "The figures that move about them seem remote, mere spots or blurs for the most part, lost in the immensity of the interiors whose dimensions they magnify by their smallness" (21).

than it first appears, plate 6 of *America* offers a small-scale rendition of this process. The text has the look of an epitaph, but there is no commemorative epitaphic function; we are not pulled into the dead past by the inscription, nor does the inscription call attention to itself. Rather, it renders in words below what the illumination above renders pictorially:

> *The bones of death, the cov'ring clay, the sinews shrunk & dry'd.*
> *Reviving shake, inspiring move, breathing! awakening!*
> *Spring like redeemed captives when their bonds & bars are burst*
> (*Am* 6.3–5)

A gap opens between the meaning of the text and its graphic or iconic context. Visually, the plate represents a liberated human power rising above a wall of words, but the meaning of the words contradicts their own epitaphic appearance, as if they too wished to rise above the lower world of obstruction, inscription, and death into the sublime of the naked human above. Conceivably, when the sublimation of the text is fully accomplished, the text per se should disappear altogether. Such sublimation (with the chemical sense of the word, "evaporation," relevant here) seems to occur in, for instance, the "Death's Door" design from Blair's *Grave*, which is obviously modeled, at least in its upper portion, on plate 6 of *America* (fig. 25). In the *Grave* design the stone lintel of the tomb replaces the borderline between text and illumination in the *America* plate, but while the transcendent human figure continues to display its naked limbs above the lintel, the expected epitaphic words below have indeed fled or evaporated, leaving in their place the signified body of death and its yawning cavern.

But at this point we need to draw back from our argument lest our theme, the sublime as text, should itself sublimate into its antithesis, the sublime as wordlessness. To represent the sublime experience without including the iconic, refractory, indeterminate elements of the signifier is not to offer the sublime at all. The "Death's Door" design, for example, visually depicts a sublime event: liberation through death's obstruction, transcendence through difficulty. There is no corresponding difficulty, however, in one's actual reading of the design. Its emblematic figures are too conventional, their schematic arrangement too pat; the design itself is not sublime. It does not provoke the differentiation of the Intellectual Powers and the Corporeal Under-

Drawn by W.Blake.

Etch'd by L.Schiavonetti.

Death's Door

but a Night, a long and moonless Night,
we make the Grave our Bed, and then are gone!

25. "Death's Door," from Blair's *The Grave*

And this, the form of mighty Hand sitting on Albions cliffs
Before the face of Albion, a mighty threatning Form.

His bosom wide & shoulders huge overspreading wondrous
Bear Three strong sinewy Necks & Three awful & terrible Heads
Three Brains in contradictory council brooding incessantly,
Neither daring to put in act its councils, fearing each-other,
Therefore rejecting Ideas as nothing & holding all Wisdom
To consist, in the agreements & disagreents of Ideas.
Plotting to devour Albions Body of Humanity & Love.

Such Form the aggregate of the Twelve Sons of Albion took; & such
Their appearance when combind: but often by birth pangs & loud groans
They divide to Twelve: the key-bones & the chest dividing in pain
Disclose a hideous orifice; thence issuing the Giant-brood
Arise as the smoke of the furnace, shaking the rocks from sea to sea.
And there they combine into Three Forms, named Bacon & Newton & Locke,
In the Oak Groves of Albion which overspread all the Earth.

Imputing Sin & Righteousness to Individuals: Rahab
Sat deep within him hid: his Feminine Power unreveald
Brooding Abstract Philosophy, to destroy Imagination, the Divine-
-Humanity A Three-fold Wonder: feminine: most beautiful: Three-fold
Each within other. On her white marble & even Neck, her Heart
Inorbd and bonified: with locks of shadowing modesty, shining
Over her beautiful Female features, soft flourishing in beauty
Beams mild, all love and all perfection, that when the lips
Recieve a kiss from Gods or Men, a threefold kiss returns
From the pressd loveliness: so her whole immortal form three-fold
Three-fold embrace returns: consuming lives of Gods & Men
In fires of beauty melting them as gold & silver in the furnace
Her Brain enlabyrinths the whole heaven of her bosom & loins
To put in act what her Heart wills; O who can withstand her power
Her name is Vala in Eternity: in Time her name is Rahab

The Starry Heavens all were fled from the mighty limbs of Albion   70

26. *Jerusalem*, pl. 70

standing that Blake holds to be the defining characteristic of his sublime art. His illuminated texts perform this task more successfully. Partly iconic themselves, they are suspended delicately between two contrasting iconic modes of the period, wordless emblems and rock-like inscriptions, avoiding sublimation into the one and hardening into the other.

Thus the etched words of Blake's illuminated books often seem to hover in space against a background of cloudy grandeur or stony height. This visual foregrounding is in itself a kind of statement of the preeminence of language, yet even in late Blake it is rarely an uncontested eminence. What kind of visual statement, for example, does plate 70 of *Jerusalem* make? The design of the huge Druidic trilithon is surely preeminent; a swollen descendant of the posts and lintel of Death's Door (fig. 26), on one level it signifies the material sublime towering high over natural man. Does this image not usurp the midway position, thrusting the text to the peripheries above and below, with the text blocks themselves functioning almost as elaborate captions? (The first words on the plate are "And this the form of," the last, "the mighty limbs of Albion." The limbs seem to be shown in petrified form here.) Yet a counterreading asserts itself against this baleful triumph of the material sublime, bringing with it different questions. How triumphantly does this image tower, when for all its "height" it does not even tower up to the top of the page? Is it not significant that language floats above the trilithon in a space precisely analogous to the space occupied by the naked youth above the lintel of Death's Door? (We are reminded of the etymology of the word *sublime*, "the lintel [raised] from beneath.") In short, the same visual schema produces antithetical readings and a see-sawing domination of rival sublimes.[5] Such equivocal competitions of text and image are of course found everywhere in Blake, and they fuel much of the energy of his composite art. But as long as an element of material "height" is present in the competition we never proceed entirely be-

5. I have elaborated on this rivalry elsewhere (see De Luca, "Sublimes" 93ff.), particularly with reference to Burke, the presiding genius of the material or petrific sublime. Blake hated the *Philosophical Enquiry into . . . the Sublime and the Beautiful*, but not so much as to refrain from using its images (which include megalithic monuments) for his own subversive ends.

yond equivocation into the transcendent certainty of the Intellectual Powers.

As his creative enterprise proceeds to its culmination in *Milton* and *Jerusalem*, Blake's own sublime becomes increasingly an affair of the text and the text alone. The reading experience supplies all the essential ingredients of the sublime experience, without reference to any external sublime. Initially offering threads of thematic and narrative continuity that lure the reader onward, the text presents a refractory iconicity, a wall or steep, that halts or dizzies the Corporeal Understanding. At the same time it displays an exuberance in its own self-referential play that provides the leap of *jouissance*, as Barthes would say, for the Intellectual Powers. In short the text provides its own golden string, its own walls, its own gates, its own heaven. I shall return presently to a further consideration of this textual heaven, but first we need a more detailed sense of the techniques employed in the late prophecies that divert the text from ordinary discourse to render it an agency of the sublime.

III

In its most developed state, Blake's sublime of the text is no longer a matter of words on walls, inscriptions on indeterminate ground, but of walls made out of words. To be sure, in the Keynes proof of the frontispiece of *Jerusalem* actual inscriptions cover the arch of the gate and the walls on either side, but Blake suppressed these inscriptions in all finished copies of the poem as if to encourage us to read the inscribed text within the work as embodying its own iconic ground. There is no danger in this kind of iconicity that the text will merge with its ground, like the letters imprisoned in stone of Piranesi's *Carceri*, for there is no material ground. The iconicity of Blake's late prophetic texts functions both as an opaque barrier to meaning and also as an exhilarating window into a textuality where riches of meaning are generated and stored.

A number of specific devices in Blake's late works contribute to this effect of words as textual walls; I shall confine myself here to mentioning four. First, visual illuminations, often occupying a block of half a plate or larger (as in *Jerusalem* 70), introduce pictorial signifiers in the midst of alphabetic ones, with the inevitable effect of inducing the eye to pictorialize the rest of a plate. The attention of the reader is diverted from a sequential pursuit of words and lines to a visual contemplation of the whole block of text as a single unit, a panel. Blake criticism is just beginning to investigate the significance of the layout of his illuminated books and to attend to such matters as the size of the designs, their situation on the plate, the intervals between them, and the patterns that combinations of these elements may produce. To look at Blake's text this way—and it is inevitable once we accept the implications of the notion of a composite art as elaborated by W. J. T. Mitchell and others—is to see it as blocks of light space, adorned with little dark figurations, played off against blocks of dark space, figured with light bounded shapes. Not only do the meanings of the individual words recede in importance in this visual perspective but so does the continuity of meaning from plate to plate; the plates become mural panels, movable units in a hundred-panelled wall.

Second, Blake frequently increases the density of inscription to the point of visual strain. *Jerusalem* provides many examples, but plate 16 is particularly notorious, crammed as it is with sixty-nine lines of verse that run virtually from one edge of the copperplate to the other, with scarcely more than a squiggle or two of visual decoration (fig. 27). To compound this impediment to easy reading, the text is packed with proper nouns, 140 of them in the lower half of the plate alone. Although such a crowding of characters and of reference inevitably irritates those who come to texts for smooth communication, the effect of this impediment to the reading eye is precisely to reify the signifier and so provoke the tension necessary for the sublime experience. Suddenly, at the turn of a page, row upon row of verses piled high strike the reader's eye, each row composed of discrete horizontal slabs of letters, like so many bricks. The text presents itself, in short, as a solid wall of words over which the eye slips, unable to find fastening. A second glance discriminates bristling ranks of capital letters, verse without syntax, nouns without predication, names without context ("Levi. Middlesex Kent Surrey. Judah Somerset Glouster Wiltshire./Dan. Cornwal Devon Dorset, Napthali" [*J* 16.45–46]). At the very start, then, the reader feels fatigue, a vertigo, and even though he may proceed through the text word by word, his ordinary, or corporeal, understanding never succeeds in comprehending or re-

Hampstead Highgate Finchley Hendon Muswell hill: rage loud
Before Bromions iron Tongs & glowing Poker reddening fierce
Hertfordshire glows with fierce vegetation; in the Forests
The Oak frowns terrible, the Beech & Ash & Elm enroot
Among the Spiritual fires; loud the Corn fields thunder along
The Soldiers fife; the Harlots shriek; the Virgins dismal groan
The Parents fear; the Brothers jealousy; the Sisters curse
Beneath the Storms of Theotormon & the thundring Bellows
Heaves in the hand of Palamabron who in Londons darkness
Before the Anvil, watches the bellowing flames: thundering
The Hammer loud rages in Rintrahs strong grasp swinging loud
Round from heaven to earth down falling with heavy blow
Dead on the Anvil, where the red hot wedge groans in pain
He quenches it in the black trough of his Forge: Londons River
Feeds the dread Forge, trembling & shuddering along the Valleys

Humber & Trent roll dreadful before the Seventh Furnace
And Tweed & Tyne anxious give up their Souls for Albions sake
Lincolnshire Derbyshire Nottinghamshire Leicestershire
From Oxfordshire to Norfolk on the Lake of Udan Adan
Labour within the Furnaces, walking among the fires
With Ladles huge & iron Pokers over the Island white.

Scotland pours out his Sons to labour at the Furnaces
Wales gives his Daughters to the Looms; England nursing Mothers
Gives to the Children of Albion & to the Children of Jerusalem.
From the blue Mundane Shell even to the Earth of Vegetation
Throughout the whole Creation which groans to be delivered
Albion groans in the deep slumbers of Death upon his Rock.

Here Los fixd down the Fifty-two Counties of England & Wales
The Thirty-six of Scotland, & the Thirty-four of Ireland
With mighty power, when they fled out at Jerusalems Gates
Away from the Conduct of Luvah & Urizen, fixing the Gates
In the Twelve Counties of Wales & thence Gates looking every way
To the Four Points: conduct to England & Scotland & Ireland
And thence to all the Kingdoms & Nations & Families of the Earth
The Gate of Reuben in Carmarthenshire: the Gate of Simeon in
Cardiganshire; & the Gate of Levi in Montgomeryshire
The Gate of Judah Merionethshire: the Gate of Dan Flintshire
The Gate of Naphtali Radnorshire: the Gate of Gad Pembrakeshire
The Gate of Asher, Carnarvonshire the Gate of Issachar Brecknokshire
The Gate of Zebulun, in Anglesea & Sodor, so is Wales divided
The Gate of Joseph Denbighshire: the Gate of Benjamin Glamorganshire
For the protection of the Twelve Emanations of Albions Sons

And the Forty Counties of England are thus divided in the Gates
Of Reuben Norfolk Suffolk Essex Simeon Lincoln York Lancashire
Levi Middlesex Kent Surrey Judah Somerset Glouster Wiltshire
Dan Cornwal Devon Dorset Naphtali Warwick Leicester Worcester
Gad Oxford Bucks Harford Asher Sussex Hampshire Berkshire
Issachar Northampton Rutland Nottingham Zebulun Bedford Huntgn Camb
Joseph Stafford Shrops Heref Benjamin Derby Cheshire Monmouth
And Cumberland Northumberland Westmoreland & Durham are
Divided in the the Gates of Reuben Judah Dan & Joseph

And the Thirty-six Counties of Scotland, divided in the Gates
Of Reuben Kincard Haddntn Forfar Simeon Ayr Argyll Banff
Levi Edinburh Roxbro Ross Judah Aberdeen Berwick Dumfries
Dan Bute Caeliness Clakmanan Naphtali Nairn Invernes Linlithgo
Gad Peebles Perth Renfru Asher Sutherlan Sterling Wigtoun
Issachar Selkirk Dumbarton Glasgo Zebulun Orkney Shetland Skye
Joseph Elgin Lanerk Kinros Benjamin Kromarty Murra Kirkubriht
Governing all by the sweet delights of secret amorous glances
In Enitharmons Halls builded by Los & his mighty Children

All things acted on Earth are seen in the bright Sculptures of
Los's Halls & every Age renews its powers from these Works
With every pathetic story possible to happen from Hate or
Wayward Love & every sorrow & distress is carved here
Every Affinity of Parents Marriages & Friendships are here
In all their various combinations wrought with wondrous Art
All that can happen to Man in his pilgrimage of seventy years
Such is the Divine Written Law of Horeb & Sinai:
And such the Holy Gospel of Mount Olivet & Calvary:

27. *Jerusalem*, pl. 16

taining the whole. The reader experiences something like Kant's sub-lime of magnitude, "for there is here a feeling of the inadequacy of his Imagination [a purely sense-related faculty in Kant] for presenting the Idea of a whole, wherein the Imagination reaches its maximum, and in striving to surpass it, sinks back into itself" (112). Frequently in *Jerusalem*, the alternative for the Corporeal Understanding to the text as spatial barrier is the text as linear labyrinth, which leads the under-standing, after much travail, back to the cold and obdurate exterior of the structure.

Third, with less dire effect, Blake enhances the iconicity of his text by favoring regular, periodic repetition of words and phrases and rec-tilinear arrangements of these reiterations on the plate:

> *And every Month, a silver paved Terrace builded high:*
> *And every Year, invulnerable Barriers with high Towers.*
> *And every Age is Moated deep with Bridges of silver & gold.*
> *And every Seven Ages is Incircled with a Flaming Fire.*
> (M 28.54–57)

> *And sixty-four thousand Genii, guard the Eastern Gate:*
> *And sixty-four thousand Gnomes, guard the Northern Gate:*
> *And sixty-four thousand Nymphs, guard the Western Gate:*
> *And sixty-four thousand Fairies, guard the Southern Gate:*
> (J 13.26–29)

> *All Human Forms identified even Tree Metal Earth & Stone. all*
> *Human Forms identified, living going forth & returning wearied*
> *Into the Planetary lives of Years Months Days & Hours reposing*
> (J 99.1–3)

The perfect vertical alignment of the repeated phrases in the first two passages is immediately apparent to the eye, indeed, more immedi-ately apparent than the meanings of the lines. In the extract from *Jerusalem* 13 verticality moves into rectangularity as the horizontal structure "And sixty-four thousand . . . guard the . . . Gate" quadru-plicates itself in symmetrically spaced columns with a variation in terms filling the lacunae like mortar. The alignments in *Jerusalem* 99 are more complex: the repetition of the word "all" at the beginning and end of the first line squares off the slab of text like a pair of quoins, but the alignments of other repeated terms are not strictly rec-tilinear. In the paired phrases "Human Forms identified," for exam-ple, the lower phrase slips slightly to the left of perfect vertical alignment. The metrically and syntactically congruent phrase "Years Months Days & Hours" in the third line echoes "Tree Metal Earth & Stone" in the first but shows a similar leftward slippage in its respective position in the line; on the other hand, "reposing" in line 3 moves to the right of a vertical alignment with the congruent "returning" in the line above. Here the effect is rather like the crosshatch layering of bricks in a wall: the mortar spaces are always obliquely aligned. More precisely, the interplay of repetition and displaced position creates a kind of visual syncopation as well as a misalignment of eye and ear (the former defeated in an expectation of periodic return that is made good for the latter). The effect is a small tension or disequilibrium that provokes, on a larger scale, the energy of the sublime experience.

The isolation of text blocks as panels in a larger visual design, the crowding of words on a plate into an opaque mass, the distribution of replicated terms along rectilinear axes all serve to induce in the text a resistance to discursive reduction. More powerful even than these three modes of inducing resistance is the massive proliferation of proper names, which we have already glimpsed in *Jerusalem* 16. Names are intrinsically irreducible, hard givens, unavailable for paraphrase. The irreducibility of the name can take two contrary forms: either it brings transparently to mind the unique signified it denotes and, in a sense, collapses into it like the epitaphic inscriptions on stone discussed earlier, or else it hides an unknown referent that cannot be made present through paraphrase or synonym, whereupon the name signifies itself as signifier and nothing else. I have argued elsewhere that Blake's manner of coining unexplained names and piling them up has the effect of granting them an autonomy, a detachment from conceptual reference ("Names" 5–22). But the particular power of the autonomous name in Blake is that in confronting its opacity we are never unaware that it also transparently denotes a unique signified whose presence is tantalizingly deferred; psychic energy is generated in the tension between the apparent opacity and the possible transparency. This tension may best be seen not in those passages in Blake where the names are pure inventions, hermetically sealed, but where the names hover at the remote margins of the known:

> A wine-press of Love & Wrath double Hermaph[r]oditic
> Twelvefold in Allegoric pomp in selfish holiness
> The Pharisaion, the Grammateis, the Presbuterion,

The Archiereus, the Iereus, the Saddusaion, double
Each withoutside of the other, covering eastern heaven
(*J* 89.4–8)

We know, vaguely, that there are real referents behind these formidable names, or rather we are induced to make that assumption because of the relative familiarity of some of them. Yet even the more familiar are orthographically distorted, estranged, as if read in a dream. Such familiarity as they have is like the faint tracing of an inscription on the cliff face of their obscurity. We labor to read but keep sliding away: a dreadful trade.

In one sense, it has been argued, the mythic names in Blake are reconstructions of the primordial language of Eternity, where an "exact congruence of name and thing" existed before sign and referent fell away from one another in the Fall (Stempel 394). But one cannot simply eliminate the arbitrary iconicity of the name as it obtrudes in the text through an invocation of its presumed transparency in Eternity, for the text also turns a face to the vegetative world and the Corporeal Understanding. Nor can one recover this transparency by retracing a linear etymology from Blake's names to their originals in supposedly primordial languages, for such a linear program leads only to an infinite regress of signifiers and never to Eternal essence. Only the intuitive leap of the Intellectual Powers can make that recovery, accomplished in the sublime moment when barriers are overcome either all at once or not at all. For this reason the two faces of language are exploited to the full in Blake's work: we are invited with open arms to recover semantic plenitude only to confront the arbitrariness of the sign. Blake's own remarks on the topic, even when they appear to assert the presence of a plenitude of meaning, are equivocal: "Every word and every letter is studied and put into its fit place" (*J* 3). This famous declaration begs more questions than it answers: what is a "*fit* place"? Why a "place"? What are the ways in which a *letter* may be "studied"? The context pertains to meter, but the reference to "every letter" eludes that context and associates the whole remark with the process of inscription and etching, with the text as spatialized form. If a mason were to say, "every stone is studied and put into its fit place," we would not find anything extravagant in the remark and would expect a good wall; we would not look for sermons in its stones. Such sermons of course may be found in many of the stones in Blake's wall of words, but these virtues do not open gates in the stones to the heaven within them, a privilege granted only to the Intellectual Powers.

IV

It is time to speak of these Intellectual Powers, and of what lies on the other side of the wall. It should be said at once that there is no other side; there is only an opacity that becomes a translucence once the intellectual order of the text is grasped. We cannot construe the phrase "Intellectual Powers" to mean a kind of higher cleverness, a hermeneutic capacity for decoding messages enshrouded in dark conceit. It has nothing to do with ratiocination or logical calculation. "The Treasures of Heaven are not Negations of Passion but Realities of Intellect from which All the Passions Emanate Uncurbed in their Eternal Glory" (E564). Intellect, then, is the matrix of desire, supplying desire's paradoxical needs—both the definite forms that are the objects of desire and an "uncurbed" freedom of play. It may seem a sleight of hand to suggest that these twin requirements of form and freedom are fulfilled by the signifier, which, as we all now know by heart, is arbitrary and which dances as often as dance it can. But the hand that moves these concepts is Blake's, not mine; in the visionary conclusion of *Jerusalem*, the delight of Eternity, the form of its fulfilled desire, is conceived as discourse—the word is Blake's own (98.35)—in which "every Word & Every Character Was Human" (98.35–36). Daniel Stempel has aptly described this famous passage depicting the Living Creatures' conversation in "Visionary forms dramatic" as one that "restores both the order and the language of eternity; the relation between words and things is immediately visible as language and representation become one" (398). I would add that what this discourse represents is not merely "things" but language itself. Discourse is not merely the matrix of vision but the object of vision as well: "I . . . *saw* the Words of the Mutual Covenant Divine" (98.41; my italics). At the far side of the sublime barrier of words are ultimate words, inscription without place.

"And the Writing / Is the Divine Revelation in the Litteral expression" (*M* 42.13–14). This is a writing whose "woven letters" compose history and fallen time, the "Woof of Six Thousand Years" (42.15). But if we detach these words from their contextual bed, allowing them to articulate the range of their syntactic and semantic possibilities, they assert a revelation about the Divine Vision itself as nothing other than transcendent writing: the Writing IS the Divine Revelation (what is revealed about the Divine); the Writing IN THE LITTERAL EXPRES-SION is the Divine Revelation (that is, the Divine Revelation inheres in the characters of the Writing, not the meaning of the Writing). God is the Word, but the Word as Written; in the Eternity every Word and every Character is human, but without losing the properties of words and characters.[6] It is thus not surprising that when Blake apostrophizes his reader in *Jerusalem* as "*lover* of books! *lover* of heaven" (3), his syntax induces us to consider the terms as appositive and the two loves as one and the same: heaven is a form of text.[7]

Behind this equation of divinity and textuality there are religious sanctions from traditional sources, both orthodox and unorthodox. The Kabbalistic tradition of creation as an emanation of the Tetragrammaton or four letters of the Divine Name is one possible source; another is the representation of the godhead as Alpha and Omega in Revelation. The Book of Revelation, furthermore, is essentially about the revelation of a book, sealed at first and opaque, then burst open to reveal a new textuality, visible letters both read and seen—a paradigm of the sublime experience that perhaps informs all its later secular versions.[8] But however much he draws on the imagery of scriptural revelation (and inscription as the revealed), Blake himself is a secularist of the sublime, if we understand "secularist" to mean one who seeks

6. Nelson Hilton articulates these points in a fundamental way: "Words," he says, "are the building-blocks of Blake's 'universe stupendous'—which is language. The words are not signs for what is seen (*idea*); rather, what appears is a *phainomenon* or showing-forth of words, a *logosophany*" (*Literal* 9). Hilton defines "literal imagination" as one that "would, in keeping with its etymology (*littera*), identify itself in letters, that is to say, in the word and in writing" (*Literal* 2).

7. In his article in this collection, Paul Mann argues the contrary position: "Eternity is bookless, a perspective from which the book is seen as a hole torn in the seamless fabric of Eternity." For Mann, all inscription is constriction and obliteration of life. One might reply that it is not so much a case of language doing violence to Eternity as of Urizen doing violence to language, by limiting its endless potentialities to reductive descriptiveness and prescriptive fiat. But the living Words of Eternity still form collectively Eternity's ideal, unfallen book.

8. On the Name of God in the Kabbalah, see Scholem, *Kabbalah* 170ff.; for a survey of older commentary on Revelation pertinent to themes mentioned here, see Wittreich, *Visionary* 3–54.

to demystify the conception of the all-creating, transcendental inscription as glowing characters suspended in the void, originating in an unapproachable Other, a mystery of mysteries. Blake understands language not only as having human origin but also as being the quintessence and the glory of our humanity. Allegory means "other-speaking," but in the state of transcendence and sublimity there is no "other." "Sublime allegory" is thus an "other-speaking" that cancels its own otherness and becomes simply speaking; "Allegory addressed to the Intellectual powers" refers therefore to a scene of self-recognition.

This is purely and simply the domain of the Romantic sublime. In Kant, again, *"The sublime is that, the mere ability to think which, shows a faculty of the mind surpassing every standard of Sense,"* and, "Sublimity does not reside in anything of nature, but only in our mind, in so far as we can become conscious that we are superior to nature within, and therefore also without us" (110, 124). For a modern, this scene in which the mind is astonished and elevated by a recognition of its own powers becomes reenacted in a recognition of the gift of language. Thomas Weiskel thought that Blake's "sublime is not the Romantic sublime" (67), but there is nothing in the operation of Blake's sublime that is fundamentally alien to anything in Kant or, for that matter, to the semiotic perspectives in Weiskel's own work. Where Blake differs from Kant, however, or from Wordsworth, is in his refusal to allow Nature a role in the propagation of the sublime experience. In those contemporaries, Nature must first tower grimly over the perceiving subject before it finally dwindles in the blazing recognition of the subject's own inner glory. But for Blake even a temporary domination by Nature is too long; long enough to suggest its otherness and something merely secondary or compensatory in the mind's eventual exaltation; there is room in such a scheme for humiliation, for a counter-tug downward to the stony Body of Death.

In Blake's sublime of the text, however, there are no such threats, though the challenges and rewards are as great as with any other form of the sublime. The Corporeal Understanding, halted before the wall of words or lost like one of Piranesi's prisoners in the labyrinths of its "hidden meanings," indeed takes comfort in the familiar opacity of Nature in the face of an opacity so much more bizarre. The Intellectual Powers, on the other hand, operate like the corresponding fac-

ulty in Kant's system, the Reason, which "requires totality [and] desires comprehension in *one* intuition," wishing to "think the infinite
as *entirely given*" (115). Blake's infinite is "entirely given" into the palm
of our hand in the form of the text before us and its potentialities. The
Intellectual Powers perceive this text as a concentration of minute particulars gathered to a presence, taking it in as a conclave of signifiers—each particular a word, each word a determinate form though
bristling with polyvalent possibilities. The words are sometimes ser-
vants of meaning, sometimes lords of their own autonomy, in kalei-
doscopically shifting patterns of order. What Weiskel has said of
Wordsworth's celebration of the power of words in book 5 of *The Prelude* is equally apt here: "The passage is evoking the penumbra of
words, the power inherent not in what they mean but in that they
mean; or, in what they are, independent of their meaning—in an earlier language, the *how* and not the *what* of sublimity. . . . Power inheres not in the perceptional form but in language or symbolicity itself" (181). The Intellectual Powers do not address themselves to
meaning as such. The text is generous in its inclusion of meanings,
which are there to be found sooner or later. Interpretation is deferred,
but delight is immediate. In that sphere of delight the wall of words
becomes a reticulated wall, and every word a window yielding pros-
pects of our sovereign powers.

A critique of Blake's sublime and an exposition of textuality's role in
his work come, then, to much the same thing. But, a final word of
critic's caution. The terminology of our present-day discourse on textuality easily lends itself to the discussion of Blake. The ease of application, however, depends largely on the fact that this terminology,
with its imagery of blocks, gaps, abysses, labyrinths, deferrals, and
the like, is itself a sublime rhetoric, one that hints at common intellectual roots between the antipositivism of Blake's time and of our own.
But a historical sense serves not only to indicate those points of *rapprochement* between Blake's theoretical concerns and our own but also
to draw the limits of their compatibility. The sublime is inherently an
idealizing mode. Although Blake would recognize much in our current discourse as part of the vocabulary of sublimity, he would see this
vocabulary as stuck in the intermediate or deprivative phase of the
sublime moment without a promise of the fulfillment that makes the
sublime worth its name. For Blake Presence is available, and the tran-

scendental subject exists; these are in fact the cornerstones of his faith. The experience of transcendence, moreover, leads him to an earnest preoccupation with other concerns currently unfashionable in some quarters—with truth and error, moral persuasion, and an unsparing analysis of the world we live in every day. The sublimity of the text is not the text's only value, and it is of no value if it serves only to lead us into an endless labyrinth of linguistic traces and differences. In that sublimity we breathe heaven's air, but as a gift to sustain us in our return to the continuities of the common day—the samphire-man back on the beach with his burden, the birds of the airy way homing in to the nest.

Envoi: "So Many Things"

GEOFFREY H. HARTMAN

Our conference produced a kind of mathematical sublime, which Hayden White might call a historicizing sublime. "So many things" have been brought to our attention that do tend, as the sublime does, to block or halt the understanding.[1] One has to react to this wealth of positions or negations, and one can react in at least two ways. One is through the clenched fist of logic, and positivism. The other is through the open or outstretched hand of rhetoric, the weltering, or floating, or swagging of indeterminacy. But, of course, the mind of the conference, if I can make such an hypostasis, triumphantly raised itself above such blockages or partial moments. I'm not sure whether *my* mind has or whether it still remains blocked by "so many things."

These impromptu remarks for the close of the conference are not meant to be a summary; they represent some of my thoughts as I listened for two days. I classify them under three headings, which have to do with conferencing generally. In a conference we discuss what is known and understood. We may also discuss what is known and not understood, and perhaps what is not known, yet understood.

Now (1) *what is known and understood* is very valuable; it is the tangible asset with which one leaves a conference. For instance, while I cannot claim there was a consensus, a general feeling emerged that Blake is not "Il Ponderoso" but rather "Homo Ludens" and that we now feel comfortable with, and very appreciative of, his laughing speech. We knew all along he was a satirist. It is just a question of

---

1. I take my title from an aside that the speaker at the "Blake and Criticism" conference may not remember. At one point Jackie DiSalvo sighed and said, "So many things"; and this is my feeling too—"so many things."

how to define that to our satisfaction: in what way are the longer poems laughing speech, despite having many tones. Blake pulls our leg. If your leg is pulled you fall on your bottom. The problem with Blake is that, to use a good Quaker expression, there is a process of unbottoming. You think you have a bottom, or you have reached the bottom, and by conversion or pressure that bottom is taken away; suddenly you sink. Some participants described that in terms of the sublime—the sublime going upward, or the sublime going downward—and everybody understands, whatever technical terms are used, how difficult it is to *ground* Blake. I'll come back to the fact that he *is* grounded, and that we have no problem responding to the experience "in" his poetry. At the same time we cannot be sure of the referentiality of his figures—of the links between metaphor and concept, or between literal and figurative in his poems.

(2) *What is known and not understood.* I should say not sufficiently understood, perhaps. An example is the text-image relation that was discussed most illuminatingly at the conference. This is known and not sufficiently understood because it is still highly extensible; it is a direction we should think about in the future. Consider not only what Blake does to the book but what he does to the page, and whether his kind of split writing—if we think of image and text as splitting the page—is comparable to Norman O. Brown's practice in *Love's Body*, or Derrida's in *Glas*, where the page is formally divided, although not into image and text, through typographical devices. The question of split writing leads to the question of polysemy, which is not only a matter of typographical or page division, although it can include that.

Another aspect of what is known and not sufficiently understood—what is still extensible—was brought to our attention by Tom Mitchell: The Dangerous Blake.[2] Anything but the English Blake! Dangerous Blake, mad Blake, dirty Blake, but please not English Blake. This aspect is not fully understood, not only because we haven't decided what the relation is between method and madness, but because we haven't even understood what is involved in the question. I can put it more dramatically by saying that even Tom Mitchell, a liberated scholar, did not mention one darker aspect of Blake, and that is Fake Blake. It is hard to gauge Blake's authority. Yes, in a con-

2. See W. J. T. Mitchell, "Dangerous Blake."

ference we are one—we all admire, appreciate, try to understand more. We are bonded together in our devotion, or at least our intellectual appreciation of Blake. But just as he wanted to pass a Last Judgment on art, can we say anything about the question of judgment? None of us did. There was no evaluation except in a highly implicit way, and I don't mean questions of "this is good" and "this is bad" and "he should have done that." I mean a judgment of the whole visionary project. Where does Blake get his authority from? Can we habituate ourselves to his oneiric mass perturbation? The question of authority is something that won't leave me as I read him. Does he have the right to parade as a kind of prophet and then take that authority away by saying, "Mine is simply the voice of honest indignation"? This is even more an issue, because his remarkable project has not been repeated (unless you compare him to Joseph Smith).

I come to my last category, the most difficult one: (3) *what is not known, yet understood*. "The eye sees more than the heart knows" is Blake's own epigraph to *Visions of the Daughters of Albion*, because he does not wish to evoke secret love or esoteric (priestly) knowledge. We have not sufficiently explored this region: that there is an understanding of Blake, of his voice, for example, which is visceral. We know that there is something physiological going on in our reponses as we read him. We do not know what it is, and I beg pardon of those who have worked on his rhythms. We do not sufficiently know what is going on.

Consequently we are still recovering the tension between the system and its minute—vocal or subvocal—articulations. I had hoped that the title of the conference, *Blake and Criticism*, would come in, that we would examine what has happened to the status of the "system"—to what Frye taught us, after Damon, or what Bloom carried through, or what Hazard Adams worked with in a different dimension. What is the status of Blake's system? Do we still believe there is one, rather than a set of fractional personifications that may or may not be capable of being integrated? The impression I receive now is that there are many overlapping integrations, and it may be a vain hope that they could become one overarching map. In fact, the general direction of the conference has been to acknowledge what Donald Ault called the "microscopic subversive detail." Many participants who discussed the text-image relation mentioned the asymmetry or gap between execution and conception. Some denied it, but every-body felt a little uneasy. There is, then, the question of whether the system is still there, or what utility for criticism Frye and Bloom have.

What of these Blakean minute particulars? The final emphasis—of the edited volume—on textuality, on the texture of the text, the mul-tiple rewriting, the over- and underdetermined names leads us into this area. There is a remarkable surface to Blake. We are unable to grapple with that surface lest we drown or get lost in its dark and dan-gerous forest. We have therefore projected ourselves out of it, like Frye, and constructed a total form. Might it be better to do for a while without the idea of total form? In the same way, some of us wish to get rid of the term *Romanticism*, however useful it is, or *Classicism*. Let's start again, and cleanse the doors of scholarly perception.

Is that even possible? Some might answer that however good or faulty Blake's execution may be, there is invention; even if we are not sure of the conception, we're damn sure that Blake is among the most inventive of artists. Who else has more invention? So at least we have the representation of an invention, but whether that represented (often re-represented) invention amounts to a conception is still not clear to me.

Most of the time I understand Blake, yet do not know what is going on. I see the mythology, I grasp the visionary characters and visionary categories that are his medium and carry him. I understand the vehic-ular energy. But I cannot get from there to experience, from symbol to experience. I can make a good guess here and there, but I can't be sure. Why can't I be sure? I'm almost always sure with Wordsworth. It cannot be because some people are born unto Wordsworth and some are not. If you will allow a short comparison, Wordsworth, even if wild and queer, pretty crazy in his own way, always *starts* on this side of the familiar: "the world which is the world of all of us." Where he *ends* I'm not sure. Blake gives me the feeling of methodically start-ing on the other side—not that he doesn't have "experience," of course he does. Perhaps it is not wishing to abandon visionary cate-gories, and feeling that so much of his project has to be mediated by them, that leads him to say things against nature and experience, and to be so tenacious of the visionary heritage. He hoards visionary expressions, aggregates their sublimity: he is *always* the poet-dreamer of *The Fall of Hyperion*: "Upon the marble at my feet there lay / Store of

strange vessels, and large draperies. . . . Robes, golden tongues, cen-
ser and chafing-dish, / Girdles, and chains, and holy jewelries." Remember the division of labor between Wordsworth and Coleridge in
Lyrical Ballads—one of them took the natural to throw an aura of the
supernatural over it; the other tried to naturalize the supernatural or
make it seem probable. In the imaginative ecology of the era, Blake is
on the side of the supernatural imagination, and everything becomes
mediated by that; therefore there is a problem of navigation, or of
readerly orientation.

I would like to end with a series of examples. Although some participants did read from Blake, I missed the *voice* of Blake. My opening
example comes from *The Four Zoas*, "Night the First." Tharmas sits
weeping in the clouds and complains:

> *Why wilt thou Examine every little fibre of my soul*
> *Spreading them out before the Sun like Stalks of flax to dry*
> *The infant joy is beautiful but its anatomy*
> *Horrible Ghast & Deadly nought shalt thou find in it*
> *But Death Despair & Everlasting brooding Melancholy*
>
> *Thou wilt go mad with horror if thou dost Examine thus*
> *Every moment of my secret hours*
>
> (4.29–35, E302)

Is Tharmas talking to a woman who has undergone psychoanalysis
and has turned it against him? I'm not sure who Tharmas is, or to
whom he is talking. The passage is what used to be called a "passion": a passionate speech movement, about which Blake said in "Auguries of Innocence," "To be in a Passion, you Good may do / But no
Good if a Passion is in you." And that would raise the question of the
cathartic effect such a passage may have. I've only cited, because of
time, the beginning. There is polysemy, on the level of voice, there
are many voices in that one voice, and what is happening seems essentially cathartic. But can we really talk about "character," or do we
have to talk about "passion"—some participants preferred "states,"
"plates," "types," and even "Process." When I asked, "What is the
hero, is there a hero," the answer was, "No, there is only Process."
But the word "passion" is a historical and human category, and it al-
lies Blake with a number of eighteenth-century concerns.

A second example of the kind of analysis that I hope is possible—

of understanding something but not yet knowing how to go about describing it so as to make it more public—would be from "Night the Ninth." Here I'm totally at a loss and just want to give myself the pleasure of quoting the first few lines of "Night the Ninth / Being / The Last Judgment."

> *And Los & Enitharmon builded Jerusalem weeping*
> *Over the Sepulcher & over the Crucified body*
> *Which to their Phantom Eyes appear'd still in the Sepulcher*
> *But Jesus stood beside them in the Spirit Separating*
> *Their Spirit from their body.*
>
> (117.1–5, E386)

The music of that is extraordinary. Even if we claim to know who Los and Enitharmon are, and even if we claim to be able to say something about why they are weeping, there is an incredibly moving tone of lamentation, and I am not satisfied, being an analytic type, to leave it alone. But I don't yet know how to *think* about such extraordinary vocal music.

I go to the third instance, more familiar, but at least as difficult as the others. It is two lines from the fifth stanza of "The Tyger." In my deconstructive or destructive moods I think, "What can I leave out?" Do we really need stanza 5? Wouldn't it be a more unified poem if we omitted,

> *When the stars threw down their spears*
> *And water'd heaven with their tears:*
> *Did he smile his work to see?*
> *Did he who made the Lamb make thee?*

The more you look at this riddle, the less sure you are of solving it, the more incongruous it is within the poem as a whole. "A Riddle or the Cricket's Cry / Is to Doubt a fit Reply." I am tempted to go directly from, "What the anvil? what dread grasp, / Dare its deadly terrors clasp!" to the last stanza's "Tyger Tyger burning bright." Then you'd have a good, horrible (Grimm) kind of nursery rhyme that has been complicated by the antithetical moment of "When the stars threw down their spears / And water'd heaven with their tears."

Would it help if we could identify the speaker? Is he *in* a passion, or is he a persona, the bard, or Urizenic questioner, as Bloom suggests? Is it someone close to innocence, or someone shocked back into innocence—many different answers have been proposed. Blake doesn't give enough cues, even if (in the longer poems) he gives you plenty of names, too many names, but who the persona is, and whether all personae are, finally, aspects of Albion, is part of the corporate mystery here.

Having given up trying to clarify the relation between passion and persona, I said to myself: in terms of its precious diction, this is a periphrasis, and scholars know the iconology or iconotropy (as Robert Graves says) of "Stars throwing down their spears."[3] Yet do they throw them down in anger, jealousy, militancy, or (what seems more likely) in surrender? The second line associates spears and tears; is it then a moment of pity or a moment of mercy; can these be distinguished? I don't know how I decided that those two lines were a periphrasis for "dawn" or "break of day." "When the stars threw down their spears, / And water'd heaven with their tears." I then associated them with that famous quotation from Blake's prose notes on *The Vision of the Last Judgment*, "Creation which was an act of Mercy," and realized that the stanza is not only antithetical to the rest of the poem, but also antithetical to the Book of Job, where the morning stars or sons of morning are present at the creation of the world, singing in *joy*. In "The Tyger" the act of creation evokes a different, or ambivalent world: "Morning"—"mourning." In the context of the lyric as a whole we have, at this point, a movement from night (night-creature or nightmare) to dawn, yet only a glimpse of dawn. As is often the case in Blake we're at the brink of *awakening*—from the Ninth or whatever Night. I don't offer this as a definitive interpretation, rather as the kind of thing I feel I understand, putting things together lightly, trying to find the "poetical" logic of Blake. If we don't find it, if we don't perceive how Blake sees *through* visionary formulas, then we have to go with Wordsworth, or with Wallace Stevens, and say, regretfully, "The solar chariot is junk"—and leave it.

3. The fullest discussion of these lines, including precise remarks on language play, image association, and the "subvocalized responses elicited by these" is Nelson Hilton's essay, "Spears, Spheres, and Spiritual Tears."

Works Cited

Adams, Hazard. "Post-Essick Prophecy." *Studies in Romanticism* 21 (Fall 1982): 400–403.

Aers, David. "William Blake and the Dialectics of Sex." *ELH* 44 (1977): 500–514.

Aers, David, Jonathan Cook, and David Punter. *Romanticism and Ideology: Studies in English Writing, 1765–1830.* London: Routledge & Kegan Paul, 1981.

Althusser, Louis. "Ideology and Ideological State Apparatuses." In *Lenin and Philosophy and Other Essays,* trans. B. Brewster, 49–53. London: New Left Books, 1971.

Arp, Hans. "Concrete Art." In *The Modern Tradition,* ed. Richard Ellman and Charles Feidelson. Oxford: Oxford University Press, 1965.

Augustine. *Confessions.* Trans. R. S. Pine-Coffin. Baltimore: Penguin Books, 1964.

Ault, Donald. "Blake and Newton." In *Epochen der Naturmystik: Hermetische Tradition in wissenschaftlichen Fortschritt,* ed. Antoine Faivre and Rolf Christian Zimmerman, 364–80. Berlin: Erich Schmidt Verlag, 1979.

———. "Incommensurability and Interconnection in Blake's Anti-Newtonian Text." *Studies in Romanticism* 16 (Summer 1977) 277–303.

———. *Visionary Physics: Blake's Response to Newton.* Chicago: University of Chicago Press, 1974.

Austin, J. L. "Performative Utterances." In *Philosophical Papers,* 220–39. Oxford: Oxford University Press, 1961.

———. *How to Do Things with Words.* Cambridge, Mass.: Harvard University Press, 1975.

Barcus, James E., ed. *Shelley: The Critical Heritage.* London: Routledge & Kegan Paul, 1975.

Barthes, Roland. "The Death of the Author." In *Image-Music-Text,* ed. Stephen Heath, 142–48. New York: Hill & Wang, 1977.

———. *Mythologies.* Selected and trans. A. Lavers. London: Cape, 1972.

———. *S/Z: An Essay.* Trans. Richard Miller. New York: Hill & Wang, 1974.

Bateson, Gregory. *Steps to an Ecology of Mind.* New York: Chandler, 1972.

Benjamin, Walter. "The Work of Art in an Age of Mechanical Reproduction." In *Illuminations,* trans. H. Zohn, 217–51. New York: Harcourt Brace, 1968.

Bentley, G. E., Jr. *Blake Books*. Oxford: Clarendon Press, 1977.

———. *Blake Records*. Oxford: Clarendon Press, 1969.

———. *Vala or The Four Zoas*. Oxford: Clarendon Press, 1963.

———. *William Blake's Writings*. 2 vols. Oxford: Clarendon Press, 1978.

Benveniste, Émile. *Problems in General Linguistics*. Trans. M. Meek. Coral Gables, Fla.: University of Miami Press, 1971.

Bindman, David. *Blake as an Artist*. Oxford: Phaidon, 1977.

Blake, William. *The Complete Poetry and Prose of William Blake*. Ed. David V. Erdman, commentary by Harold Bloom. Newly revised ed. Berkeley and Los Angeles: University of California Press, 1982.

———. *The Book of Urizen*. See Easson, Kay Parkhurst, and Roger R. Easson.

———. *Notebook*. See Erdman, David V.

Bloom, Harold. "The Pictures of the Poet." *New York Times Book Review* (3 January 1982): 2.

Borges, Jorge Luis. "The Library of Babel." In *Labyrinths: Selected Stories and Other Writings*, 51–58. New York: New Directions, 1964.

Boswell, James. *The Life of Samuel Johnson, L.L.D.* 2 vols. London: J. M. Dent, 1949.

Bradbury, Malcolm. *The History Man*. London: Secker & Warburg, 1976.

Brewster, Ben, Stephen Heath, and Colin McCabe. "Comment on Julia Lesage's 'The Human Subject—You, He, or She?'" *Screen* 26, no. 2 (Summer 1975): 83–90.

Brisman, Leslie. *Romantic Origins*. Ithaca: Cornell University Press, 1978.

Brooks, Peter. "Freud's Masterplot." In *Literature and Psychoanalysis: The Problem of Reading: Otherwise*, ed. Shoshana Felman, 280–300. Baltimore: Johns Hopkins University Press, 1983.

Burke, Edmund. *A Philosophical Enquiry into the Origin of Our Ideas of the Sublime and Beautiful*. 2d ed. London, 1759.

———. *Reflections on the Revolution in France*. Ed. C. C. O'Brien. London: Penguin Books, 1968.

Butler, Marilyn. *Romantics, Rebels, and Reactionaries: English Literature and Its Background, 1760–1830*. New York: Oxford University Press, 1982.

Carr, Stephen Leo. "William Blake's Print-Making Process in *Jerusalem*." *ELH* 47 (1980): 520–41.

Cassirer, Ernst. *Language and Myth*. Trans. Susanne K. Langer. New York: Harper and Brothers, 1946.

———. *The Philosophy of the Enlightenment*. Trans. C. A. Koelin and J. P. Pettegrove. Boston: Beacon Press, 1955.

———. *Substance and Function and Einstein's Theory of Relativity*. Trans. W. C. Swabey and M. C. Swabey. Reprint ed. New York: Dover Publications, 1953.

Coleridge, Samuel Taylor. *The Notebooks of Samuel Taylor Coleridge*, vol. 1. Ed. Kathleen Coburn. Princeton: Princeton University Press, 1957.

Connolly, Thomas E., and George R. Levine. "Pictorial and Poetic Design in Two *Songs of Innocence*." *PMLA* 82 (1967): 257–69.

Cozens, Alexander. *A New Method of Assisting the Invention in Drawing Original Compositions of Landscape.* London: the author, [1785].

Creech, Thomas, trans. *The Works of T. Lucretius Carus.* Reprinted in Robert Anderson, ed., *The Works of the British Poets,* vol. 13. London, 1795.

Culler, Jonathan. *The Pursuit of Signs.* Ithaca: Cornell University Press, 1981.

Cunningham, Allen. *The Lives of the Most Eminent British Painters and Sculptors.* Vol. 2. 1830. Reprint ed. New York, 1959.

Curran, Stuart, and Joseph Anthony Wittreich, eds. *Blake's Sublime Allegory: Essays on "The Four Zoas," "Milton," "Jerusalem."* Madison: University of Wisconsin Press, 1973.

Damon, S. Foster. *A Blake Dictionary: The Ideas and Symbols of William Blake.* 1965. Reprint ed. New York: Dutton, 1971.

———. *William Blake: His Philosophy and Symbols.* 1924. Reprint ed. Gloucester, Mass.: Peter Smith, 1958.

Damrosch, Leopold, Jr. *Symbol and Truth in Blake's Myth.* Princeton: Princeton University Press, 1980.

Darwin, Erasmus. *The Botanic Garden: A Poem, in Two Parts. Part I. Containing the Economy of Vegetation. Part II. The Loves of the Plants. With Philosophical Notes.* 1791. Facsimile reprint; Menston, Eng.: Scolar Press, 1973.

Davies, Paul. *Other Worlds: Space, Superspace, and the Quantum Universe.* New York: Simon and Schuster, 1982.

De Luca, V. A. "Blake and the Two Sublimes." In *Studies in Eighteenth-Century Culture,* vol. 11, ed. Harry T. Payne, 93–105. Madison: University of Wisconsin Press, 1982.

———. "Proper Names in the Structural Design of Blake's Mythmaking." *Blake Studies* 8 (1978): 5–22.

De Man, Paul. *Blindness and Insight: Essays in the Rhetoric of Contemporary Criticism.* 2d ed., revised. Minneapolis: University of Minnesota Press, 1983.

Dennett, Daniel C. *Brainstorms: Philosophical Essays on Mind and Psychology.* Cambridge, Mass.: MIT Press, 1981.

Derrida, Jacques. "Differance." In *Speech and Phenomena,* trans. David B. Allison, 129–60. Evanston, Ill.: Northwestern University Press, 1973.

———. *Dissemination.* Trans. Barbara Johnson. Chicago: University of Chicago Press, 1981.

———. "Force and Signification." In *Writing and Difference,* trans. Alan Bass, 3–30. Chicago: University of Chicago Press, 1978.

———. "Freud and the Scene of Writing." Trans. Jeffrey Mehlman. *Yale French Studies* 48 (1972): 73–117. Also in *Writing and Difference,* 196–231.

———. "Limited Inc a b c . . . ." *Glyph* 2 (1977): 162–254.

———. "Living On: Border Lines." Trans. James Hulbert. In Harold Bloom et al., *Deconstruction and Criticism,* 75–175. New York: Seabury Press, 1979.

———. *Of Grammatology.* Trans. Gayatri Chakravorty Spivak. Baltimore: Johns Hopkins University Press, 1981.

———. *Positions.* Trans. Alan Bass. Chicago: University of Chicago Press, 1981.

———. *Speech and Phenomena, and Other Essays on Husserl's Theory of Signs.* Trans. David B. Allison. Evanston, Ill.: Northwestern University Press, 1973.

———. *Spurs: Nietzsche's Styles.* Trans. Barbara Harlow, introduction by Stefano Agosti. Chicago: University of Chicago Press, 1978.

———. "White Mythology: Metaphor in the Text of Philosophy." Trans. F. C. T. Moore. *New Literary History* 6 (1974): 5–74.

Dundes, Alan. *Analytical Essays in Folklore.* The Hague: Mouton, 1975.

Eagleton, Terry. *Criticism and Ideology: A Study in Marxist Literary Theory.* London: Verso Editions, 1978.

Easson, Kay Parkhurst, and Roger R. Easson, eds. *The Book of Urizen.* Boulder, Colo., and New York: Shambala and Random House, 1978.

Eaves, Morris. "Blake and the Artistic Machine: An Essay in Decorum and Technology." *PMLA* 92 (1977): 903–27.

———. *William Blake's Theory of Art.* Princeton: Princeton University Press, 1982.

Eco, Umberto. *The Role of the Reader: Explorations in the Semiotics of Texts.* Bloomington: Indiana University Press, 1979.

Edwards, Gavin. "Mind-Forg'd Manacles: A Contribution to the Discussion of Blake's *London.*" *Literature and History* 5, no. 1 (Spring 1979): 87–105.

———. "Politics and Characterisation." *Essays in Criticism* 28, no. 3 (July 1978): 254–59.

Ehrenzweig, Anton. *The Psycho-Analysis of Artistic Vision and Hearing.* New York: George Braziller, 1965.

Eitner, Lorenz. "Cages, Prisons, and Captives in Eighteenth-Century Art." In *Images of Romanticism: Verbal and Visual Affinities,* ed. Karl Kroeber and William Walling. New Haven: Yale University Press, 1978.

Eliade, Mircea. *Cosmos and History: The Myth of the Eternal Return.* Trans. Willard Trask. New York: Bollingen Foundation, 1954.

———. *Images and Symbols.* Trans. Philip Mairet. New York: Sheed and Ward, 1969.

Ellis, Edwin John, and William Butler Yeats, eds. *The Works of William Blake, Poetic, Symbolic, and Critical.* 3 vols. London: Bernard Quaritch, 1893.

Erdman, David V. *Blake: Prophet Against Empire.* 3d ed. Princeton: Princeton University Press, 1977.

———. *The Illuminated Blake.* Garden City, N.Y.: Anchor Press/Doubleday, 1974.

———, ed. *The Notebook of William Blake: A Photographic and Typographic Facsimile.* Oxford: Clarendon Press, 1973.

Erdman, David V., et al., eds. *A Concordance to the Writings of William Blake.* 2 vols. Ithaca: Cornell University Press, 1967.

Erdman, David V., and John Grant, eds. *Blake's Visionary Forms Dramatic.* Princeton: Princeton University Press, 1970.

Essick, Robert N. "Review of *Blake Books.*" In *Blake: An Illustrated Quarterly* 43 (1978): 178–99.

————. *The Separate Plates of William Blake: A Catalogue.* Princeton: Princeton University Press, 1983.

————. *William Blake, Printmaker.* Princeton: Princeton University Press, 1980.

Everest, Kelvin, and Gavin Edwards. "William Godwin's *Caleb Williams*: Truth and Things as They Are." In *1798: Reading Writing Revolution*, ed. Francis Baker et al., 129–46. Colchester, Eng.: University of Essex, 1982.

Feyerabend, Paul. *Against Method: Outline of an Anarchist Theory of Knowledge.* London: New Left Books, 1975.

Fish, Stanley. *Is There a Text in This Class?* Cambridge, Mass.: Harvard University Press, 1980.

Flexner, Eleanor. *Mary Wollstonecraft: A Biography.* Baltimore: Penguin Books, 1973.

Fogel, Aaron. "Pictures of Speech: On Blake's Poetic." *Studies in Romanticism* 21 (1982): 217–42.

Foucault, Michel. *The History of Sexuality*, vol. 1: *An Introduction.* Trans. Robert Hurley. New York: Random House, 1980.

————. *Power/Knowledge: Selected Interviews and Other Writings, 1972–1977.* Ed. Colin Gordon. Brighton, Eng.: Harvester, 1980.

————. "What Is an Author?" In *Language, Counter-Memory, Practice*, ed. Donald F. Bouchard, trans. Bouchard and Sherry Simon, 113–38. Ithaca: Cornell University Press, 1977. Also in *Textual Strategies*, ed. Josué V. Harari, 141–60. Ithaca: Cornell University Press, 1979.

Freud, Sigmund. *Civilization and Its Discontents.* Trans. James Strachey. New York: W. W. Norton & Co., 1962.

————. *Moses and Monotheism.* Trans. Katherine Jones. New York: Random House, 1967.

————. "Some Psychical Consequences of the Anatomical Distinction Between the Sexes." In Vol. 19 of *The Standard Edition of the Complete Psychological Works of Sigmund Freud*, ed. James Strachey, 248–58. London: Hogarth Press, 1953–77.

————. *Inhibitions, Symptoms and Anxiety.* Vol. 20 of *The Standard Edition.*

————. *Studies on Hysteria.* Vol. 2 of *The Standard Edition.*

————. *Three Essays on the Theory of Sexuality.* Vol. 7 of *The Standard Edition.*

————. *Totem and Taboo.* Vol. 13 of *The Standard Edition.*

————. "The Unconscious." Vol. 14 of *The Standard Edition*, 159–215.

Frye, Northrop. *Fearful Symmetry: A Study of William Blake.* 1947. Reprint ed. Princeton: Princeton University Press, 1969.

Fry, Paul H. "The Absent Dead: Wordsworth, Byron, and the Epitaph." *Studies in Romanticism* 17 (Fall 1978): 413–34.

Gallant, Christine. *Blake and the Assimilation of Chaos.* Princeton: Princeton University Press, 1978.

George, Diana Hume. *Blake and Freud.* Ithaca: Cornell University Press, 1980.

George, Margaret. *One Woman's "Situation": A Study of Mary Wollstonecraft.* Urbana: University of Illinois Press, 1978.

Gernet, Louis. *Les Grecs sans miracle: Textes réunis*, ed. Riccardo di Donato. Paris: Maspero, 1983.

Girard, René. "Differentiation and Reciprocity in Lévi-Strauss and Contemporary Theory." In *"To double business bound,"* 155–77. Baltimore: Johns Hopkins University Press, 1978.

Glazer-Schotz, Myra, and Gerda Norvig. "Blake's Book of Changes: On Viewing Three Copies of the *Songs of Innocence and of Experience.*" *Blake Studies* 9 (1980): 100–121.

Gleckner, Robert F. *The Piper and the Bard.* Detroit: Wayne State University Press, 1959.

Glen, Heather. "The Poet in Society: Blake and Wordsworth in London." *Literature and History* 1, no. 3 (March 1976): 2–28.

———. *Vision and Disenchantment: Blake's 'Songs' and Wordsworth's 'Lyrical Ballads.'* Cambridge: Cambridge University Press, 1983.

Godwin, William. *Memoirs of the Author of a Vindication of the Rights of Woman.* 2d ed. London: Joseph Johnson, 1798.

Grant, John. "Mother of Invention, Father in Drag." *Blake Newsletter* 6/7 (1968): 29–32, 50–54.

———. "Recognizing Fathers." *Blake Newsletter* 2 (1967): 2–28.

Guralnick, Elissa S. "Rhetorical Strategy in Mary Wollstonecraft's *A Vindication of the Rights of Woman.*" *Humanities Association Review* 30 (1979): 170–79.

Guthke, Karl S., ed. *Henry Fuseli: Remarks on the Writing and Conduct of J. J. Rousseau.* Augustan Society Reprint no. 82. Los Angeles: Augustan Reprint Society, 1960.

Hamlin, Cyrus. "The Temporality of Selfhood: Metaphor and Romantic Poetry." *New Literary History* 6 (1974): 169–93.

Harper, George Mills. "Mary Wollstonecraft's Residence with Thomas Taylor the Platonist." *Notes and Queries* 207 (1962): 461–63.

———. *The Neoplatonism of William Blake.* Chapel Hill: University of North Carolina Press, 1961.

Hartman, Geoffrey H. *Beyond Formalism.* New Haven: Yale University Press, 1970.

———. *The Fate of Reading.* Chicago: University of Chicago Press, 1975.

———. "From the Sublime to the Hermeneutic." In *The Fate of Reading*, 114–23.

———. "The Loom and the Shuttle: Language from the Point of View of Literature." *The Review of Metaphysics* 23, no. 2 (December 1969): 240–58.

Hertz, Neil. "The Notion of Blockage in the Literature of the Sublime." In *Psychoanalysis and the Question of the Text*, ed. Geoffrey H. Hartman, 62–85. Baltimore: Johns Hopkins University Press, 1978.

Hilton, Nelson. *Literal Imagination: Blake's Vision of Words.* Berkeley and Los Angeles: University of California Press, 1983.

———. "Spears, Spheres, and Spiritual Tears." *Philological Quarterly* 59, no. 4 (Fall 1980): 515–29.

Hirsch, E. D. *Innocence and Experience.* New Haven: Yale University Press, 1964.

Hofstadter, Douglas R. *Gödel, Escher, Bach: An Eternal Golden Braid.* New York: Random House, 1980.

Holt, J. C. *Magna Carta.* Cambridge: Cambridge University Press, 1967.

Howard, John. "An Audience for *The Marriage of Heaven and Hell.*" *Blake Studies* 3, no. 1 (Fall 1970): 19–52.

Humboldt, Wilhelm von. *An Anthology of the Writings of Wilhelm von Humboldt: Humanist Without Portfolio.* Trans. Marianne Cowan. Detroit: Wayne State University Press, 1963.

Ingarten, Roman. *The Cognition of the Literary Work of Art.* Trans. Ruth Ann Crowley and Kenneth R. Olson. Evanston, Ill.: Northwestern University Press, 1973.

Jakobson, Roman. *Shifters, Verbal Categories, and the Russian Verb.* Cambridge, Mass.: Russian Language Project, Harvard University, 1957.

———. "Why 'Mama' and 'Papa'?" In *Selected Writings*, vol. 1, 538–45. The Hague: Mouton, 1962.

Jameson, Fredric. "Imaginary and Symbolic in Lacan: Marxism, Psychoanalytic Criticism, and the Problem of the Subject." *Yale French Studies* 55/56 (1977): 338–95.

———. "Interview." *Diacritics* (Fall 1982): 72–91.

———. *The Political Unconscious.* Ithaca: Cornell University Press, 1981.

Janson, H. W. "Fuseli's *Nightmare.*" *Arts and Sciences* (Spring 1963): 26–28.

Jensen, M., ed. *English Historical Documents*, vol. 9. London: Eyre and Spottiswoode, 1955.

Johnson, Barbara. "Poetry and Performative Language." *Yale French Studies* 51 (1977): 140–58.

Johnson, Samuel. *Samuel Johnson on Shakespeare.* Ed. W. K. Wimsatt. New York: Hill & Wang, 1960.

Joyce, James. *James Joyce: The Critical Writings.* Ed. Ellsworth Mason and Richard Ellmann. New York: Viking Press, 1964.

———. *Finnegans Wake.* New York: Viking Press, 1957.

Kafka, Franz. *Parables and Paradoxes.* New York: Schocken Books, 1974.

Kanner, Leo. "A Philological Note on Sex Organ Nomenclature." *Pyschoanalytic Quarterly* 14 (1945): 228–33.

Kant, Immanuel. *Critique of Judgment.* Trans. J. H. Bernard. London: Macmillan, 1914.

Keynes, Geoffrey. *William Blake's Songs of Innocence and of Experience.* Oxford: Oxford University Press, 1967.

King, James. "The Meredith Family, Thomas Taylor, and William Blake." *Studies in Romanticism* 11 (1972): 153–57.

Kierkegaard, Søren. *Philosophical Fragments or a Fragment of Philosophy.* Trans. David F. Swenson, rev. Howard V. Hong, 1936. Reprint ed. Princeton: Princeton University Press, 1962.

Knowles, John. *The Life and Writings of Henry Fuseli*, vol. 1. London, 1831.

Kubler, George A., ed. *Historical Treatises Abstracts and Papers on Stereotyping*. New York: n.p., 1936.

Kristeva, Julia. *Desire in Language: A Semiotic Approach to Literature and Art*. Ed. Leon Roudiez, trans. Roudiez, Thomas Gora, and Alice Jardine. New York: Columbia University Press, 1980.

———. *Polylogue*. Paris: Editions du Seuil, 1977.

———. "Psychoanalysis and the Polis." *Critical Inquiry* 9, no. 1 (September 1982): 77–92.

———. Σημειωτιχὴ: *Recherches pour une sémanalyse*. Paris: Editions du Seuil, 1979.

Lacan, Jacques. "Desire and the Interpretation of Desire in *Hamlet*." *Yale French Studies* 55/56 (1977): 11–52.

———. *Écrits: A Selection*. Trans. Alan Sheridan. London: Tavistock, 1977.

———. *Feminine Sexuality*. Ed. Juliet Mitchell and Jacqueline Rose. Trans. Rose. New York: W. W. Norton & Company, 1982.

———. "Fonction et champ de la parole et du langage en psychanalyse." In *La Psychanalyse*, vol. 1 (1956). Republished in *Écrits*, Paris: Editions du Seuil, 1966. Published in English as *The Language of the Self*, trans. Anthony Wilden (New York: Dell Publishing Co., 1968).

———. *The Four Fundamental Concepts of Psychoanalysis*. Ed. Jacques-Alain Miller. Trans. Alan Sheridan. London: Hogarth Press, 1977.

Land, Stephen K. *From Signs to Propositions: The Concept of Form in Eighteenth-Century Semantic Theory*. London: Longman Group, 1974.

Laplanche, J., and J.-B. Pontalis. *The Language of Psychoanalysis*. Trans. D. Nicholson-Smith. New York: W. W. Norton & Co., 1973.

Leader, Zachary. *Reading Blake's Songs*. London: Routledge & Kegan Paul, 1981.

Lévi-Strauss, Claude. *L'Homme nu*. Paris: Plon, 1971.

Locke, John. *An Essay Concerning Human Understanding*. Ed. P. N. Nidditch. Oxford: Clarendon Press, 1975.

MacCabe, Colin, ed. *James Joyce: New Perspectives*. Sussex and Bloomington: Harvester Press and Indiana University Press, 1982.

[Macklin, Thomas.] *Poetic Description of Choice and Valuable Prints, Published by Mr. Macklin, at the Poets' Gallery, Fleet Street*. London: T. Bensley, 1794.

Macpherson, James. *The Poems of Ossian*. 1762. Reprint ed. Edinburgh, 1896.

McGuire, J. E. "Force, Active Principles, and Newton's Invisible Realm." *Ambix* 15 (1968): 154–208.

McNeil, Helen T. "The Formal Art of *The Four Zoas*." In *Blake's Visionary Forms Dramatic*, ed. David V. Erdman and John E. Grant, 373–90. Princeton: Princeton University Press, 1970.

Manuel, Frank E. *The Religion of Isaac Newton: The Fremantle Lectures, 1973*. Oxford: Clarendon Press, 1974.

Márquez, Gabriel García. "Chronicle of a Death Foretold." Trans. Gregory Rabassa. *Vanity Fair* (March 1982): 105–249.

Mason, Eudo. *The Mind of Henry Fuseli: Selections from his Writings, with an Introductory Study.* London: Routledge and Kegan Paul, 1951.

Milton, John. *Paradise Lost.* Ed. Merritt Y. Hughes. New York: The Odyssey Press, 1962.

Mitchell, W. J. T. *Blake's Composite Art: A Study of the Illuminated Poetry.* Princeton: Princeton University Press, 1978.

———. "Dangerous Blake." *Studies in Romanticism* 21, no. 3 (Fall 1982): 410–16.

———. "Poetic and Pictorial Imagination in Blake's *The Book of Urizen.*" *Eighteenth-Century Studies* 3 (Fall 1969): 83–107.

Moers, Ellen. "Vindicating Mary Wollstonecraft." *The New York Review of Books* (19 February 1976): 38–41.

Morris, W., ed. *The American Heritage Dictionary of the English Language.* Boston: Houghton Mifflin Co., 1969.

Murry, John Middleton. *William Blake.* 1933. Reprint ed. New York: McGraw Hill, 1964.

Newton, Isaac. *Sir Isaac Newton's Mathematical Principles of Natural Philosophy and His System of the World*, 2 vols. Ed. Florian Cajori, trans. Andrew Motte. Berkeley and Los Angeles: University of California Press, 1934.

Nietzsche, Friedrich. *The Birth of Tragedy.* Trans. Walter Kaufmann. New York: Vintage Books, 1967.

———. *The Birth of Tragedy and The Genealogy of Morals.* Trans. Francis Golffing. Garden City, N.Y.: Doubleday & Co., 1956.

Nurmi, Martin Karl. *William Blake.* London: Hutchinson, 1975.

Ostriker, Alicia. Review of Janet M. Todd, ed., *A Wollstonecraft Anthology. Blake: An Illustrated Quarterly* 14 (1980): 130.

Paine, Tom. *The Rights of Man.* Ed. Henry Collins. London: Penguin Books, 1969.

Paley, Morton D. Review of David V. Erdman and John Grant, eds., *Blake's Visionary Forms of Dramatic. Blake Studies* 4, no. 1 (Fall 1971): 93–105.

Peirce, C. S. *Collected Papers.* Cambridge, Mass.: Belknap Press, 1965.

Phillips, Michael, ed. *Interpreting Blake.* Cambridge: Cambridge University Press, 1978.

Piaget, Jean. *Structuralism.* London: Routledge and Kegan Paul, 1968.

Plowman, Max. *An Introduction to the Study of Blake.* 2d ed. London: Cass, 1967.

Pope, Alexander, trans. *Homer's Iliad: Books 1–12.* Ed. Maynard Mack et al. Vol. 7 of The Twickenham Edition. London and New York: Methuen and Yale University Press, 1967.

Punter, David. *Blake, Hegel and Dialectic.* Amsterdam: Rodopi, 1982.

Raine, Kathleen. *Blake and Tradition*, 2 vols. Bollingen Series, no. 35, vol. 11. Princeton: Princeton University Press, 1968.

Reiman, Donald H., and Christina Shuttleworth Kraus. "The Derivation and Meaning of 'Ololon.'" *Blake: An Illustrated Quarterly* 16, no. 2 (Fall 1982): 82–85.

Ricks, Christopher. "Clichés." In *The State of the Language*, ed. Leonard Michaels and Christopher Ricks, 54–63. Berkeley and Los Angeles: University of California Press, 1980.

Riffaterre, Michael. *Text Production*. Trans. Terese Lyons. New York: Columbia University Press, 1983.

Sandys, George. *Ovid's Metamorphoses, Englished, Mythologized, and Represented in Figures by George Sandys*. Ed. Karl K. Hulley and Stanley T. Vandersall. Lincoln: University of Nebraska Press, 1970.

Santa Cruz Blake Study Group. Review of *The Complete Poetry and Prose of William Blake*, newly rev. ed., ed. David V. Erdman. *Blake: An Illustrated Quarterly* 18, no. 1 (Summer 1984): 4–31.

Sartre, Jean-Paul. *Literature and Existentialism*. Secaucus, N.J.: The Citadel Press, 1980.

Saussure, Ferdinand de. *Course in General Linguistics*. Trans. Wade Baskin. New York: McGraw-Hill, 1966.

Schiff, Gert. *Johann Heinrich Füssli: 1741–1825*, 2 vols. Zürich: Berichthaus, 1973.

Schleiermacher, Friedrich D. E. *The Christian Faith*. Trans. of 2d German edition, ed. H. R. Mackintosh and J. S. Steward. Edinburgh: T. T. Clark, 1928. Reprint ed., 1976.

Scholem, Gershom. *Kabbalah*. New York: New York Times Book Company, 1974.

Schorer, Mark. *William Blake: The Politics of Vision*. New York: Henry Holt, 1946.

Serres, Michel. *Hermes: Literature, Science, Philosophy*. Ed. Josué V. Harari and David F. Bell. Baltimore: Johns Hopkins University Press, 1982.

Shaviro, Steven. "'Striving with Systems': Blake and the Politics of Difference." *Boundary 2* 10, no. 3 (Spring 1982): 229–50.

Sherry, Peggy Meyer. "The 'Predicament' of the Autograph: 'William Blake.'" *Glyph* 4 (1978): 131–55.

Simmons, Robert E. "*Urizen*: The Symmetry of Fear." In Erdman and Grant, eds., *Blake's Visionary Forms Dramatic*, 146–73.

Simpson, David. *Irony and Authority in Romantic Poetry*. London and Totowa, N.J.: Macmillan and Rowman & Littlefield, 1979.

———. *Wordsworth and the Figurings of the Real*. London and Atlantic Highlands, N.J.: Macmillan and The Humanities Press, 1982.

Smart, Christopher. *Jubilate Agno*. Ed. Karina Williamson. Oxford: Clarendon Press, 1980.

Smith, John Thomas. *Nollekens and His Times*, 2 vols. London: Henry Colburn, 1828.

Spivak, Gayatri Chakravorty. "Displacement and the Discourse of Woman." In *Displacement: Derrida and After*, ed. Mark Krupnick, 169–95. Bloomington: Indiana University Press, 1983.

———. "French Feminism in an International Frame." *Yale French Studies* 62 (1981): 154–84.

Starobinski, Jean. *Trois fureurs*. Paris: Gallimard, 1974.

Stempel, Daniel. "Blake, Foucault, and the Classical Episteme." *PMLA* 96 (May 1981): 388–467.

Stevens, Wallace. *The Collected Poems.* New York: Alfred A. Knopf, 1955.

Sunstein, Emily W. *A Different Face: The Life of Mary Wollstonecraft.* New York: Harper and Row, 1975.

Swedenborg, Emanuel. *Apocalypse Revealed.* Trans. A. S. Sechrist. New York: Swedenborg Foundation, 1968.

———. *Treatise on the Earths in the Universe.* London, 1745. Reprint ed. [*Earths in the Universe*], New York: Swedenborg Foundation, 1970.

Tannenbaum, Leslie. *Biblical Tradition in Blake's Early Prophecies: The Great Code of Art.* Princeton: Princeton University Press, 1982.

Taylor, Thomas. *A Dissertation on the Elusinian and Bacchic Mysteries.* Amsterdam [*sic*]: n.p., n.d. [ca. 1790–91].

———. *Thomas Taylor the Platonist: Selected Writings.* Ed. Kathleen Raine and George Mills Harper. Bollingen Series, no. 88. Princeton: Princeton University Press, 1969.

———. *A Vindication of the Rights of Brutes.* 1792. Reprint ed. Boston, 1795.

Thass-Thieneman, Theodore. *The Interpretation of Language.* Vol. 2: *Understanding the Unconscious Meaning of Language.* New York: Jason Aronson, n.d. [1973].

Thompson, E. P. "London." In *Interpreting Blake*, ed. Michael Phillips, 5–31. Cambridge: Cambridge University Press, 1978.

Thorslev, Peter L., Jr. "Some Dangers of Dialectical Thinking, with Illustrations from Blake and His Critics." In *Romantic and Victorian: Studies in Memory of William H. Marshall*, ed. Paul W. Elledge and Richard L. Hoffman. Rutherford, N.J.: Farleigh Dickinson University Press, 1971.

Tomory, Peter. *The Life and Art of Henry Fuseli.* New York: Praeger, 1972.

Tyson, Gerald P. *Joseph Johnson: A Liberal Publisher.* Iowa City: University of Iowa Press, 1979.

Viscomi, Joseph. *The Art of William Blake's Illuminated Prints.* [Manchester, England]: Manchester Etching Workshop, 1983.

Wardle, Ralph M. *Mary Wollstonecraft: A Critical Biography.* Lawrence: University of Kansas Press, 1951.

Wasser, Henry H. "Notes on the *Visions of the Daughters of Albion* by William Blake." *Modern Language Quarterly* 9 (1948): 291–93.

Weiskel, Thomas. *The Romantic Sublime: Studies in the Structure and Psychology of Transcendence.* Baltimore: Johns Hopkins University Press, 1976.

Welch, Dennis M. "Blake's Response to Wollstonecraft's *Original Stories.*" *Blake: An Illustrated Quarterly* 13 (1979): 4–15.

Wellek, René, and Austin Warren. *Theory of Literature.* New York: Harcourt, Brace and Co., 1956.

White, Hayden. "Michel Foucault." In *Structuralism and Since: From Lévi-Strauss to Derrida*, ed. John Sturrock, 81–115. Oxford: Oxford University Press, 1979.

Wilson, F. P., ed. *The Oxford Dictionary of English Proverbs.* Revised ed. Oxford: Oxford University Press, 1970.

Wittreich, Joseph Anthony, Jr. *Visionary Poetics: Milton's Tradition and His Legacy.* San Marino, California: Huntington Library, 1979.

Wollstonecraft, Mary. *Mary* and *Maria, or The Wrongs of Woman.* Ed. James Kinsely and Gary Kelly. Oxford: Oxford University Press, 1980.

———. *Original Stories from Real Life.* 2d ed. London: Joseph Johnson, 1791.

———. *A Vindication of the Rights of Man.* 1790. Facsimile reprint, Gainesville, Fla.: Scholars' Facsimiles and Reprints, 1960.

———. *A Vindication of the Rights of Woman.* London: Joseph Johnson, 1792 [cited in text as *Vindication*].

Wordsworth, William. *The Prelude.* Ed. Jonathan Wordsworth, M. H. Abrams, and Stephen Gill. New York: W. W. Norton & Co., 1979.

Wright, John W. *William Blake's "Urizen" Plate Designs.* Ann Arbor, Mich., 1980.

Contributors

Donald Ault, Vanderbilt University, is the author of *Visionary Physics: Blake's Response to Newton* (1974) and *Narrative Unbound: Re-Visioning Blake's "Four Zoas"* (in press), as well as a number of articles on Blake.

Stephen Leo Carr, University of Pittsburgh, has published articles on *Macbeth*, Berkeley, Mill, and Blake and is completing a study of reproduction and representation in Blake's graphics. He is an advisory editor of *Pretext*.

V. A. De Luca, Erindale College, University of Toronto, is the author of *Thomas de Quincey: The Prose of Vision* (1980) and many articles on Blake. He is the editor of the nineteenth-century section of the forthcoming *Oxford Anthology of Poetry in English*.

Gavin Edwards, Saint David's University College, has recently completed a book on Crabbe. His article on "London" appeared in *Literature and History*.

Robert N. Essick, University of California at Riverside, is the author of *William Blake's Relief Inventions* (1978), *William Blake, Printmaker* (1980), and *The Separate Plates of William Blake* (1983).

Geoffrey H. Hartman, Yale University, has written books and articles on a variety of subjects, including *The Unmediated Vision* (1954), *Wordsworth's Poetry* (1964), *Beyond Formalism* (1970), *Criticism in the Wilderness* (1980), and *Saving the Text: Literature / Derrida / Philosophy* (1981).

Nelson Hilton, University of Georgia, has recently published *Literal Imagination: Blake's Vision of Words* (1983) as well as articles on Blake and other topics. He is review editor for *Blake: An Illustrated Quarterly*.

Paul Mann lives and writes in San Francisco.

David Simpson, Northwestern University, is the author of *Irony and Authority in Romantic Poetry* (1979), *Wordsworth and the Figurings of the Real* (1982), *Fetishism and Imagination: Dickens, Melville, Conrad* (1982); his edition of *Ger-*

man Aesthetic and Literary Criticism: Kant, Fichte, Schelling, Schopenhauer, Hegel appeared in 1984.

Thomas A. Vogler, Cowell College, University of California at Santa Cruz, organized the "Blake and Criticism" Conference held there in May 1982. He is the author of *Preludes to Vision* (1970) and articles on various eighteenth- to twentieth-century writers and topics.

Index

Compositor: Wilsted & Taylor
Text: 10/13 Palatino
Display: Palatino
Printer: Malloy Lithographing, Inc.
Binder: John H. Dekker & Sons